A
TREASURY
OF
YIDDISH
POETRY

YID

A TREASURY OF DISH POETRY

EDITED BY

IRVING HOWE

AND

ELIEZER GREENBERG

HOLT · RINEHART AND WINSTON

NEW YORK · CHICAGO · SAN FRANCISCO

SBN-03-066425-x
Printed in the United States of America

ACKNOWLEDGMENTS

It is a pleasure to acknowledge the help of two splendid institutions. The first is the National Translation Center in Austin, Texas, which provided a subvention that was used entirely to improve the always-inadequate fees paid to translators. (It is impossible to overpay them.) The second is YIVO, the Institute for Jewish Research, in New York City, which provided us with rare texts and bibliographical help. Especially do we wish to thank Dina Abramovitch, the YIVO librarian, whose love of things Yiddish made her an ideal colleague and helper.

THE EDITORS

TO THE YIDDISH WRITERS
DESTROYED BY
HITLER AND STALIN

CONTENTS

II | DIE YUNGE AND THEIR CONTEMPORARIES   85

V | MODERN YIDDISH POETRY IN AMERICA   243

VI | YIDDISH POETS IN ISRAEL   347

A
TREASURY
OF
YIDDISH
POETRY

INTRODUCTION

In fiction, Yiddish literature finds its fulfillment almost at the very beginning. During the last third of the nineteenth century there appear in Eastern Europe the three masters of Yiddish fiction—Mendele Mocher Sforìm Peretz, and Sholem Aleichem—who set the main patterns of sensibility and style for the work of later writers. Important novelists and story writers follow them; some achieve innovations in subject and technique; but it is at least an open question whether later Yiddish fiction, even that composed by writers as distinguished as David Bergelson, Moshe Kulbak, and Isaac Bashevis Singer, represents a radical break from the tradition established by the founding trio. With Mendele's didactic satire, Peretz' folk-like yet sophisticated tales, and Sholem Aleichem's humorous monologues, Yiddish fiction strikes its most authentic note, so much so that one can say that almost everything which follows is a variation on the opening "classical" phase.

The development of Yiddish poetry is very different. It comes to its maturity a bit later than does Yiddish prose. The romantic verse of Peretz and the nationalist lyrics of S. Frug have a historical interest; but it would be an exaggeration to say that in such early figures there is already present the essential materials of a literary tradition. As it develops in the twentieth century, Yiddish poetry goes through a series of rather abrupt changes and inner revolutions; it draws both upon the cultural resources of the Jewish past and the surrounding modern literatures of Europe and America; and it bears the imprint of the American immigrant experience more strongly than does Yiddish fiction. The writers of Yiddish novels and stories who came to America during the early years of this century could still use the *shtetl* (Jewish village) as their dominant locale, while the Yiddish poets who settled in America were more open to the inducements and onslaughts of literary modernism as it was then developing in Europe and America. Nor is the reason for this difference hard to discover: the story writer retained in his imagination a complete old-country milieu, remembered in common with his audience, while the poet, composing in briefer forms, had immediately to confront a fragmented and uncertain experience.

By the 1890's Yiddish fiction was firmly established in Eastern Europe. Yiddish poetry, by contrast, was still feeling its way and beginning simultaneously to appear in several parts of the globe. One of these, perhaps surprisingly, was the United States, where a group of "sweatshop poets" arose who were recent immigrants but whose work already betrayed a distance, even a rupture, from Old World Yiddish culture. Bringing socialist and anarchist ideologies with them from Russia, yet soon overwhelmed by their experience as immigrants, these sweatshop poets produced exhortatory and descriptive verse that was only slightly influenced by the Yiddish poets of Eastern Europe. On the contrary, it was the often crude work of the sweatshop poets in New York that would influence many of the Yiddish poets to come, both those who would immigrate to the United States and those who would remain in Europe. In the cramped and brief existence of Yiddish literature, the historical line of poetry is discontinuous, like an erratic zigzag.

We have therefore divided this anthology into a number of groupings, some of them obviously required by the nature of the material itself, and others improvised for the sake of convenience. The amount of space we have given the poets suggests, *very roughly*, both their standing in the Yiddish world and our own estimate of their value. There are poets central to the Yiddish tradition who defy translation, and these we have had to omit. With some, the references in their work are so esoteric or culturally "internal," requiring so intimate a knowledge of Jewish history and lore, that an English version would be all but meaningless. With others, the language is so rich in Hebraic components or local vernacular as to make translation impossible. And with still others, their characteristic work is in lengthy narrative and reflective forms, impossible to include in an anthology of this kind. (Among the important poets who fall into one or more of these categories are Abraham Lyessin, Menahem Boraisha, and Isaac Katzenelenson.) The early figures in the history of Yiddish poetry, we are frank to acknowledge, have here been scanted, mainly because translation would be tantamount to misrepresentation. Nevertheless, most of the main figures of modern Yiddish poetry can be found in these pages.

1 · THE LANGUAGE AND EARLY LITERATURE

For the Jews, Hebrew has always been *loshon hakodesh,* the sacred tongue. At least, however, since the time of the Second Temple, Hebrew has had to compete or coexist with a variety of languages and dialects that drove it out of the market place, if not the house of prayer. During the period of the Second Temple, Aramaic was the daily language of the Jews. After the fall of the Temple, the Jews remaining in Palestine began to adopt Greek as their mundane tongue. Many Jews in the Near East and North Africa have spoken Arabic for centuries. The Sephardic or Spanish Jews have used Ladino, a Spanish-derived language, in daily speech, while the Ashkenazic or Eastern Jews have used Yiddish. This bilingualism has not always made for peace in the Jewish community, since the orthodox have repeatedly fought against the penetration of the vernacular, which they took to signify, and with some reason, a threat of the profane. But since Jewish life has itself been so persistently torn between the urge to the sacred and the pressures of the profane, bilingualism has been almost inevitable—indeed, an indispensable means for regulating the tension between the two.

Yiddish first began to develop in the Rhine region between the tenth and twelfth centuries. Gradually the Jews adapted the High German of that time and place to their own needs, developing a language that, despite numerous detractors within and without the Jewish world, is a distinct linguistic entity. At the beginning, this language consisted mainly of German words transliterated into Hebrew characters; then the original German underwent changes in pronunciation and in meaning and syntax. Meanwhile, Hebrew was there, a resource from which to draw, a treasury of sanctified memories and associations.

Since the Jews were usually confined to narrow spaces for large portions of their lives, a new vocabulary reflecting their special experience was inevitable. And since the Jews of Europe, whatever their status in one or another country, always tried to maintain some relations with one another, foreign words from both West and East, from the Romance and Slavic groups, were gradually introduced. After the large-scale Jewish migrations eastward, to Poland and Russia, there followed a major infusion of Slavic elements into the language, so that to this day Slavic ranks only behind Hebrew and German as a source or component of Yiddish.

By the end of the thirteenth century, Yiddish was well on the way to being a language in its own right. In the eyes of the Jewish community, to be sure, it did not enjoy full equality with Hebrew; it served rather as a crutch with which to make one's way across the treacherous Diaspora. This uneasy relationship between languages would be maintained among European Jews until the beginning of our century. Yet Yiddish would prove itself to be remarkably virile and stubborn, and its survival over the centuries reflects the miracle of Jewish survival itself. Eclectic, endlessly assimilative, yet never allowing its identity to be destroyed, Yiddish continued to draw from almost every European and Near Eastern language; after the mass migration of Jews to America in the late nineteenth and early twentieth centuries, it gained a new and rich reinforcement from English.

Whatever the tensions between them, Yiddish and Hebrew were intimately linked. The comparison sometimes made between Jewish bilingualism and the bilingualism of European countries where Latin served as the language of the church is not really very useful. For Latin did become a dead language, relegated mainly to priests and scholars, while even at the lowest points of Jewish experience, when ignorance and poverty blighted the ghettos, Hebrew was known and used by considerable numbers of Jews. The Jewish community was never ready to accept the idea that religious discourse is a proper area for specialization, and every Jew, it was assumed, would know at least enough

Hebrew to recite his prayers and perhaps read a passage of the Talmud.

Under alien and temporal pressures, Hebrew was pushed out of "the week" and back into the Sabbath, but this in no way decreased the veneration the Jews felt toward it; on the contrary, the language was thereby raised to a still more honored place.* Very probably, this was the only way Hebrew could be preserved through centuries of dispersion. But preserved it was, and when Yiddish came, it was not as a replacement but an addition.

Like the language itself, the early literature in Yiddish can be traced to three major sources: traditional pietistic writings in Hebrew; secular writings and folk materials of the surrounding gentile cultures; and the experience of dispersion, exile, and persecution.

The very earliest Yiddish literature of which we have some traces is an oral and manuscript literature. Among the medieval Jews there grew up bardic recitations, derived from the German *Spielmann* stories. Such popular German romances as the *Hildebrand Lied* and *Dietrich von Bern* were adapted into Yiddish and recited or sung by Jewish troubadours. Gradually and subtly, these epics, romances, and stories were given a somewhat Jewish flavor. References to Christian myth and ceremony were cut out, physical violence and struggle underplayed, the value systems of chivalry subjected to humane modulation, and at times seemingly incongruous elements of tragic feeling, barely present in the originals, were introduced into the Yiddish adaptations.

The Jewish troubadours and scribes drew from their own culture as well. A few Yiddish lyrics have survived this early period; they express, with homely earnestness, the burden of sustaining Jewish religious life in exile. Such poems, together with translations of and glosses on Biblical passages, were sometimes collected in manuscript anthology by prosperous Jewish women. Though of limited intrinsic value, these writings, which waver between predictable piety and glimpses of folk experience, represent the first efforts to use Yiddish as a literary vehicle.

* In one of Peretz' stories, "Devotion Without End," the hero is punished for overbearing pride, and the worst punishment Peretz can conceive for him is that, at one stroke, he forgets all the Hebrew he knows.

Dr. Max Weinreich divides Yiddish poetry into several con-
venient periods:

Old Yiddish, 1400–1800, drawing linguistically mainly from German
and marked by folk simplicity, a kind of pre-literary verse;

East European, 1800–1900, containing the following materials: Ha-
sidic legends: indigenous folk songs; *Maskilishe folkslieder* or verses
composed by individual writers under the influence of the Haskalah
(Enlightenment), which are soon absorbed into the folk culture;
and the popular troubadour and *Badkhen* (marriage entertainer)
songs;

Modern Yiddish, composed by self-conscious artists, starting with
Peretz, Frug, and Abraham Reisen in Eastern Europe and the
"sweatshop poets" in the United States.

Dr. Weinreich warns against the simplified and widespread view
that "the older literature was religious and the newer worldly.
That is not right. . . . Old Yiddish writing was strongly char-
acterized by worldly elements,"* just as modern Yiddish poetry,
though emerging from a secularist atmosphere, still contains
strong religious elements.

Perhaps the first sustained work in Yiddish that has distinct
literary merit is the *Shmuel Bukh (Samuel Book),* which ap-
peared in the mid-sixteenth century, though its unknown author
wrote it at least a hundred years earlier. This epic poem elabo-
rates the Biblical stories of King David, celebrating feats of
Jewish heroism in a manner that makes David into a blend of
ancient monarch and medieval knight.

This shuttling between borrowed and indigenous materials is
characteristic of Yiddish writing in the early period: it seems to
reflect a lingering uncertainty as to the possibilities of the lan-
guage, an unformulated question as to its capacity for inde-
pendent life when flanked on one side by Hebrew and on the
other by the languages of Europe. After the invention of printing,
however, the use of Yiddish increased tremendously, both in
adaptations of stories and poems from adjacent cultures and as
a means of religious instruction and folk expression.

It was to the Jewish woman that most of these early printed
works were directed. For her there was no loss of dignity in read-

* Max Weinreich, *Bilder fun der Yiddisher Literaturgeshikhte.*

ing simplified Biblical commentaries in Yiddish, or in reciting the Psalms in homely Yiddish translation, or in mulling through the immensely popular *Tsenna Urenna*, a late sixteenth-century compendium of Biblical paraphrases in Yiddish prose and verse, together with homely exegesis, wise comments from contemporary sages, all woven into one text. It was not even considered unseemly for the Jewish woman to read something as frivolous as the Yiddish recasting of the King Arthur stories, which appeared in the sixteenth century.

The distinction we have suggested here, between borrowed and indigenous materials—between, say, the Yiddish version of the King Arthur stories and the *Tehinot*, collections of women's prayers in Yiddish that began to appear at the end of the sixteenth century—is strongly insisted upon by many Yiddish critics who wish to establish a clear line of Jewish tradition in the literature. Thus S. Niger, a leading Yiddish critic, makes a crucial distinction between two widely read Yiddish works of the sixteenth century. One of these is the *Bova Bukh*, by a gifted writer named Elijah Bokhur. A verse narrative in *ottava rima*, it consists of a free version of an Italian romance, itself an adaptation of the English tale of Bevys of Hampton. The other is the famous *Maase Bukh (Story Book)*, a collection of more than 250 tales drawn mainly from Talmudic sources but also including European folk material. Both were extremely popular and probably read by the same audience, but Niger insists that such translated romances as the *Bova Bukh* "are alien to the Jewish life-style, the Jewish cultural tradition. . . . They created readers or listeners for Yiddish; they did not create a Yiddish literature. They were greatly loved by Jewish women and the Jewish folk; but not every book that is popular is a folk book. . . . The alien *Bova Bukh* was popular, but the homely *Maase Bukh* was a folk book."* In any case, these two works mark the high point of Yiddish writing during the period of Old Yiddish.

In the middle of the eighteenth century, with the rise of Hasidism and during the early years of the nineteenth century, with the penetration of the Haskalah into Eastern Europe, there began an imposing renaissance of Yiddish literary imagination.

Hasidism helped prepare the way for modern Yiddish writing

---

* S. Niger, *Die Tsveishprakhikeit fun Unzer Literatur.*

by validating the language, by raising it to a plane of esteem as the companion of Hebrew within the Jewish world. Its use of Yiddish was spontaneous, natural, earthy, in sharp contrast to those Jewish intellectuals who a few decades later made gingerly efforts to turn from Hebrew, Russian, and German to Yiddish. Hasidic leaders like the Baal Shem Tov and Rabbi Nachman of Bratzlav were genuinely inspired poet-sages whose allegories and parables raised the tradition of Yiddish storytelling to a new level of moral and literary value. But the unique contribution of Hasidism to Yiddish literature was not merely that it lent prestige to the language or gave the Yiddish writers a reservoir of folk material; it was rather that by the twentieth century the Hasidic stories still seemed fresh, so that when Peretz turned to them he could feel the peculiar excitement that comes from drawing upon folk material already secure in the tradition yet still quick with the pulse of life. And for the succeeding poets, the Hasidic figures and stories have been a major source of dramatic interest.

By the late nineteenth century, when modern Yiddish literature came to the forefront of Jewish life, the folk imagination was still vivid. Yiddish literature is distinctive for its closeness to folk sources; it borrows heavily from folk sayings, folk legends, folk humor. The literature itself, written by self-conscious artists, cannot properly be said to be a folk literature, but much of its special charm comes from the fact that its moment of "classicism" in the late nineteenth century occurred when the folk materials were still alive for the literary imagination, yet the idea of self-conscious craft had begun to fascinate writers. A meeting of traditional and modern Yiddish literature draws simultaneously from the Hasidic wonder tales and nineteenth-century Russian fiction; from the homely verse of nineteenth-century Yiddish troubadours traveling from *shtetl* to *shtetl* and the romantic poetry of Heine and Pushkin, Byron and Lermontov.

During the nineteenth century there grew up in Eastern Europe a notable school of popular Yiddish minstrels and bards who composed their own verses, ranging in subject from vivid genre sketches to Haskalah-inspired satire of bigotry. One such minstrel, Velvl Zbarzher, moved beyond the usual domestic themes of the *badkhonim* to write lyrics on communal and political topics. At first he would appear in private homes, singing his ditties about love, wine, and pleasure; later he would perform professionally at inns and wine cellars. Contemporaneous with Zbarzher were the *Broder Zinger*, the Singers of Brod, who not only composed their own songs but also used pantomime and simple skits in their performances—a source of Yiddish poetry and Yiddish theater. Itzik Manger, the Yiddish poet who employed the traditional ballad with great skill and sophistication, acknowledged the *Broder Zinger* as a major source of his work.

Perhaps the most popular of these minstrels is Eliakim Zunzer, a bard from Vilna who composed some 600 songs. Beginning as a *badkhen*, he strove to transform the Yiddish minstrel into a more dignified figure, one whose verses would contain satiric and poignant comment on the plight of the exiled Jews. Inspired at first by the Haskalah, Zunzer moved in his later years to Zionism, and at the turn of the century came to America, where he composed songs about the life of the immigrants. Some of Zunzer's songs have been so popular as, in effect, to achieve the status of folk songs.

The Yiddish folk song has been an enormous influence on Yiddish poetry. Some of Abraham Reisen's lyrics were quickly put to music and adopted by the people as their own; the story is told that Reisen, once attending a Jewish gathering, remarked to his neighbor that he, Reisen, had written the song that was being sung, whereupon the neighbor indignantly rejected the notion that any single person, let alone one so modest in appearance, could have composed so beloved a song. In the lyrics of Mani Leib, the Yiddish folk song is consciously turned to sophisticated ends; and even in the modernist poetry of Jacob Glatstein one can still hear its echoes. *Rozhenkes mit mandln, die goldene pave, dos goldene tzigele* (raisins and almonds, the golden peacock, the golden little goat)—these presences of folk song,* known to anyone with the slightest Jewish background, weave their way through Yiddish poetry from start to finish.

Another element of Jewish folk lore that is precious to many

---

* The difficulty of drawing a clear line between Yiddish folk songs and those composed by individual lyricists is suggested by the fact that the enormously popular *Rozhenkes mit mandln*, which has achieved the status of folk song, was actually written by an individual writer, Mark Warshawsky.

Yiddish poets is the legend of Elijah. The most lovable character of Jewish faith and legend, Elijah descends to earth in humble dress and with mild speech; he cares only to help suffering men; he anticipates the Lord's coming, as well as seeming a partial recompense for His failure to come. To many Yiddish poets, including some, like Mani Leib, who are not explicitly religious, Elijah is a figure who can be made to stand for their emotional attachment to beliefs they no longer entirely accept; to other poets, like Itzik Manger, Elijah presents himself mainly as a familiar figure of Jewish domestic life—a friend of the afflicted.

The value of folk motifs in Yiddish poetry is somewhat equivocal. It has been all too easy for mediocre talents to fall back upon such familiar materials, as if the mere invocation or reference were enough to do the poet's work; but for the gifted writers, these motifs provide a wonderful resource for nuance, complication, and irony.*

2 · YIDDISH LITERATURE: SOME GENERAL OBSERVATIONS

As it makes its appearance in the late nineteenth century, Yiddish literature can be seen as the outcome of a meeting—at once affectionate and violent—between the traditional religious culture of the Eastern European Jews and the humanist Enlightenment that had gradually stumbled eastward in the preceding decades. Dr. Weinreich makes the point that both the Haskalah and Hasidism, though one was a movement of Enlightenment tinged with secularism and the other a movement of religious enthusiasm tinged with fundamentalism, served to hasten the breakdown of traditional Jewish life:

> There appeared a new epoch of struggle. Two enemies, the Haskalah and Hasidism, bombarded from opposite sides the fortress of a stultified past: the first with the weapons of mind, the second in the name of the heart.

Had secularist values not been brought to the Eastern European Jews through the Haskalah and later Zionism and Social-

* We have borrowed some passages in the preceding section from our Introduction to *A Treasury of Yiddish Stories* (New York: The Viking Press, 1954).

ism, it is doubtful that Yiddish literature—at least Yiddish litera-
ture as the work of self-conscious artists—could have developed
or survived. Yiddish would have continued to serve as the
mundane or street language of a people regarding itself as driven
into exile and looking upon that language as fit enough for the
weekday but to be brushed aside when the Sabbath brought a
fragile sanctification of Hebrew.

The truly orthodox understood that a crack in the monolith of
belief would sooner or later bring deep fissures, perhaps dis-
astrous splits, within the Jewish world. Isaac Bashevis Singer
describes the response of his father upon discovering that he,
Isaac, meant to be a secular writer:

> It was a great shock to my parents. They considered all the secular
> writers to be heretics, all unbelievers—they really were, too, most
> of them. To become a *literat* was to them almost as bad as becom-
> ing a *meshumed,* one who forsakes the faith. My father used to
> say that secular writers like Peretz were leading the Jews to heresy.
> He said everything they wrote was against God. Even though
> Peretz wrote in a religious vein, my father called his writing
> "sweetened poison," but poison nevertheless. And from his point of
> view, he was right. Everyone who read such books sooner or later
> became a worldly man and forsook the traditions. In my family, of
> course, my brother [the Yiddish novelist I. J. Singer] had gone first,
> and I went after him. For my parents, this was a tragedy.

One need only add that by the time the defenders of orthodoxy
had risen in alarm and complaint, the virus of skepticism had
already spread across the body of Eastern European Judaism. It
was too late.

If, however, the trend toward secularism had succeeded in
completely dominating the life of the Eastern European Jews, it is
again doubtful that Yiddish literature as we know it would have
been able to develop or survive. For a complete triumph of the
Enlightenment would have been possible only if those socio-
political handicaps that had been thrust upon the Eastern
European Jews had been utterly removed; and only if the tradi-
tion of faith and rabbinical authority had been completely de-
stroyed. That would have meant, in a sense, the "Americaniza-
tion" of Jewish life without a need to take the long journey to
America. But, in fact, nothing of the sort did or could happen.

There followed, instead, a curious and in some ways a wonder-

ful interregnum in the life of the Jews: the period of *Yiddishkayt,*
in which the opposing impulses of faith and skepticism stand
poised, locked in opposition yet sharing a community of culture.
This interregnum, which began about the middle of the nine-
teenth century and has not yet come to an end, found its setting
in czarist Russia, Poland between wars, and in various points of
Western exile and immigration, notably the United States. While
always aware of its precarious state, the spokesmen and artists of
Yiddishkayt—a cultural movement in which all the competing in-
tellectual tendencies were brought together under conditions
of maximum pressure—nevertheless had to assume as a premise
of their existence that the survival of Yiddish culture was not in
question. Today we know that its existence was very much in
question, indeed, that its very nature made survival problematic.
Only the ways in which it would actually be destroyed—through
the brutalities of Nazism and Stalinism, and also the gentleness
of American assimilation—could not quite have been foreseen.

One condition for the rise of Yiddish literature was that to the
rising young Jewish intelligentsia of Warsaw, Lodz, Vilna, and
the numerous *shtetl* peripheries the traditional religious culture
should remain powerful yet seem more and more inadequate,
both as ethical faith and social norm. At the same time, the
winds of the Enlightenment, sweeping across the airless streets
of the Pale, were promising secular freedom—yet were in reality
not strong enough to bring that freedom. The Jews had there-
fore to live in a historical moment characterized by frustration
and anxiety; the past could not die, nor the future come to birth.
The past remained vivid, even beautiful to many of those who
found themselves attacking it as obsolete, while the future en-
ticed, almost against their will, many of those who declared
themselves defenders of the past. It was a condition of Eastern
European Jewish life that every idea emerging out of it be brought
to absolute extreme and raging climax, even while, and probably
because, few of its ideas could be realized in actuality.

Orthodox believers knew themselves to be profoundly threat-
ened by the rise of secular writing, yet it would take a heart of
stone or a willful closing of Jewish ears not to be charmed by the
humor of Sholem Aleichem or the pathos of Abraham Reisen.
Who could resist them, even among the most fanatic of the ortho-

dox? Meanwhile, the younger writers making their pilgrimages to Warsaw, where Peretz opened his door and his heart to them, were often the sons of rabbis and learned men, often themselves *Yeshiva bokhurim* (religious students) in both physical and cultural flight from their youth. Even as they discussed Marx, Heine, and Nietzsche, they were still caught up, much more than they knew, in the tunes of prayer and the dialectic of Talmud. Had there been an atmosphere of true socio-political freedom, such as the Jews were more or less to find in America, there would surely have occurred a full-scale split between believers and skeptics. But in Eastern Europe, no matter how much they quarreled, sons against fathers, apostates against believers, they were still pressed together in poverty and danger. They *had* to live with one another. As a social experience this exacted a severe price—let us beware of romanticizing oppression and poverty! But for Yiddish literature it was a boon, making for density of feeling, sharpness of engagement, and an overwhelming, sometimes even claustrophobic, seriousness.

What this tense coexistence of past and future within the prison cell of the present often led to was a blend of tradition and experiment, faith and skepticism: only in analysis, only in the coolness of retrospect, can the two be distinguished. In the daily work of Yiddish literature there was an effort—remarkable because undertaken with so much self-awareness—to extract the best from, and perhaps create a new synthesis of, past and future. (Every literary generation may regard itself as transitional, but few have been so completely devoted to the idea of the transitional as the early Yiddish writers.) In his Hasidic and *folkstimmlikhe* stories, Peretz undertook this fusion of two modes of Jewish experience, trying to connect the folk voice of the past with his problematic vision of the future; and this is one reason, as one can now see, why he stood at the center of Yiddish cultural life.

Peretz became the commanding figure of the Yiddish world because, with his unique generosity of spirit and mind, he offered a worked-out idea: the idea of Jewish humanism. In all his invocations of Jewish tradition, in all his demands that the young Yiddish writers steep themselves in the Jewish tradition, Peretz was really urging a stringent kind of selectivity, such as would

lead to conscious choices and possible exclusions regarding the
inherited culture of the Jews. As a rule, tradition is most likely
to be invoked by those literary men who experience or feel threat-
ened by a loss of tradition. By contrast, those within the Jewish
community who had maintained an organic connection with the
religious past had no need to invoke the Jewish tradition. The
idea Peretz spoke for may now seem fragile and precarious, but
it was an idea that inspired, for example, the famous Yiddishist
conference held in Czernowitz, Romania, in 1908 at which an
array of Yiddish writers (Peretz, Reisen, Asch, Nomberg, Zhitlov-
sky, and others) came together, programmatically to declare their
adherence to Yiddish, not merely as a language meriting respect
in its own right but as the agent of a national-cultural ideal.
("The first conference devoted to the Yiddish language recog-
nizes Yiddish as a national tongue, the language of the Jewish
people, and demands for it political, communal, and cultural
equality. . . .")

Unavoidably, Jewish humanism would be fragmented and, in
its most ambitious goals, unfulfilled—mostly because it remained
and had to remain an idea, cut off from the possibilities and
complications of social power. It came into being because the
conditions for realizing it in the life of the Eastern European
Jews were just barely beginning to appear; yet had these condi-
tions been fully present or readily available, it might not have
survived for long. The sense of being trapped in a cultural-na-
tional limbo which the Jews, with a unique outburst of creative
ingenuity, would transform into an arena of fulfillment—this gave
urgency, drama, tension to the moment in which modern Yiddish
literature was born. For if Jewish humanism could seldom achieve
its realization in the day-to-day life of the Eastern European
Jew, and if, indeed, it had often to cast itself as a kind of inspired
luftmensh dreaming impossible dreams, then it found in Yiddish
literature a haven of affection, a surrogate home enabling it to
survive as a cultural value long after its historical matrix had
been shattered.

It was along these lines of speculation that the Yiddish critic
B. Rivkin advanced the theory that Yiddish literature, more
through necessity than choice, must function as a substitute for
a "would-be territory," a nation struggling to be born. This meant

that many of the communal needs which for other peoples were met by the nation had somehow, among the Jews, to be satisfied by literature. In the interregnum during which the hold of religion had begun to weaken and the idea of nationality not yet found its grip, Yiddish literature became a central means of collective expression for the Eastern European Jews, satisfying some of the needs—through yearning and vicarious statement—of both religion and the idea of nationality. In the absence of a free and coherent national life, Yiddish literature had to provide the materials for a sense of national identity. And even as, in honesty, it reported the realities of both *shtetl* and city, realities often deeply shocking and depressing, it had also to nurture and exalt collective aspirations. From many points of view, this was an impossible task for any literature, let alone one as frail and youthful as Yiddish; yet something of the moral seriousness—though little of the metaphysical boldness—that we admire in nineteenth-century Russian writing is also to be found in Yiddish poetry and prose.

Yiddish literature released a profound yearning for a return not to the supremacy of Hebrew as a language but to those conditions of life that would make possible a revival of Hebrew: that is, for an end to the dispersion. During most of the life span of Yiddish writing, this hope could not be realized—and the distinctive ground note of Yiddishism is one that brings together, as a kind of ironic double-stop, both hope and hopelessness. The Yiddish writer did not work in a culture sufficiently at ease with the world, or even with itself, to allow for the kind of art that abandons any effort to reform—or perhaps even to reflect—the world in which it appears. The sense of aesthetic distance that allows writers to direct their energies toward formal problems of literature was not available to Yiddish writers, certainly not during the early "classical" period, and as it would turn out, not even in those later moments when Yiddish poets struggled earnestly to achieve a "pure art." From birth the Yiddish poet was an "engaged" writer, and in that sense, if none other, he had indeed been chosen. He knew to whom his heart was pledged.

It was pledged neither to the world nor to God, but to the people who believed in God or had only yesterday believed, or for whom the vision of God was inseparable from the vision of peoplehood. This is one reason that a recurrent theme in Yiddish poetry is the quarrel with God *(krign zich mit Got)*, a quarrel undertaken with intimacy, affection, and harshness. If God had lapsed in His obligation toward the Jews, the Yiddish writers would not lapse in their role as spokesmen for the Jews addressing God: and this role, it should be stressed, was assumed both by believers and skeptics. The tradition of *krign zich mit Got* goes straight back to the famous chant of Rabbi Levi Yitzkhok of Berditchev, an eighteenth-century leader of Hasidism, who addresses to God an utterly loving indictment:

> Good morning to You, Lord of the Universe!
> I, Levi Yitzkhok, son of Sarah of Berditchev,
> Have come with a claim against You
> On behalf of your people Israel.
> What do you have against your people Israel?
> Why do you afflict your people Israel?
> And I, Levi Yitzkhok, son of Sarah of Berditchev, say:
> I shall not stir from here.
> From this spot I refuse to stir,
> There must be an end to this,
> The exile must come to an end!
> Magnified and sanctified be His Name!

Levi Yitzkhok appears later in a poem by Itzik Manger, who imagines the Hasidic rabbi after the holocaust, angered with God and silent in his anger. A somewhat similar note is struck by H. Leivick—a kind of muted Prometheanism—in the excerpt from his poetic drama *Job* which appears in this volume. And in the remarkable group of poems written by Jacob Glatstein after the holocaust one can again hear echoes of Levi Yitzkhok's quarrel with God, this time as the poet commiserates with a desolate God and embraces his shoulders as a fellow-survivor. *Der Got fun mein umgloybn iz prekhtig,* the God of my disbelief is magnificent, writes Glatstein.

In the historical moment when Yiddish literature begins to flourish, the question of belief as a formulated problem seems barely to signify in the fiction and poetry themselves despite the ferocity with which it is discussed in the culture. God might be denied by many writers, yet He continued to inhabit their work, equally real to believers and disbelievers. For once mere opinions are left behind, the experience of the Jews in the last 150 years is so overwhelming, so beyond discussion or even comprehension, that for poets writing in Yiddish there can only be a return, again and again, to the crushing fact of that experience itself.

3 · THE EARLY POETS: FOLK, NATIONAL, LABOR

Modern Yiddish poetry begins to appear almost simultaneously in Eastern Europe and the United States. Perhaps the more interesting, both intrinsically and as an influence upon the later writers, is the work of the pioneer "sweatshop" or labor poets who wrote in the United States during the last years of the nineteenth century.

The first volume of Yiddish poetry to be published in this country appeared in 1877, the work of a somewhat unorthodox rabbi named Jacob Sobel, who had been influenced both by the Haskalah and Jewish radicalism. Composed in poor Yiddish, with a heavy German adulteration, Sobel's poems are only of historical interest, reflecting the confusions of a whole generation of Jews uprooted from Old World styles of life yet sadly unsettled in the new world.

The large-scale immigration of Eastern European Jews began in the 1880's, and it was then that, for the first time, there grew up a Jewish working-class in major American cities. Previously, the small number of Eastern European Jews coming to New York had scraped out a living at marginal businesses, such as "customer peddling" or door-to-door selling of dry goods. By and large the immigrants of the late 1800's came from the lower social and cultural levels of the Eastern European Jewish world; they found in America relief from persecution and escape from conscription, but also conditions of life that were usually wretched; and the great majority of them were doomed to waste their lives in the sweatshops as ill-paid garment workers. Ties with old-country life were ruptured if not entirely broken—in part because there were still not enough immigrants here to form a self-confident and self-sufficient community, and in part because Eastern European Jewish life remained comparatively secure, not yet threatened by the loss of its most vigorous young people to the New World. And while many immigrants clung to the religious

forms they had inherited, these proved difficult to maintain with
the old dignity and conviction. Both in response to their life in
America and because they had brought across with them some
of the new political ideologies, these immigrants were often at-
tached to a severe and intransigent sort of radicalism. Yiddish
newspapers, some socialist or anarchist in opinion, sprang up in
the cities, speaking to the trials of the immigrants.

The circumstances of these immigrant Jews were ripe for a new
kind of literary expression, a fiction and poetry that would be
blunt in speech, tendentious in politics, breaking away from the
quiet passivity of traditional Jewish folk material, unsophisticated
in tone and technique but stormy in speech, and directed toward
the surging emotions of the Jewish masses. The sweatshop or
labor poets who now came to the forefront and for almost two
decades dominated Yiddish writing were men of varying skill
and education, but about one thing there can be no doubt: they
arose organically from Jewish immigrant life. They spoke fiercely
to the sentiments of large numbers of Jewish workers, and their
tremendous popularity rested on the directness, the urgency with
which they satisfied the needs of their readers. As the Yiddish
critic B. Rivkin writes: *

> Despite European influences, American Yiddish literature [at the
> end of the nineteenth century] had a largely autonomous begin-
> ning. . . . A huge mass of potential Yiddish readers was gathering
> in the cities. Even if they had not wished to, they really had no
> choice but to read Yiddish. Yiddish was the only language that
> could gradually lead them into the life of the new country. Those
> who came from the *shtetl*, where you could count the number of
> people at a glance, and where most were known acquaintances—
> these immigrants felt themselves lost in a "desert" where men
> seemed like grains of sand and the new language, English, was
> difficult to learn. So they naturally turned back to Yiddish. . . . Even
> complete illiterates—and there were quite a few among the early
> immigrants—as well as the numerous half-literates, who could spell
> out a few words in the Hebrew prayer books, now troubled to learn
> the alphabet in order at least to be able to read a daily paper in
> Yiddish.
>
> The first immigrant generation and most of the writers were Jews
> without Jewish memories or traditions. . . . Even the few who did

* B. Rivkin, *Die Grunt-Tendentsen fun Yiddisher Literatur in America.*

maintain traditions forgot them in their flight from the pogroms. . . .
They shook them off in the boat when they came across the seas.
They emptied out their memories. If you would speak with dis-
respect, they were no more than a mob. If you would speak with
respect, they were a vigorous people.

Within a few years of arriving in America, as their lives set-
tled into some kind of routine, the Jewish immigrants began to
acquire strong cultural appetites. Rivkin continues:

> Poems and stories helped them to understand their new environ-
> ment, the people about them, and most of all themselves. They
> sought in literature the same thing they wanted in a newspaper:
> a way of becoming somewhat less of a "greenhorn," a way of es-
> caping a little from their loneliness. And when poem and story gave
> them a certain enlightenment about mankind in general, the green-
> horns began to feel they were becoming a little Americanized—
> soon they might feel at home here, just as in the old country. They
> began to search out the "literary evening" which offered poetry
> readings and storytelling and would soon become a major folk
> institution. And then the newspaper brought the "literary evening"
> directly to their homes.

Four writers stand out in the sweatshop school (though only
one, Rosenfeld, is included in this collection), and each is sharply
distinctive. Morris Winchevsky—*der Zeyde* (the grandfather)—
was the only one among them to bring a rich Jewish culture to
America. Speaking in the accents of a *Maskil,* or Enlightener,
Winchevsky bridged the gap between the Haskalah and Jewish
Socialism. For a time he worked in the German socialist move-
ment, then became a friend of William Morris, and like many
other immigrants, found in London a political and cultural way
station where he began to write the declamatory odes—calls to
international Socialism and justice for the oppressed—that made
him enormously popular with the Yiddish public. In 1894 he
arrived in the United States, already known among Yiddish read-
ers as a tribune of the people. Winchevsky employed complicated
rhyme schemes and sometimes gave vent to his gift for satiric
comment; some of his poems offer rather generalized pictures of
Jewish poverty (he composed a Yiddish version of Thomas Hood's
"Song of the Shirt"); but in the main his poetry shows little dis-
tinctively Jewish quality. He was a writer of the moment.

A very different and more poignant figure is David Edelstadt.

In him the disintegration of traditional Jewishness, already under way in both Eastern Europe and immigrant America, was all but complete. As a youth he knew no Yiddish at all, but instead wrote Russian verses. Only after coming to the United States did he learn Yiddish, and never with complete mastery. An ardent anarchist, he wrote strictly political and tendentious poems; his main concern was to stir his fellow-workers to rebellion. In Edelstadt's poems language, form, rhythm are all inferior, and at best derivative; yet, at least in Yiddish, they yield a distinctive pathos, for they are entirely indigenous, almost as if they came out of the collective audience itself, feverish with trouble and idealism. Dead at twenty-six, this fiery rebel—"even his nightingale," remarks Rivkin, "sings anarchist proclamations"—is that rarity of rarities: a genuine working-class poet.

The most popular of the sweatshop poets and probably the most popular Yiddish poet ever to write in the United States was Morris Rosenfeld, a man of large talents and flaring personality. Endowed with a gift for dramatic rhetoric, as well as for dramatizing the sufferings of the Jewish immigrant, Rosenfeld was a poet of major potential. His radicalism was not as ideological as that of Winchevsky, nor as selfless as that of Edelstadt; it was the radicalism of the Jewish masses brought to a high pitch of pathos, the outcry of a generation that felt lost and cared more about its plight than its programs. Later in his career Rosenfeld would turn from Socialism to Jewish nationalism. The distinction between the two, clear to us now, was by no means always clear at the turn of the century. Both ideologies were efforts to cope with a collective experience at once bewildering, tragic, and hopeful.

"I sing about what moves me," said Rosenfeld, and often he would recite with florid gesture and sing aloud his poems before audiences of adoring Jewish workers. The *badkhen* tradition of an Eliakim Zunzer could still be seen in his declamation, though given a new urgency by Rosenfeld's immersion in the immigrant experience. The Yiddish critic A. Tabachnick remarks that where a poet like Winchevsky "went to the Jewish masses, Rosenfeld came from the Jewish masses," and where Winchevsky wrote socialist-internationalist hymns, Rosenfeld wrote "Jewish-social" outcries, authentic outpourings of the immigrant experience. In

Rosenfeld, writes Tabachnick, there was already present an in-cipient "I-poet," that is, a poet of personal lyricism, but the time for such a writer had not yet come. "To become a major poet in Rosenfeld's day one needed to have, or know how to develop in oneself, the poetic strength, the stylistic resources, by means of which to express what was essentially social. . . . Until the twentieth century, the lyrical 'I-poem' was a second- and indeed third-class genre in Yiddish poetry."

For a decade Rosenfeld worked in a sweatshop, sharing the miseries of the Jewish proletariat. His most famous poems, set to stirring music and once known to every Yiddish reader through-out the world, still communicate a somewhat sentimental elo-quence and force. He was the first Yiddish poet to achieve fame beyond the Jewish world, and like a number of later Yiddish writers he found it an unsettling experience. Early in the twen-tieth century his poems were translated by Leo Weiner, a pro-fessor of Slavic history at Harvard and one of the earliest historians of Yiddish literature. For a time Rosenfeld even enjoyed a certain vogue among English readers and upper-class Jews of German origin, who helped him financially and patronized his readings. But he soon had to return to the world of Yiddish, where he now tried to earn his living by working for the newspapers. Unstable and capricious, first the spoiled darling of the ghetto and then bitterly having to confront his unpopularity when a later genera-tion of Yiddish poets declared his work coarse and obvious, Ro-senfeld experienced the tragedy of a writer who speaks only for his own generation. Yet there is truth in the praise given him by Moishe Leib Halpern, one of the Yiddish poets who at first had joined in mocking him:

> Rosenfeld is in the blood of every one of us. Thousands of voices of the awakened proletariat echoed his every utterance. His lan-guage is not as refined as that of the later poets, but finally that does not make them better. . . .

The fourth of the sweatshop poets, Joseph Bovshover, arrived in America at the age of eighteen, became a furrier, and joined the anarchist movement. He soon was composing revolutionary verses, somewhat in the manner of Edelstadt, but with a psychic distance that would result in a sharply different course as a poet.

Bovshover learned English, studied American literature briefly at Yale, came under the spell of Shelley, and began to translate his own poems into English for the anarchist magazine, *Liberty*. Not a natural fighter like the other sweatshop poets, he experienced severe emotional difficulties even as a young man. One critic has called him "the first Bohemian in Yiddish poetry." Though best known for his radical verse, Bovshover began to show in his later work outcroppings of individuality, a romantic estrangement from all collective enterprises. In his late twenties he was removed to a hospital because of severe depression, and there remained until his death in 1915.

For twentieth-century readers brought up on modern literature, the work of these sweatshop poets may not prove satisfying. It emerged from the life of the Jewish masses, as part of a genuinely popular culture, and it never found a secure resting place between folk expression and sophisticated literature. The sweatshop poets are naive writers, but naive in ways that yield, within the Jewish tradition, a certain cumulative strength. Arising out of the immigrant experience, and reflecting the losses that followed on the rupture with traditional Jewish culture, these poets must be read with a greater tolerance for sentiment and a stronger belief in the idea of the poet as collective spokesman than many readers are now likely to possess.

Nothing could, in any case, be more mistaken than to confuse their crude but genuine verse with the kind of "proletarian writing" that appeared, both in English and Yiddish, during the thirties. Edelstadt and Rosenfeld wrote directly out of their own experience, even if thereby revealing the limitations of their culture. At their most sentimental and propagandistic, they were never middle-class intellectuals engaged in poetic slumming. Winchevsky and Edelstadt would never have claimed they were sacrificing a poetic gift to a political cause: such a distinction would have seemed unreal to them. For Rosenfeld and Bovshover the idea of a poetic career apart from "the movement" may have begun to seem a tempting prospect; but they saw little choice, they felt themselves caught in the urgencies of their situation. And if these writers did indeed sacrifice their talents, they seldom complained, for they still saw the fate of the individual writer as inseparable from that of the collective culture.

There were of course growing connections between Yiddish

poetry in America and Yiddish poetry in Eastern Europe. Books published on one continent were bought and read on the other— at this point, most Yiddish book publishing was still in the old country. In 1894 there appeared in the New York *Arbayter Tseitung*, a Yiddish radical paper, a poem by Peretz clearly indicating that he had been following the sweatshop poets with interest: "A poem one can write/ That will move stones and mountains/ That will ring through all of Poland/ That will make the whole world tremble./ Rhymes and ideas I have in plenty/ But regretfully I have no hero." Winchevsky soon answered: "In our midst/ Your wise and beautiful muse/Would find a true hero/ In a proletarian blouse."*

The interweaving of socialist and national themes—both desperate responses to the crisis of Jewish life at the turn of the century—found its strongest expression in a group that may be regarded as "transitional" Yiddish poets. Abraham Lyessin, Yehoash, and Abraham Reisen were poets of greater self-consciousness than the sweatshop poets. The simple exhortation and didacticism of the earlier writers is now abandoned, and the slogans of socialist internationalism are looked upon with a somewhat more critical, even ironic, eye. Lyessin, Yehoash and Reisen are deeply grounded in the traditions of the Jewish past and the knotty immediacies of the Jewish present: they represent a healing of the rupture between Old and New World Jewish life. All of them strive for a greater melodiousness, a purer diction, a less obtrusive metric than their predecessors.

Lyessin was primarily a poet of ethical declamation, admired for the seriousness of his tone—no longer, like Winchevsky, a journalist in verse, but rather an essayist in verse, forever returning to the glories of the Jewish past. As a poet, Yehoash was caught between the clashing impulses of past and present, traditional lyricism and modernist lyrics, folk-like singing and idiosyncratic speech. Sometimes he wrote pure nature poems, perhaps the first in Yiddish to apprehend the external world as an object of beauty in its own right, and certainly the first to yield to romantic pantheism. Sometimes he composed lyric exotica, as in the Chinese poems that appear in this book. Sometimes he ventured into topical verse. But always he was an unsettled writer. His finest achievement is the first complete translation of the

* This exchange is quoted and discussed in S. Niger's book on Peretz.

Old Testament into Yiddish, a work in which he could submit himself to the discipline of a great text and thereby escape the conflict of impulses that went on within him.

Abraham Reisen is the first major lyricist in Yiddish. His lyrics, most of them employing simple rhyme patterns and a regular four-beat metric, draw heavily upon Yiddish folk songs and poetry. Though an educated man who knew and loved Heine, Pushkin, and Nekrasov, and who would remain under the spell of nineteenth-century romanticism throughout his long career, Reisen was ultimately, and at his best, a poet crystallizing the feelings and values of *Yiddishkayt*. Anyone who wishes to grasp the world outlook of the Eastern European Jew, both in the *shtetl* and in the immigrant world, must turn to Reisen. The anti-heroism, the anti-Prometheanism of *Yiddishkayt* finds in Reisen's prose sketches and poems—fragile in structure and composed, as it were, in profile rather than full face—its classical expression. The sanctity of the poor, the celebration of *dos klayne menshele* (the little man), the urgency and pathos of revolt, the transcience of beauty, the shy budding of a puritan romanticism, the ingathering of familiars: these are Reisen's themes. Few Yiddish writers knew so well the secret life of the *shtetl*, the psychology of the Jewish householder, the nostalgia of the Jewish immigrant. So thoroughly is Reisen immersed in his culture, so completely does he find himself at home in its limits, that both his poems and stories depend heavily on the tacit cooperation of an audience expected to fill in the details he supposes them completely to possess. It is an economy possible only to a writer in the most fundamental rapport with his audience; the economy of a writer with a sense of identity so firm and unasserted as to make the explicit seem almost an indelicacy. No wonder many of Reisen's lyrics were soon put to music and accepted by Yiddish audiences as if they were folk songs! Jacob Glatstein writes about Reisen that Jewish audiences would lovingly applaud his appearances even before he began to read, for something of his ironic affection seemed to shine out of his face. And this relation to the audience is not at all that of a Rosenfeld, who is, finally, a "natural" arising out of the folk and never really moving beyond the folk. Nor is it the relationship which, only a few years after Reisen appears on the American scene, will develop between the modernist Yiddish poets and a Jewish readership ill-prepared to receive them. The miracle of a Reisen is not that he derives from the people, but that he remains at harmony with them, coming and leaving them, always distinct from yet always able to return to their inner life. Precisely because he regards being a Jew as a "natural" condition of life, beyond query or challenge, his poems and stories take his culture utterly for granted: they neither explain nor justify.

Reisen's poems emanate from a quiet flash, a brief perception, an ironic turn—what is called in Yiddish a *kneytch,* literally, a crease, but suggestive of a slight surprise, a sudden turn of sadness or twist of bitterness. His poems grow subtler in technique as he keeps writing—he is enormously productive, and sometimes succumbs either to flatness, mere genre notations, or to self-imitations, a predictability of tone. He learns to soften his rhymes and modulate his music—at times, very slightly, he reminds one of Robert Burns in his simplicity and A. E. Housman in his melancholy; but essentially he remains throughout his career a unified sensibility: tender but not at all soft, free from romantic illusion but not at all given to Promethean gesture.

The first-person singular figures strongly in Reisen's poems, and there is a distinctive tone, a mixture of sweetness and tartness, in his verse; but it is still an impersonal "I." One could no more imagine Reisen indulging in a poetic confession of personal sin than admitting into his work the violence and perversity that obsess the modernist writer. Admired by those who come after him, he is a powerful influence, yet an influence strongly resisted, like a father beloved but denied. The poets who follow him, as B. Rivkin writes, "those who are more individualistic than collective, could take Reisen as their model only for a short while, because . . . they had to create for themselves a lyric through their personal struggle, and for this Reisen could not completely be their guide."

4 · MODERN YIDDISH POETRY: DIE YUNGE

The beginnings of a distinctively modern Yiddish poetry can be dated with precision. In 1907 a group of immigrants, new to America and feeling their isolation very strongly, started to publish a small periodical called *Yugend (Youth).* Some of these

young men had begun to write while still in Europe, but none
had yet developed a distinctive style or literary personality. They
had of course been influenced by earlier Yiddish writing, espe-
cially by the lyric verse of Reisen; but what would soon make
them a revolutionary force within Yiddish literature was that they
refused the burdens of political commitment and denied the
obligation to speak in behalf of national ideals or as the voice of
collective sentiments. Never to be at home with either America or
the English language, these ambitious young men nonetheless
turned to world literature and, most of all, to the ideas of aesthetic
autonomy and symbolist refinement then sweeping through it.
In the tenements of the Lower East Side, while hurrying to and
from work in the shops, they read with eagerness the modern
European poets, the romantics, impressionists, and symbolists.
Though sharing the lot of millions of Jewish immigrants and in
their poems and fiction never able completely to detach them-
selves from the preoccupations—if you wish, the provincialism—
of the immigrant world, these young men really lived, when they
were most free imaginatively, in the lofty spaces of European
poetry. As one of them, Reuben Iceland, would later recall:

> Most deeply satisfying to us were the alien poets we were then en-
> countering for the first time; we learned the most from the Russian,
> German, Polish, and French moderns. Baudelaire, Verlaine, and
> Rimbaud, whom we could read only in translation, became our
> daily poetic fare, and so too did Sologub, Bryusov, and Blok, and
> Liliencron, Dehmel, Rilke, and Hofmannsthal. With Stefan George
> and Theodor Storm we became acquainted somewhat later. . . .

Meeting together in cafés after work, these young writers soon
developed a common aesthetic position, to which some of them,
as collaborators in annuals and little magazines, would remain
faithful throughout their lives. In poetry the leading figures were
Mani Leib, Zisha Landau, Reuben Iceland, Joseph Rolnick, and
Moishe Leib Halpern; in prose Joseph Opatashu, David Ignatow,
and A. Raboy. At first *Die Yunge* (The Young Ones) was a term
of contempt bestowed by the older Yiddish writers; but after a
year or two they accepted this label with the pride of the dis-
sident literary group which wishes above all else to establish its
distinctiveness. Some important Yiddish poets, like Halpern and
Leivick, merely brushed against *Die Yunge* and then went their

own ways; but what they all shared for a time was a rejection of the earlier tendentious writing. *Die Yunge* directed their main polemical fire against the idea of submerging Yiddish poetry in political journalism and national declamations; they wished to free it from the crushing weight of ethicism; and they felt, as Landau wittily remarked, that until their appearance Yiddish poetry had been little more than "the rhyme department of the Jewish labor movement."

These young poets had been touched, like most intelligent Jewish youth in Eastern Europe, by the socialist ideals of the Bund and the revolutionary ferment of Russia; but they came to America after the failure of the Russian revolution of 1905, when moods of defeat swept through the Jewish intelligentsia. The rejection of inflated rhetoric was therefore not merely a sound aesthetic response; it also reflected, if not disillusion with political ideals, then a sense of weariness and resignation in a bad time. One of Mani Leib's most beautiful lyrics, *Shtiller, Shtiller* (translated in this book as "Hush and hush—no sound be heard"), is simultaneously a credo in behalf of a poetry of nuance, a kind of allegorical reflection on the state of modern Jewish life and a statement about the Messianic expectation that runs through Jewish life: a statement, as Iceland remarks, in which "resignation is raised to heroism."

Though leftward in political sympathies, most of *Die Yunge* kept apart from the polemics and journalistic excitements of the immigrant Jewish world. If occasionally they did serve as the voice of collective aspirations, it was not by intent but simply because they were being loyal to their own experience. Their Jewishness was essentially cultural; they drew heavily on traditional materials: Mani Leib on folk songs and legends (especially the Elijah motif) and Landau on Hasidic tales. From Reisen they borrowed simple lyrical forms and the first-person singular as a legitimate presence in Yiddish verse; but finally they had to go beyond Reisen, transforming his generic and impersonal "I" into a distinct and personal "I." With *Die Yunge* the voice of the poet —his voice in its own right, quite apart from Jewish problems or destinies—comes through in fullness: the voice of the poet as it might reflect moodiness or sensual pleasure, despair or boredom, sanctioned or illicit responses.

If by now commonplace in Western literature, the literary program of *Die Yunge* was revolutionary within the Yiddish world. The aesthetic of self-sufficiency is one that could never be fully realized by *Die Yunge*. But when it was announced in the years before the First World War, it met with much resistance from older Yiddish writers, who were frightened by the innovations of Mani Leib and Landau, as also from Yiddish publicists, who sensed that these muted poets, more concerned with a musical phrase than a popular incitement, were never likely to appeal to the ordinary reader. And indeed a public raised on Winchevsky and Edelstadt was ill-prepared for Mani Leib. *Die Yunge* were the first, though by no means the last, Yiddish writers who accepted as an unavoidable condition of their creative lives that they had to remain cut off from the mass of Yiddish readers.

Deliberately setting out to purify the Yiddish language, *Die Yunge* expelled from their poems both newspaper vulgarisms and *Deutschmarish*, those Germanisms beloved of earlier writers that made for effects of oratorical sententiousness. They were chary in employing Hebraisms because they knew that for a Yiddish writer, employing a Biblical phrase or rabbinical locution can often be a lazy substitute for creating his own image. They faced, in short, the problem not merely of creating a modern poetry but of simultaneously creating the very language of that poetry, since both in America and Europe Yiddish was still in a state of uncertainty and flux.

As prosodists, *Die Yunge* were not very unorthodox. They were devoted to metrical regularities and proprieties; they experimented not so much with forms (though a few tried their hand at European stanzaic patterns) as with language, playing upon the infinitely flexible Yiddish vocabulary in a way no earlier poets had dreamed of doing. They were much concerned, more than most American or European twentieth-century poets, with the musicality of verse, constantly revising their poems to make them smoother and more melodious, a pattern of modulated sound that was meant to be pleasing in its own right. In retrospect, it seems clear that they were entirely right in this emphasis: for while most of them expressed a thoroughly romantic sensibility, drawing heavily upon nineteenth-century European models, they did not have strong classical predecessors in Yiddish against whom to thrust themselves in reaction and rebellion. It was therefore necessary for *Die Yunge,* even while proclaiming their modern distinctiveness, also to establish their own poetic models and boundaries; they had, in a sense, to do the work of both classicism and romanticism. It is not by chance that in the critical essays of Iceland, the theoretician of the group, the term "limitation" appears over and over again.

At least in one important respect, the program of *Die Yunge* was at odds with the poetry they actually wrote. They claimed to be largely indifferent to the demands of subject matter, but it now seems clear that what they really meant was that they were in rebellion against the subject matter of past Yiddish poetry: its heavy didacticism and social utilitarianism, its smothering ethicism and romantic-heroic bombast such as could be recited "with stirring effect" at public gatherings. They wished to write a personal and muted poetry—chamber music coming after brass bands. They understood that this seemingly modest desire would bring them into permanent opposition to dominant voices in a community not only obsessed with its destiny but still marked by strong puritanical reticence and ethical strictness. As late as 1925, when the original cadre of *Die Yunge* was publishing a literary journal called *Der Inzel (The Island),* a title taken, not by accident, from a periodical issued by the German symbolists, Landau would still feel obliged to remark in his caustic way: "We suffer from an epidemic of profound subject matter [in Yiddish poetry]. It is considered a scandal to wife and child if we so much as treat an ordinary event." And in a passage that could have been duplicated in almost every language of the world, he polemicized:

> The prophet, the preacher, the politician have distant goals; distant and often obscure. And frequently calculation takes the place of goals. Only we, the aesthetes, have no goals and no purposes. Certainly no calculations. The tree blooms—the tree is beautiful. . . . Everything that is here is beautiful; and beautiful because it is here. Ugly is what is still to come, still to be born. This is the truth known to all who live with their senses.*

Live with their senses: the phrase, by now so commonplace in Western culture and even a crutch for the mindless and the in-

---

* Zisha Landau, "Far'n Kuvit fun Vort," *Der Inzel,* March 1925.

dolent, could still arouse discomfort in the Yiddish world. It seemed to suggest something frivolous and gentile, even "decadent." Indeed, the term "decadent" was often used against *Die Yunge* by hostile critics, though, as it must seem today, with complete irrelevance. If anything, these poets are now likely to strike us as writers of singular purity and even innocence. Despite a mild Bohemianism and a wish to endow their harried lives with a romantic flavor, *Die Yunge* never broke away, never really could break away, from the common patterns of Jewish immigrant life.

What they said, and the ways in which they wrote their poems, did signify, however, a new relationship between Yiddish poets and Yiddish audience. *Die Yunge* were no longer folk heroes, as Rosenfeld had been and Reisen still was. Like modern poets of every culture, they suffered the burden of isolation, the pain of ridicule and neglect. At least in the early years, the Yiddish newspapers were closed to them and Jewish institutions indifferent. They had no choice but to publish their annuals and short-lived magazines; indeed, the little magazine as an institution in Yiddish literary life begins mostly with *Die Yunge,* first with *Yugend* in 1907, then with *Shriften* in 1912, and finally, in the twenties and thirties, with a considerable number of journals.

Yet if the formal claims of *Die Yunge* now seem mainly an echo of the programs issued in such abundance by groups of writers throughout Europe and America during the first few decades of this century, their situation was notably and poignantly different. They dreamed of being pure poets; they saw themselves as distant and unrecognized cousins to the great European poets from Pushkin to Rilke (they had little knowledge of American poetry, which in any case was not exactly flourishing during the years before the First World War). But they were also poverty-stricken immigrants, and some would remain workers for the bulk of their lives. Mani Leib was a shoemaker and for a time a laundryman, Landau began as a house painter, Leivick worked for many years as a paper hanger, and Halpern was a waiter and Jack-of-all-trades.

Nothing else could underscore more sharply the uniqueness of their position and the reason they finally could not become "pure poets" in Yiddish. Imagine in any other literature the turn to impressionism and symbolism being undertaken by a shoemaker and a house painter, a paper hanger and a waiter; the dismissal of the social muse led by men who themselves labored in factories every day! Proletarian aesthetes, Parnassians of the sweatshop—this was the paradox and the glory of *Die Yunge*. As late as 1934, when Leivick had become a world-recognized poet with work translated into most European languages, he could be seen in the streets of New York carrying his paint bucket and wall paper. And the Bohemianism of these poets, tame enough by later standards, had still to be enacted within the tight confines of the immigrant Jewish world. As Iceland would recall: *

> The majority of *Die Yunge* were shop workers. To miss a day's pay often meant not to have a pair of shoes for one's child or be short three dollars toward the rent. Yet when we came into The Basement [a café on East Broadway], we found the gang, though we knew each of us should be in the shop. Several of *Die Yunge* were paper hangers and upholsterers, and it wasn't unusual that in the midst of his work one of them would step off the ladder and come to the café flecked with paint on his clothes and face. Many a day I had my lunch in the shop out of fear that if I went out to eat in the café I would not have the strength of will to complete the day's work.

Nor were they lacking a sense of the difficulties of their situation, the way in which it would deny and destroy them. Mani Leib would later say:

> An immigrant, bringing with me native landscapes, ideals of Socialism and humanity, nebulous artistic impressions of German romanticists and French symbolists, of Russian writers from Pushkin to Blok, and then thrust into a sweatshop and poverty, with little time to write, what was there I could do? But the little I did do is my own. . . .

In their early verse *Die Yunge* yielded too much, perhaps, to their desire for elegant versification, chiming melodiousness, painterly harmonies. Infused with a new artistic scrupulosity, they achieved a purified, idiomatic Yiddish.† Their own earlier verse may now seem somewhat thin, lacking in verbal thrust and

---

* R. Iceland, *Fun Unzer Frieling.*
† They translated widely from foreign literatures, Mani Leib from Slavic songs, Landau from Old English and Scottish ballads, Russian symbolist and German impressionist poetry, I. J. Schwartz from medieval Hebrew verse and Shakespeare's plays, B. Lapin from Shakespeare's sonnets.

dramatic marrow. But as they continued to write, it became clear they could never fully turn away from the realities of Jewish experience and the pressures of Jewish tradition. They were modern poets, but more important, modern *Yiddish* poets. More than they knew or supposed, they shared in the experience against which they rebelled. Their poetry, as it must be, is Jewish through and through—in reference, spirit, and tonality.

5 · A FEW CENTRAL FIGURES

The leading poet among *Die Yunge* was Mani Leib, a handsome and romantic figure who loved Pushkin, Blok, and the Yiddish folk song. About Mani Leib's position in Yiddish literature one could say what Dryden said about Edmund Waller: "The excellence and dignity of rhyme were never fully known until Mr. Waller taught it; he first made writing easily an art. . . . Unless he had written, none of us could write."

Into the unsettled and half-cultivated world of American Yiddish literature Mani Leib brought his love of language and a sensibility of high refinement. Where did he acquire these traits, this self-taught immigrant who spent years in the shops, who had no formal literary training, and among modern languages knew well only Yiddish? In part, from that intense love the Eastern European Jewish intelligentsia had developed for nineteenth-century Russian poetry; in part, from the inner Jewish tradition of *edelkayt,* a term signifying both nobility and delicacy.

Mani Leib, writes the poet Itzik Manger, "was the Joseph among the brothers of Yiddish poetry." And as if to support this vivid characterization, the critic Tabachnick writes in detail about the ways in which Mani Leib purified Yiddish poetry, demanding that it shake off bombast, dialect, and journalese, and insisting that Yiddish poets adhere "to the principle of strict word choice." The poem as self-contained object, the poem as subtly modulated arrangement of image and idea, the poem as pattern of musical harmonies, the poem as taut structure melding theme and connotation ("he set boundaries for Yiddish poetry," writes Tabachnick, and only those steeped in literature will fully appreciate the weight of this remark)—all this finds its first Yiddish fulfillment in Mani Leib's lyrics. In American Jewish life, and perhaps in the whole of modern Jewish life, Mani Leib represents a new type: the single-minded literary man, the writer who lives solely for the word.

Mani Leib was not an experimental poet. Through most of his life he continued to use a conventional quatrain of rhymed iambics, or a number of other set lyrical forms with traditional rhyme and metrical schemes. He believed in the idea of "beauty" as something self-contained, perhaps separable from the matter of the poem, and to be created through diction and sound—that is, he believed in what eighteenth-century English critics would have called "decorum." At times his themes may be disturbing, but his poems are rarely disturbed; they are marked by that clarity and serenity he invoked in one of his loveliest lyrics, "Come, Serene Plainness" (p. 89). He was a writer for whom the idea of becoming a poet was a sacred obligation. "Poetry," he would recall at the end of his life, "was for us [Die Yunge] the meaning of life. Poetry lit up our gray days of hard physical labor at the sewing machines. . . ." In his lyric, "I Am" (p. 87), he brought together his pride as worker and pride as poet, and here the two sides of his sensibility, the one deriving from his life as immigrant Jew and the other from nineteenth-century European romantic verse, achieved a triumphant fusion. In the work of Mani Leib we see telescoped a whole sequence of human aspiration and cultural development. His earlier poems, it is true, are sometimes marked by thinness, a lack of force and substance, as a result of his self-conscious aestheticism. But for men like him the struggle for assurance and autonomy as poet could never be fully won or come to an end.

At the close of his career Mani Leib composed a series of sonnets that even his detractors in the Yiddish literary world acknowledge to be the best of their genre in Yiddish. His language now became firmer, thicker, juicier—with less space, so to say, between the words. The immigrant experience breaks through more freely, since he no longer feels so strong a need to be "literary." While the language is still as refined as in the earlier poems, the sensibility informing these sonnets is more complex and mature—in a sense, more mature because more Jewish. A ripe wisdom, half of it the resignation with which Die Yunge began their work and half a passionate turning-back to the appearances and surfaces of the physical world, moves quietly through these final poems.

Where Mani Leib purified Yiddish poetry, Moishe Leib Halpern coarsened and invigorated it with salty Yiddish idiom. Where Mani Leib was a poet of aesthetic detachment, Halpern was a poet of psychic turmoil. And where Mani Leib was a writer of modulated temper, Halpern was a writer of explosive temperament.

Moishe Leib Halpern is perhaps the most original poet in Yiddish: not its central figure, not its most beloved voice, not its most fulfilled writer, but its fiercest and most forceful. In his abrasive poems, half song and half curse, Halpern brought together the traditional resources of *Yiddishkayt,* the satiric thrust of Mendele, and the characteristic sensibility of modernism. A rebel against his poverty-stricken life, he grew into a rebel against his own rebelliousness: "Help me, O God," he wrote, "to spit on the world and on you and on myself." Halpern brought into Yiddish poetry the disgust, the raging imprecation, the livid self-assault we associate with modernist literature. "Poet and anti-poet," a Yiddish critic has called him, and the phrase quickly places him in the vortex of urban tumult and malaise.

Halpern was a master of grotesquerie. A demon races through his lines, the demon of self. In his weaker pieces this often causes a drop into self-pity and predictable irony; but in the strong ones it becomes objectified and distanced through a brilliantly sustained *persona—Moishe Leib der takhshit,* Moishe Leib the rascal. At best there is a cruel interplay between narrative voice and caustic *persona,* between the speaker and *der takhshit,* whom he often addresses. Moishe Leib the wolf tearing at his own self; Moishe Leib the buffoon dancing in Coney Island or warning his son that, whatever else, he is never to become a poet (see "The Will," p. 112); Moishe Leib becomes the name of his torment.

Halpern steadily approaches, but in his best poetry transcends, the mode of romantic irony and all the pitfalls it too readily sets up; but in the dialectical spiraling of his mind there is no fixed point at which his irony is allowed to settle into ease. "Everywhere a stranger," he writes about himself, he keeps "struggling anxiously like my brother Don Quixote with windmills." Overcome by nostalgia for the old country, he turns to his *shtetl* Zlochev, but then remembers its ugliness and wretchedness, and ends with a superb curse: "This is the only solace to me:/That I won't be buried in thee—/My home, Zlochev." And in his soured fantasia, "The Bird" (p. 104), he creates an ultimate self-assault on the moral and psychic impoverishment of the immigrant world.

Nihilism eats into Halpern, but he remains a Yiddish poet wandering from city to city in search of bread and working at a great number of jobs. For a few years he turns to the Yiddish communist paper *Freiheit;* he is the first Yiddish poet to approach it, in 1921, and angrily, the first to leave. What keeps him from misanthropy is a recurrent tenderness of spirit he can never quite suppress, as if Moishe Leib the wolf becomes Moishe Leib the lamb, as if the city poet summoning the powers of darkness still finds half-hidden within himself one of Reisen's *edele layt,* or refined souls. And what saves him from chaos is a hopelessly unbreakable tie with the Jewish immigrant masses whom he can neither abide nor abandon. In another culture he might become a desperado like Rimbaud or an aristocrat of letters like Stefan George; but here he has no choice, he dies in the East Bronx.

Yiddish critics have compared Halpern to Baudelaire. It is a useful comparison, but mainly insofar as it points up enormous differences. Halpern lacks Baudelaire's obsession with the idea of sin; he has a playfulness, a gift for blessed fooling, which Baudelaire lacked; in his poems he loves to clown, dance, croon, murmur. He introduces into Yiddish poetry not merely the mode of the grotesque, but the whole idea of the self as drama, chaos, fire. Each of his poems is a field upon which the battle of impulses is endlessly fought. Yet he cannot find a solace in beautiful words, or ugly ones either, though he frequently uses these as a weapon of self-defense; for him art is a sacred plague, and he is envious of all those who can gain relief in the business of daily life. He writes in a 1922 letter—and this Baudelaire would have understood:

> The most ordinary ignoramus, the tough on the street, does not make a *tsimmis* of his woes. He neither transfers them to parchment nor decks them out with a Torah cover. When his anger reaches the boiling point, he isn't ashamed to show that stones can fly like birds. But when the artist gets angry, he runs home and fusses with

words until he grows sick of himself. I would like to believe that
those artists who still retain some humanity must carry their art
as if it were a boil under their arm. And their whole longing is to
be redeemed from it.

In the end he is lost. His struggle with self is beyond resolu-
tion, and it sours into a barrage of self-contempt, an impatience
with beauty, culture, mind. It is as if, together with all other
Yiddish poets, he feels the absolute urgency that the Messiah
come; but that if He were to come He would not be welcome;
and in any case, we may depend on it, He will not come. Yet
precisely this conclusion Halpern finds unbearable.

Halpern's mastery of Yiddish is radically different from that of
his predecessors: he breaks contemptuously from refinement,
mellifluousness, smoothness. His images are like glass crushed in
one's hand. His language is nervously idiomatic, stylized impreca-
tion, a thrust of shock against the family sweetness of Yiddish
culture. His rhythms are broken, startled. Like Mayakovski, he
stamps "on the throat of his poems."

The third major Yiddish poet to begin writing shortly before
the First World War is H. Leivick, a visionary figure who stands
at the center of modern Yiddish poetry. Born in Russia, sentenced
in his youth to six years' imprisonment for activity in the socialist
Bund, and later driven to a wretched Siberian exile, Leivick
came to the United States in 1913, where he was quickly recog-
nized as a gifted Yiddish writer but nevertheless had to continue
struggling for livelihood. After years of hard work, he developed
tuberculosis and in the early thirties spent three years in a
Denver sanatorium. All his life Leivick aspired toward pain, for
the most part not gratuitously but as a way of sharing in the
ordeal of his generation and his people. Throughout his volumi-
nous writings—realistic plays, poetic dramas, psychological verse
narratives, sonnets, lyrics of every kind, and prose autobiography
—the theme of suffering runs like a channel of blood.

In Leivick's poetry a major element of modern Jewish experi-
ence is isolated and raised to a feverish and apocalyptic intensity.
Suffering—suffering exalted, suffering celebrated, suffering raised
to mystique, suffering as token of redemption. Of all Yiddish
writers he most closely approaches the religiosity of Dostoevski
as it declares the necessity of receiving pain in order to be ready

for grace. Though not as complex a writer as Dostoevski—he lacks Dostoevski's saving gift for comic self-mockery—Leivick shares with him a belief in the sanctity of the passive. Like Dostoevski he sees the Crucifixion as the common lot, though to say this is not at all to suggest that his outlook is derived from Dostoevski. It is merely to remark that if pushed far enough all religious exaltations of pain come to seem alike. Some of Leivick's Yiddish critics have attacked his obsession with suffering as "masochistic" and in certain of his inferior works there is in fact a reveling in self-torment; but this obsession derives not from any literary or alien source, nor is it a mere posture of cultural display; it stems from a complete immersion in the Jewish experience, a willed defenselessness—for Leivick this is what it means to be "chosen"—before the agonies of our century.

Though he has declared that the figure of Jesus is attractive to him—"I saw in him simply the prisoner"—Leivick writes mainly out of the ethos of the Eastern European Jews. If at times he veers beyond the perimeter of strict Jewish belief, it is for reasons that a writer like Isaac Bashevis Singer, in tone and feeling so radically different, also veers beyond that perimeter: the sheer intolerableness of Jewish life in the last hundred years, the endless and senseless accumulation of blood. In his refusal of violence, in his belief that force is the path to injustice, in his pulsing identification with all those cut by the lash—Leivick is the poet of *galut* or exile, the *galut* as it is raised to an ecstatic mystique of martyrdom. In the spectrum of Jewish values he stands at the opposite pole from the *sabra*.

Speaking in 1957 at a Jerusalem conference of writers, Leivick recalled a traumatic incident of his childhood. One day after having been beaten on the street by a drunken Pole, he entered *kheder* or Hebrew school:

> The teacher began the lesson for the day, the verses about the sacrifice of Isaac. Isaac accompanies his father Abraham to Mount Moriah, and now Isaac lies bound upon the altar waiting to be slaughtered. Within me my heart weeps even harder. It weeps out of great pity for Isaac. And now Abraham raises the knife. My heart is nearly frozen with fear. Suddenly—the angel's voice: Abraham, do not raise your hand against your son; do not slay him. You have only been tested by God. And now I burst into tears. "Why are you crying now?" the teacher asked. "As you see, Isaac was not slaugh-

tered." In my tears I replied, "But what would have happened had the angel *come one moment too late?*" The teacher tried to console me with the reassurance that an angel cannot be late.

This image of the angel delayed would receive a large-scale embodiment in Leivick's ambitious verse drama *Job*. The very sheep who replace Isaac at the altar cry out against the common feeling that, Isaac having been spared, all is now well. Just as Dostoevski was haunted by the thought of the single child who might have to be slaughtered to set the world aright, so Leivick kept returning to the thought that somehow, somewhere, still another victim would be found.* The idea is perhaps extreme and barely manageable this side of the morbid; but it is developed by Leivick with that groping and ruthless intensity which is the mark of the visionary who cares not a damn that to ordered, or ordinary, minds he may seem ridiculous.

During his lifetime Leivick became a culture hero within the Yiddish-speaking world. What had earlier been dismissed as his neurotic excesses or inclinations toward un-Jewish heresies, came to seem, in the years of the holocaust, a profound anticipation of modern reality. In Leivick's work the Yiddish reader could find an extreme version of his own forebodings about Jewish destiny, an ecstatic invocation of the apocalypse that must always be present to those who live by Messianic expectation.

Leivick wrote in almost every poetic genre available to the modern Yiddish writer, and his work, because it is put to the service of so passionate and distraught a sensibility, is often marred by obscurities. There are points at which one senses in his poems a gap between the visionary strained beyond endurance and a craftsman who cannot achieve a disciplined embodiment of his theme. His lyrics generally run in two directions, those in which he manages a complete fusion of motive and act

---

* The Yiddish critic Shlomo Bickel remarks: "In Leivick's commentary on Job, the complaint of the innocent man of suffering remains a central motif, but Leivick brought into play another revealing motif. Job says:

> Blessed be the man of suffering
> Who calls God Himself to judgment.

But what of Job himself, he who demands judgment? As soon as his sorrows are quieted, his complaints are stilled. Thereby he allows the need for judgment to lapse."

—poems concentrated, gnarled, and quivering—and those in which he fails to escape the perils of declamation.

To the alien or unprepared reader, Leivick presents considerable barriers, and in translation, no matter how skillful, these are not likely to be entirely surmounted. There are poets who stand at the center of their culture—Pushkin is the obvious example—yet are all but inaccessible to outsiders. Whoever has not penetrated the poetic vision of Leivick has not really come to the heart of modern Yiddish poetry.

Like most literary groups, *Die Yunge* were important less for what they said than for what they discarded. Only a few poets —Mani Leib, Landau, Iceland—would remain faithful to their original program and continue to function as a distinctive group, but their insistence upon the autonomy of literature helped others who went off in a great many poetic directions. Halpern and Leivick never subscribed to the stricter notions of *Die Yunge,* yet it is doubtful that they could have found their own voices without the group's aesthetic credos.

Other notable poets, both older and younger, appeared simultaneously or in friendly association with *Die Yunge:* I. J. Schwartz, who composed long verse narratives and dramatic vignettes about the immigrant experience in the American provinces; Joseph Rolnick, one of the most authentic lyricists in Yiddish and notable for evocations of country life that bear an odd resemblance to some of Frost's poems; J. I. Segal, a voluminous writer who made of the simplicities and details of ordinary Jewish life in the new world an endless source of observation and interest.

6 · IN ZICH: EXPERIMENT AND INNOVATION

While *Die Yunge* validated the idea of the poem as autonomous creation and brought into the narrow precincts of Yiddish poetry some awareness of modern European literature, they cannot be said to have been "modernists" in any strict sense of the term. For self-conscious experimentation with form and theme, we must turn to a new group of Yiddish poets who began to make their presence felt shortly after the First World War. Led by Jacob Glatstein, Aaron Glanz-Leyeles, and N. B. Minkoff, the *In Zich* or introspectivist group pushed Yiddish poetry about as far as it could go toward the kinds of writing composed both in Europe and America during the years directly after the war.

The *In Zich* poets directed their rebellion mainly against *Die Yunge*, since by 1920 the latter were the dominant tendency in American Yiddish poetry. Yet, for all the notable differences between the two groups, it seems plausible in retrospect to see the *In Zich* poets as heirs of *Die Yunge*, at least insofar as they continued the inexorable movement away from didactic verse and toward modernist individuality. To see this partial continuity is an advantage of hindsight; but at the time when Glatstein and his colleagues first appeared on the scene, there were hot debates in Yiddish literary circles about the step or two they proposed to take beyond *Die Yunge*. In a peppery essay that appeared in the first issue of the little magazine, *In Zich*, Glatstein showed small affection and not much more respect for writers like Mani Leib and Landau; he felt them to be too "poetic," too cut off from the blunt realities of Jewish experience, too devoted to the poem as a smoothed-out and nicely rounded form that was fixed once and for all. The usual rebellion of sons against fathers—even and especially fathers who had cleared the way for the sons—was again taking place, and many years would have to pass before there could be a reconciliation. And the reconciliation would occur only after it had become clear that in his maturity Glatstein no longer held strictly to the *In Zich* program, any more than a writer like Mani Leib held in his later years to the original program of his group.

There were differences other than aesthetic. Most of *Die Yunge* had been immigrant workers, at least in their earlier years chained to the shops, no matter what their aesthetic pretensions or Bohemian inclinations. The *In Zich* poets, though still sharing in the poverty of immigrant life, had nevertheless received a certain amount of education in America, some of them having gone to college here. Few of *Die Yunge* ever mastered English, and most of them were in imagination forever linked to European literature; but writers like Glatstein, Glanz-Leyeles, and Mink-off had read, or would soon be reading, Pound, H.D., Eliot, and Stevens. The *In Zich* poets had a strong sense of the contemporary cultural movement, and it is in their work that the impress of American poetry first makes itself felt.

It is hard to determine to what extent the *In Zich* poets were influenced by the notions of contemporary American modernism and to what extent they developed along independent but parallel lines. Experimentation with meter and language, innovations in subject matter and tone were in the literary air throughout the world, and young men as sophisticated as the *In Zich* poets were probably responding to the moment pretty much as were their equivalents in English. Where *Die Yunge* still conformed to the norms of metrical regularity and verbal decorum, the *In Zich* poets turned to free verse, were quite happy to play with incongruities of diction and sound, and were more concerned with a fierce individualistic expressiveness than with literary niceties. The poetry of Whitman seems to have had some effect upon them, but writers like Glatstein insist that the cadenced verse of the Bible was by far the greater formative influence.

In 1920 there appeared the journal *In Zich*, which offered not merely examples of the new writing but also a declaration of aesthetic principles notably similar to those put forward by the imagists in America and other modernist groups in Europe. Poetry, they wrote,

> . . . is not merely a matter of feeling and rationality but also, and perhaps primarily, the art of expressing adequately both feeling and the rational. . . . What happens in the soul of the poet when he finds himself under the influence of certain phenomena? In the language of *Die Yunge* this creates a mood. The poet, according to them, has to express and transmit this mood. But how? In a concentrated and well-rounded form, without which the poet's mood cannot have a general effect or, to employ the language of our older poets, an eternal value. . . . Such poems are at best ornaments, verbal decor. At worst they ring false bells.

> We introspectivists want, first of all, to present life as it actually is, with precision, to the extent that it reflects itself within us. . . . In what form? Does the complexity of verse come out of the moods we have just discussed? . . . It comes in the form of association and suggestion, the two elements we consider the most important

in poetic expression. . . . We know that poets of all times have made use of association and suggestion, yet we emphasize these because we think they are best suited to express the complicated feelings of present-day man. . . .

Most poets make too much use of ready-made images and materials. . . . When the poet or anyone else looks at a sunset, he may see in it the most modern things, which superficially have nothing to do with the sunset. The picture reflected in his soul is only one in a series of far-reaching associations of what his eye has seen. . . .

To the knowledgeable reader, all this may seem familiar. But we must remember that it is familiar because forty-five or fifty years ago it was new, and that in the world of Yiddish such views struck home with a special force. The *In Zich* group continued:

Form and content are one. A poem that can be paraphrased is no poem. Its major characteristic is rhythm. We come to a question that has disturbed poets in many languages, the problem of free verse. For introspectivist poetry free verse is not a "must." One may write an introspectivist poem in a regular meter. We believe however that free verse is best suited for our individuality of rhythm, and that is why we prefer it to other forms. . . .

When non-poets take to writing free verse, however, they have no easier time of it than when using iambs, trochees, and anapests.

What was most disturbing to the Yiddish public was the way in which the *In Zich* manifesto pushed to an extreme the earlier views of *Die Yunge,* relieving Yiddish poets of national-social obligations:

For us there does not exist the sterile question as to whether the poet should write about national or social or personal problems. We make no distinction between poetry of the heart and poetry of the mind.

In regard to our *Yiddishkayt,* we would point out that we are Yiddish poets by virtue of the fact that we are Jews and write in Yiddish. Whatever a Yiddish poet may write about is *ipso facto* Yiddish. One does not need specifically Jewish themes. . . .

It is not the task of the poet to prove his *Yiddishkayt.* Only in two ways are we definitely Yiddish—in our affection for Yiddish as a language and in our respect for Yiddish as a poetic instrument.

None of the *In Zich* poets would remain with these views for very long. Glanz-Leyeles soon began to experiment with traditional French forms, the villanelle and the rondeau, as part of his restless effort to multiply the possibilities of Yiddish verse. Glatstein went on to become a major Yiddish poet, ranging freely across a wide range of styles and subjects. Yet in the history of Yiddish poetry the *In Zich* group marks an important turning point, one at which Yiddish poetry almost—*almost*—joins the mainstream of twentieth-century world poetry. For younger Yiddish writers, both in America and Europe, the *In Zich* group completes the coming-of-age begun by *Die Yunge*.

7 · YIDDISH POETRY IN THE SOVIET UNION

By 1920 there had developed at least three major cultural and geographical centers of Yiddish poetry: the United States, Poland, and the Soviet Union. These were not merely distinct in space, they also represented sharply different possibilities for Yiddish writing: the American toward increasing worldliness, the Soviet toward a Marxist stress and the repudiation of traditional *Yiddishkayt*, and the Polish toward an autonomous and organic Yiddish culture, tied to the past but also responsive to modern European experience.

In 1912 and 1913 a group of Yiddish writers began to form in Kiev, sharply different from the traditional masters who had lived in the Ukraine a few decades earlier. Influenced by Russian and Western European impressionists and symbolists, these young men in Kiev sought to create Yiddish works that would be more sophisticated than those of their fathers. The leading figures in Kiev were the novelists David Bergelson and Der Nister, and the poet David Hofstein.

During the First World War Yiddish culture suffered crippling blows in Russia, mainly through government censorship and proscription. Once, however, the February 1917 revolution broke out, there followed a rapid upsurge of Yiddish cultural activity. Many newspapers in Yiddish, as well as a variety of literary publications, sprang up in Petrograd, Minsk, Kharkov, and Kiev; Jewish political parties became active; a new generation of Yiddish writers, inspired by the revolutionary turmoil, felt hopeful

that the "new Russia" might bring a better life to the Jews—
though what the "new Russia" would be no one yet knew.

Together with such veterans as Bergelson and Hofstein, there
now appeared a remarkable number of talented Yiddish novelists
and poets. It is no exaggeration to say that in these early years
of Soviet life, approximately until 1924, there occurred a major
flowering of Yiddish poetry and prose, as well as of critical and
philological scholarship. The atmosphere was relatively free.
While one could not safely write against the Bolshevik regime,
the pressures to compose verses flattering a Beloved Leader
were not yet irresistible. Many of the younger Yiddish writers
were genuinely sympathetic to the Soviet cause, and some were
its active partisans, seeing in Socialism not only an escape from
the pogroms of Czarism and the stagnation of the *shtetl,* but also
a way of breaking past the dilemmas of the Polish Jews who, for
all their superb political organization and cultural vivacity, were
still trapped under repressive and often anti-Semitic governments.

In the Soviet Union of these early years it was still possible,
for both Russian and Yiddish writers, to employ "neutral" sub-
jects, themes free of political implication or tendentiousness. And
the problem of censorship was not yet overwhelming. Between
1917 and 1921 approximately 850 Yiddish books were published
in the Soviet Union, a number that would be impressive at any
time but seems quite remarkable for a period of hunger and civil
war. The Yiddish theater, under the brilliant guidance of Shlomo
Mikhoels, was full of energy and experiment. Kiev, the major
center of Yiddish culture, had two dailies in Yiddish, as well as
several publishing houses. And a number of high-level literary
journals were published in Yiddish, among them *Der Shtern (The
Star)* and *Shtrom (Stream).* When *Shtrom* appeared in Moscow in
1922, it declared itself open to contributions from Yiddish writers
throughout the world, thereby proclaiming a "heresy" that would
cost Yiddish writers dearly: the "heresy" that there existed an
international Yiddish literature with norms and themes not neces-
sarily determined by the Russian revolutionary experience.

In the early twenties Russian literature itself was experiencing
a brilliant rebirth, a modernist phase enlivened by playfulness,
experiment, impudence, and raw energy. The chants of Mayakov-
ski, the lyrics of Pasternak, the stories of Babel and Pilnyak—

these marked a period in Russian literature second, perhaps, only to that of the mid-nineteenth century; and Yiddish literature, in part under the influence of the contemporary Russians and in part through its own inner development, enjoyed a similar flare of talent.

In Yiddish poetry there were new motifs, new voices, new tones. The poets repeatedly dealt with the clash, both as objective fact and subjective trouble, between a received Jewish tradition and their embroilment in the revolutionary world. Violently and ostentatiously, sometimes with a rude sneer, the Yiddish writers turned their backs on the self-preoccupation and petty languors of the *shtetl;* yet often—especially is this true for the older poets —they cast a lingering look across their shoulders at the remembered world of their childhood and youth. One Yiddish poet, Leib Kvitko, tells the older Jews to be "on their way," to get lost in the darkness of oblivion, but also murmurs the hope that during the journey they will "be well."

The new Soviet Yiddish writers identified the *shtetl* with religious obscurantism, social stagnation, moral decay. *Shtetl* idyllicism or romanticism, so important a motif in earlier Yiddish writing, became the butt of caustic attack and ironic dismissal. For these new poets—Feffer, Markish, Kvitko, Charik, Kushnirov —the idea of the future, the gesture of revolt, became the driving force in their poetry: probably not enough to sustain writers for a long time but certainly enough to set them into enthusiastic motion.

Eager to live out their convictions, some of the Yiddish writers fought on the Bolshevik side during the civil war. They looked upon Yiddish not as the language of *galut,* since to acknowledge the idea of exile may imply hope for return to a Jewish homeland, but simply as a language that happened to be theirs and which in time would be absorbed by a new socialist culture in Russia. Apart from sentiment, they really had no strong reason for insisting upon the survival of Yiddish. And as a result—though also because of pressure from the communist authorities—they began to cut themselves off from Yiddish culture abroad. While creating a worldly literature of their own, they did not accept the more extreme stylistic innovations of the younger Yiddish poets in Poland and America. And as Stalinism tightened its grip on Russian society, they fell behind the Yiddish writers of other countries, lapsing into an ideological and literary provincialism of their own.

But the achievement of the early years remains a high point in Yiddish writing. The most colorful, if not the most disciplined, of the new Yiddish poets was Peretz Markish, the kind of poet who seems forever to be discovering the world as if he were its first inhabitant. In the free verse of his early period there is something of the chaos and wildness that marks the poetry of Mayakovski during these same years. Markish pours out quantities of lyrics, dramatic monologues, plays: it is as if the old mustiness of Jewish life were being swept away and replaced by pleasure in the air and fields, an embrace of the possibilities of vigor. Markish is not a mere rhymester of slogans; like Mayakovski, he is half in love with the chaos of the early twenties, drawn to the idea of a new life but also to the actuality of destruction. By contrast, David Hofstein is a more restrained poet, drawing both upon his immersion in the Jewish past and his interest in the modernist poetry of early twentieth-century Russia. His poems are terse, enigmatic, and sometimes elliptical, their very form reflecting a fine intelligence.

There were other notable poets: Leib Kvitko, a popular lyricist whose children's poems were extensively translated into Russian; Itzik Feffer, who began with sardonic assaults on the *shtetl*, dropped into sycophantic paeans to Stalin, and ended with the broken cry, "I am a Jew"; and Samuel Halkin, a quieter, less political poet, close to the Hebrew tradition and distinguished for his verbal control and meditative tone.

The decades of nightmare began in the late twenties. Political censorship tightened intolerably. Yiddish commissars masquerading as critics hounded the poets and novelists: they cling to traditional themes, they remain subject to Zionist ideology, they do not incorporate non-Jewish "positive heroes" into their work— complaints and denunciations that paralyzed the Yiddish writers. Several of them went into temporary exile, but all felt cut off from their cultural roots, and within a few years they returned to Russia.

The rest of the story, one of the most tragic in modern Jewish life, is by now too well known to require detailed telling: harassment and humiliation, recantations of ideological error and shamed revisions of texts. Like Pasternak, many Yiddish writers turned for relief and survival to translation, rendering Goethe, Shakespeare, and Balzac into Yiddish. But there was no exit for them, no escape. In the late thirties the poets Charik and Kulbak, as well as the literary historians Israel Tsinberg and Max Erik, were arrested and destroyed in the purges.

The Second World War brought a moment of reprieve. Writers like Markish completed fervent long poems full of patriotic sentiment; Feffer, a high-pitched poem called "Shadows of the Warsaw Ghetto." Aaron Kushnirov, veteran communist and Yiddish poet, went off to fight on the front, though he was already past fifty. Little of the writing done in this period has much literary value, since it was by now completely tailored to the demands of the state. The Yiddish poets were of course utterly sincere in rallying the Russian Jews to the war against Hitler, but their earlier individuality had long been suppressed, and even their command of Yiddish, from which they had been forced by party decree to expel Hebraic components, was by now often impoverished.

The dark age begins in the late forties. In January, 1948, the actor-director Mikhoels is murdered by the secret police. On August 12, 1952, some thirty writers—including Bergelson and Markish—are shot. An authoritative estimate by the Yiddish literary historian, Elias Shulman, indicates that more than 500 additional Yiddish writers are sentenced to concentration camps, there to meet death. What Hitler had left undone, Stalin completed.

During these terrible years the Yiddish poets realize their days are numbered. Some behave with dignity, a few with deceit. David Hofstein, a man of courage, writes a poem that begins with the traditional Hebrew phrase, "For learning issues from Zion," and for this he is mercilessly attacked. He continues to write—"for the drawer"—private reflections on the fate of the Jews in Hitler's Europe. Kushnirov, whose son had been killed in the war, is called upon to speak at a public gathering and denounce the sins of his fellow Yiddish poets. "On reaching the platform," writes Charles Madison, a historian of Yiddish literature, he "was struck dumb; his lips moved spasmodically, but no voice came."

Yiddish poetry composed in the Soviet Union is a poetry of

great aspiration, brilliant flashes, but not true fulfillment. It begins with modernist flame and ends with conformist ashes. Its relationship to recent Yiddish culture is inherently problematical, since it both draws upon and denies its sources in the Jewish tradition, some of the Soviet Yiddish writers being genuinely convinced communists and others "marranos," forced converts who must suppress their inner Jewish sentiments. Soviet Yiddish poetry had neither time nor freedom: it is a crushed spark. But read now with historical awareness, it seems endlessly poignant in its rash hopefulness and its assumption that through sheer will men can undo their past.*

8 · EUROPE BETWEEN WARS

During the years between the two world wars, Yiddish culture was most firmly rooted in Eastern Europe, especially in Poland and Lithuania. Warsaw was the center of Jewish worldly life, Vilna (the "Jerusalem of Eastern Europe"), the center of Jewish learning. Though living for the most part under repressive and authoritarian regimes that severely restricted their political and economic rights, the Jews of Poland and Lithuania were usually allowed to conduct their cultural affairs as they wished. There was enough repression to make the idea of assimilation seem impractical, but not so much repression as to make an autonomous culture impossible. In these cramped but lively and even feverish circumstances, the Jews of Poland and Lithuania maintained until the very outbreak of the Second World War a vigorous and often brilliant cultural life, resting almost entirely on Yiddish as the language of both secular discourse and artistic expression. Daily newspapers, literary journals, large-scale publishing houses, scholarly research centers (such as YIVO, which would later transfer its resources to New York), serious theatrical groups (most notably the Vilna Company) flourished until the moment they were destroyed by the Nazi and Stalinist terrors.

---

* For some of the material in this section we are indebted to the valuable anthology *A Shpigl Oif a Shtayn (A Mirror on a Stone)*, edited by K. Shmeruk and published in Tel Aviv in 1964. This 800-page volume contains both a careful selection from the leading Soviet writers and an authoritative history of their literary careers and personal fates.

The strength of Eastern European Yiddish culture rested on the fact that it managed to bring into an uneasy but fruitful relationship the Jewishness of the past—laden with traditional lore and religious material—and the Jewishness of the present—secular, radical, cosmopolitan. It was in Poland during the twenties and thirties that the socialist Bund thrived as the strongest secular institution in Jewish life. Characteristically, it was a movement devoted to Yiddish as both the language of the masses and the medium of the culture it wished to preserve.

This uneasy union of past and present emerges powerfully in the work of M. Kulbak, one of the most gifted Yiddish writers of the twentieth century. For a time Kulbak, who was well-educated in Jewish matters, served as a teacher in a Yiddish school in Vilna, and in both his poetry and prose fiction, the sense of the Jewish past is heavy with memory and pain. In his long poem "Vilna" (p. 216) Kulbak addresses the city directly:

> You are a psalm, spelled in clay and in iron.
> Each stone a prayer; a hymn every wall,
> As the moon, rippling into ancient lanes,
> Glints in a naked and ugly-cold splendor.
> Your joy is sadness—joy of deep basses
> In chorus . . .
>
> You are a dark amulet set in Lithuania.
> Old gray writing—mossy, peeling.
> Each stone a book; parchment every wall.
> Pages turn, secretly open in the night,
> As, on the old synagogue, a frozen water carrier,
> Small beard tilted, stands counting the stars.

It was perhaps unavoidable that Kulbak be seized by the demons of his generation, the restlessness of the post-war years and the political and cultural impulses sweeping the continent. In the early twenties he went to Berlin, there to savor the excitements of Weimar Germany; later he composed a brilliant sequence of short poems called "Childe Harold" (p. 205) in mock imitation of Byron and reminiscent in tone of the expressionist drawings of George Grosz. Bitingly, nervously he counterposes his background as green Jewish youth from the *shtetl* to the cultural decadence and political battles of Berlin.

Berlin nights.   The floor is jumping.
He is near the jazz band.
Berlin nights.   The girlies topless.
What could be more cultural?
Wizards of the surplus market . . .

The jazz band cries.   Voices from the colonies,
Black fires of the Negro dance.

Drawn to the communist idea, Kulbak tried to resolve his inner
discords by going to the Soviet Union; but the satiric fiction he
wrote there about the early years of Communism made him po-
litically suspect and in the late thirties he vanished in the purges.

The younger poets in Eastern Europe who began to write in
the mid-twenties and early thirties were similarly open in feeling,
chancy in style, rambunctious in tone. One interesting group,
which appeared in Warsaw, called itself *Die Khaliastra* (The
Gang), and was largely expressionist in temper. The main figures
were Peretz Markish, then a visitor from Russia, Melech Rawitch,
who would become a world traveler finding harbor in Canada,
and Uri Zvi Greenberg, later to be a major Hebrew poet in Israel.
Die Khaliastra gained a moment of notoriety: they would give
tumultuous recitations in large halls before eager audiences of
Jewish youth, shouting their poems, declaring themselves to be
anti-Establishment, anti-religion, anti-Bund, indeed hostile to the
whole humanist tradition of Jewish resignation as well as to
Jewish politics. In their raw and rasping poems attacking all fixed
beliefs, they wished to capture the chaos of their moment. They
did, and that is precisely the limitation of their work.

A group of more lasting literary significance appeared during
the early thirties, called *Yung Vilna* (Young Vilna). Apart from
being a center of learning, Vilna figured with special prominence
in the development of Yiddish culture during these years, mainly
because here there was still a Yiddish-speaking and -reading
youth—a rising generation that spontaneously and "naturally"
used Yiddish as its first language. Within this cultural context, the
Jewish youth of Vilna was strongly influenced by leftist ideas and
cosmopolitan styles. Straining to break past the inhibitions of a
confined ghetto life, it responded with enthusiasm to the new
young poets—Chaim Grade, Abraham Sutzkever, Lazer Wolf,
and many others—who in the late twenties and early thirties

began to write in Yiddish. More restrained in tone and less concerned with mere gestures of defiance than the *Khaliastra*, the *Yung Vilna* poets were bound together not so much by an aesthetic creed as by a shared predicament. In a short while, both as poets and men, they would go their separate ways, but for a few years they shared the excitement of self-discovery and public acceptance.

The *Yung Vilna* poets really had no unifying aesthetic credo or practice. Lazer Wolf wrote expressionist, sometimes almost surrealist lyrics, with jangling rhythms and images, which deal with themes of boredom and deracination; his dominant tone of voice is satiric but in a suppressed, almost cryptic way. Sutzkever, in his early phase, showed himself a virtuoso of Yiddish prosody and stanzaic improvisation. His poems are gentle and smooth in texture, personal and musing in stress, and intensely responsive to the colors and shadings of the physical world. During the war, while trapped in Poland, he fought with the underground, and from that point until his permanent settlement in Israel, his poetry underwent a major change. He composed a long narrative in verse about the Warsaw resistance, and in Israel, while retaining his earlier virtuosity, he came back somewhat to the traditional themes of Yiddish poetry. Chaim Grade, by contrast, was from the outset a national poet. Influenced by Bialik and Leivick, far more deeply educated in traditional Jewishness than most Yiddish poets, Grade inclined almost from his earliest work toward a prophetic stance, composing verse of great emotional thrust and frequent verbal excess. He too had been overwhelmingly shaken by the holocaust—he managed to escape from Vilna to the Soviet Union, where he met and shared the ordeals of the Yiddish poets, and then after the war to make his way to the United States.

In their mature work all these poets have gone along sharply different ways, yet what Grade wrote about his development is by no means unique to him:

> In recent years I have often longed for the darkness from which I came, for that isolation which formed my life-style . . . but I know: to those nightmares I dare not return. My path is toward the community, to its problems and goals. . . . Art is for men, like Sabbath rest, even though the rabbis used to try to persuade us that the

Jew was created for the Sabbath. . . . Perhaps never before has Yiddish literature been fated to engage so completely with its national tasks.

9 · AFTER THE HOLOCAUST

About the ultimate preoccupation of Yiddish poetry there can be no doubt. After the Second World War all the schools, groups, and tendencies melt away; disputes as to poetic direction must now seem trivial; every Yiddish writer finds himself under the most crushing and sacred of obligations. The memory of cataclysm is decisive.

Lyrics continue, of course, to be written on the usual range of topics, but Yiddish poetry now returns—it must return—to its original concern with the collective destiny of the Jewish people. The future of Yiddish, now the language of martyrdom as well as of daily life, becomes an obsessive theme, with the poets oscillating between fierce gestures of persistence and sorrowful questions about the future. To an overwhelming extent Yiddish poetry becomes a *Khurbn* or holocaust poetry. What the critic S. Niger wrote in 1947 remains true for the years to follow:

> The tendencies characteristic of Yiddish poetry in the last few years have more to do with motives, ideas, and thematic material than with artistic form or style. This is not because they no longer strive to create works of art. On the contrary. It is fair to say that no representative of Yiddish literature today has attempted to make it solely into an instrument of ideological expression. Ideas and a variety of psychological and ethical matters are for Yiddish literature, as for any other, now as always, the raw material which requires expression in pictorial, lyrical, or rhythmic structure. But this is something Yiddish writers have recently ceased to emphasize. . . . Insofar as Yiddish writers are conscientious—and they are—they no longer want to be reckoned with as artists or "mere" artists. It is as if they feel guilty that their people's and their own tragedy has become no more than a "theme" for their poems and stories.

In the desolation of memory, Yiddish poets find themselves turning back to the old Jewish God, not so much the God of orthodoxy or even the God their fathers had worshiped, but a

God inseparable from Jewish fate, a God with whom one pleads and quarrels. It is as if, in a depopulated world, there must at least be someone to talk with: some figure or force, even if projected through images of denial and in accents of reproach, in whom the sheer possibility of meaning continues to reside.

There is also a recurrent doubt, even guilt, about the very act of continuing to write verse, continuing to care about meters and rhymes, images and phrases. Aaron Zeitlin, a Yiddish poet in whom traditional religious values are strong, remarks:

> Were Jeremiah to sit by the ashes of Israel today, he would not cry out a lamentation, nor would he drown the desolate places with his tears. The Almighty Himself would be powerless to open up his well of tears. He would maintain a deep silence. For even an outcry is now a lie, even tears are mere literature, even prayers are false.

And in the moving lines of Zeitlin's long poem "I Believe":

> Can I then choose not to believe
> in that living God whose purposes
> when He destroys, seeming to forsake me,
> I cannot conceive;
> choose not to believe in Him
> Who having turned my body to fine ash
> begins once more to wake me?

Such dilemmas are experienced both by believers and skeptics. It is a time for silence, but silence is impossible; nothing can be said, but everything must be spoken; and from the impermissibility of words comes powerful speech. The seasoned Yiddish poets have kept returning to the *Khurbn* again and again: they can neither stay with it nor away from it. And since it is impossible or perhaps useless to talk to men, they steadily turn back to the God who has been silent yet may still be listening.

Leivick implores Him:

> O, who on the steps of the path to Treblinka
> Will forgive me the sins of my song?

Kadia Molodowsky bitterly demands:

> O God of Mercy
> For the time being
> Choose another people.
> We are tired of death, tired of corpses,

We have no more prayers.
For the time being
Choose another people.

It is in the poems of Jacob Glatstein—poems remarkable for
their fusion of anger and resignation—that the dialogue with the
unheeding God is conducted most brilliantly. In one beautiful
poem "My Wagon Brother," Glatstein turns back to a theme first
employed by the famous Hebrew poet Bialik, who after the
Kishinev pogroms had shown God as a helpless, indeed another
suffering, Jew. "Forgive your God, you shamed ones," Bialik had
written. Glatstein goes further:

. I love my sorrowful God,
My wagon brother.
I love to sit down with him on a stone
And talk my heart out to him.

.   .   .   .   .

And here he sits with me, my friend, clasping me
And sharing his last bite with me.

And then, as if from regained distance, he writes:

The night is endless when a race is dead.
Earth and heaven are wiped bare.
The light is fading in your shabby tent.
The Jewish hour is guttering.
Jewish God!
You are almost gone.

For the Yiddish novelists and story writers, the destruction of
European Jewry has brought difficulties almost beyond over-
coming. Few of those living in the United States can write with
any great authority about Jewish, or non-Jewish, life in this coun-
try; and the life of the Jews in Eastern Europe, whether in *shtetl*
or city, is now little more than a memory, no longer able to yield
fresh or immediate experience. For the poets, however, precisely
this constriction of subject matter has been a major, and in a
tragically perverse way, fruitful theme. During the decades since
the Second World War, Yiddish poetry has been all but de-
stroyed in Eastern Europe and feebly audible in Russia; but in
the United States it has had a moment of late glory.

At least a few of these contemporary poets should be men-
tioned. Kadia Molodowsky is a vivid and forceful writer who in

her earlier poems was one of the first to break past the reticence traditionally imposed on the Jewish woman. Writing with great charm and playfulness, she can bring together in a poem like "White Night" (p. 288) a seeming innocence of voice with a tough grasp of experience. Rachel Korn is a poet of personal sensibility, rich in the detail with which she explores impulse, memory, and desire. Aaron Zeitlin is the most religiously orthodox voice in modern Yiddish poetry, holding fast to traditional feelings, denying all deniers, still adoring the Jewish God.

Another notable poet of these recent years is Itzik Manger, balladist and satirist who derives mainly from the tradition of Yiddish folk singers and tavern entertainers. Masquerading as a primitive but full of wit and slyness, Manger has bridged the gap between traditional motifs and modern forms: he writes with bounce and swing, an earthiness rare in Yiddish, and a temperamental inclination toward lightheartedness. Sharply in contrast is Chaim Grade, one of the few Eastern European Yiddish poets to survive the war. Almost everything he writes is haunted by memories of the holocaust; his poems embody the price of recall and are written with an unnerving intensity, sometimes at a pitch so high as to make them perilous for an alien readership.

In the poetry of Jacob Glatstein, Yiddish finds a particularly rich expression. Now long beyond the aesthetic restrictions of his early poems, which were marked by such luxury motifs as the difficulty of sustaining a personal self in the modern city, Glatstein has become pre-eminently a national poet. Through his long and weighty lines, he has given his verse more intellectual body than the traditional Yiddish lyric could allow. Whether subjective lyrics or dramatic monologues, his poems are marked by cognitive power, an avoidance of folk rhetoric, a gift for dramatizing reflective materials within compact stanzaic forms, and a readiness to subordinate the melodic line of his verse to the demands of his thought. A technical master, he has tried his hand at almost every poetic genre except the long verse narrative. He has written symbolic lyrics as nuanced as those of Stevens; he has written brilliant pictorial vignettes; he has made the poetry of statement—indeed, of imprecation—distinctively his own. In his later poems he returns again and again to the quarrel with God, the meaning of survival, the problem of justice. He has celebrated, yet not idyllicized, half-forgotten places and vanished ways of life. He has written out his despair over the incomprehensibility of the martyrdom. In what are perhaps the two greatest portions of his work—the Hasidic monologues, loving in tone and rich in humor, and the holocaust poems, jeremiads of shattering force— he has yoked together the two sides of modern Jewish life. And in the end, what else can a Yiddish poet do?

Beyond the holocaust, a few stalks of life. Among the small and rather isolated group of Yiddish poets in Israel, the horrors of yesterday cannot be forgotten, but they are put aside a little. These poets deal with the precariousness of things in Israel; they test out the hope for new life on the soil; they look quizzically upon the distance between themselves and the young *sabras*. Such fine poets as Aryeh Shamri, who works on a *kibbutz*, M. Yungman, and Jacob Friedman write quietly about the slowly recognized pleasures of being in one's own vineyard, near holy places. Their imaginations are stirred to humor and pleasure by the closeness they can feel to figures of the Bible, who seem to them like neighbors on the land, spirits in the air. Abraham Sutzkever remains a virtuoso of Yiddish phrasing, employing his gifts, as in the sequence called "Spiritual Soil" (p. 351), for a poetry of kaleidoscopic association: pictures, memories, encounters, colors, possibilities, but most of all, nightmares. Shamri is a husbander of words, gnomic and enigmatic. Freed a little from the burdens of anguish and breathing a softer air, the Yiddish poets in Israel contribute a fresh note to Yiddish literature, not merely in their tone but also in their diction, which takes on a heavy component of Hebrew.

10 · A FEW CONCLUSIONS

The course of development which in other poetries takes centuries is for Yiddish packed into a few decades. The emergence of a classical phase, the drama of a romantic reaction, the leap into modernist skepticism, the compulsive progress into undefined possibilities of subject and method—all these, part of the inner development of Western poetries, occur in Yiddish across a single century, which in effect means: *almost simultaneously.* What, for the ends of exposition, has to be ordered into a linear development, is in reality a jumble of contemporaneous happenings. As a result, everything is compressed and nothing quite fulfilled: no literary phase or period able to develop with leisure and internal sweep, and all of them, through the abrasions of space and time, forced into mixed and overlapping forms.

Yet it must be stressed that we are not dealing with the poetry of a backward people suddenly thrust into the center, or along the edge, of modern history. Yiddish poetry emerges out of—and in its deepest impulse, remains continuous with—an old and rich culture. It has for a major source the most influential book humanity has ever read; indeed, not to know the Bible is to stumble hopelessly in one's encounters with Yiddish writing. At the very moment of its birth, Yiddish poetry draws from a multitude of internal Jewish sources and Jewish languages. Intimately tied to the folk, blessed with a rich store of folk materials, Yiddish poetry nevertheless bears the ethos of a people at once far advanced in its history, traditionally reflective in its moral existence, and experienced, all too experienced, in its relations with the surrounding world. The stress a poet like Itzik Manger places upon the folk ties of Yiddish poetry is entirely correct, indeed essential for a grasp of its major works; but if left in isolation, or allowed to lapse into a cozy self-sufficiency, this stress would be largely misleading. Yiddish poetry is not a folk poetry; it is a modern poetry frequently employing folk themes and especially close to folk life. Within its own precinct and limit, it achieves spontaneously what Yeats and Synge tried programmatically to do with Irish poetry.

Yiddish poetry is at once universal and provincial. Its ultimate sources are among the richest in human culture, its immediate sources an experience often cramped and deprived. It speaks out of high moral claims—indeed, one reef on which some Yiddish poets, like some Yiddish prose writers, dash themselves is that of excessive moral demands; yet at the same time it speaks through a culture trying desperately to escape from enforced confinement, most violently in Eastern Europe but also visibly in the United States. Yiddish poetry bears the stamp, on its every word and for believer and skeptic alike, of a profoundly religious cul-

ture. In the actual composition of lyrics or ballads or dramatic
monologues, this proves to be an endless resource of images, ref-
erences, fables, and characters; yet by the very fact of its appear-
ance, by the fact that young men recently graduated or escaped
from the Yeshiva should now concern themselves with iambs and
trochees or read Lermontov and Eliot, it signals the disintegration
of a total religious faith. Yiddish poetry can never break away
from the traditions of this faith; yet neither can it return to the
wholeness of perception, the integrated world-view, which, un-
wittingly or not, it has helped to destroy. It yearns for what it
denies, it denies what it yearns for.

Yiddish poetry, for good or bad, largely escapes the twentieth-
century polarity between high and low culture. In the rootedness
of their historical moment—even if that moment had always to be
insecure—the major Yiddish poets look back to the song of their
grandfathers and forward to the sophisticated poetry of Russia,
Germany, France, and the United States. Between lapsed or
almost-lapsed faith and corrosive skepticism, they find an un-
comfortable resting place, a home for the ethical style of *Yiddish-
kayt*. That the culture of *Yiddishkayt* is transient they know; but
they write as if there were a specific Jewish time untroubled by
the tyranny of the clock; they make of their brief moment a
foundation for a complex way of living, past and present jumbled
into one, a place where the Baal Shem Tov and Baudelaire can
meet.

By collapsing the distinctions of history, Yiddish poetry bridges
the gap between eternity and time. The prophet Elijah steps
into the pages of Yiddish verse with the assurance he must have
felt in crossing the plains of Palestine; he jostles greenhorns on
the Lower East Side, Yemenites in Israel, rabbinical students
disputing in Vilna. The central premise of Jewish survival is a
defiance of history; the costs are beyond measure. And what can-
not be carved out in the actuality of space and time, such as an
assured nation or the fellowship of the helpless, is carved out in
the images and rhythms of poetry. As against the crumbling of
history, poetry is declared an unsleeping witness.

Yiddish poetry is strongly influenced by the poets of surround-
ing cultures, and to the reader who approaches it as a stranger,
through the necessarily coarse medium of translation, much of it
may seem familiar and even derivative. Beware the parochialism

of sophistication! For in reality, even when not on the highest literary level, everything in Yiddish is distinctive: finally, Yiddish romanticism is not the same as the romanticism of the various European cultures, and Yiddish modernism, precisely because it is Yiddish and therefore boxed into a particular destiny, can never become as free, as unburdened, as gratuitous as the modernism of Europe and America. In some cases this Yiddish distinctiveness makes for a unique achievement: there really are no poets in other languages quite like the main figures in this anthology, for no matter what the parallels in the development of techniques, the poets of other languages do not have to confront the destiny of Jewishness. It is a historical distinctiveness that may also, of course, make for special literary failures: the lugubriousness, the self-protectiveness, the threadbare declamations of much Yiddish poetry.

Yiddish literary life can never develop a full-scale aristocracy of aesthetes, and even its occasional ventures into Bohemianism are doomed to mildness. It is inescapably a plebeian culture, a culture of *folksmassen*, with all the gains and losses that may entail. Aestheticism is a luxury, and detachment a rarity: not that Yiddish poets do not repeatedly yearn for these, but that their immediate condition of life, as also their final situation as Jews, denies them such possibilities. Is there another Western literature in which the major poets, including those who within the spectrum of Yiddish can be called pure poets, spend their early years, and in some instances the whole of their lives, as shop workers?

Yiddish poetry comes to its language not as a finished reality, an inheritance waiting to be exploited, but as a range of untested possibilities. The process of "creating" a language which in English takes centuries is here pressed into a few years; or more precisely, the process of "creating" a literary language, approximately bounded and available for a variety of uses ranging from high rhetoric to demotic idiom, occurs toward the end of the nineteenth and the beginning of the twentieth centuries, long after Yiddish has gone through its own historical development. The refinement of diction, the denial of alien vocabularies, the alignment of punctuation, the settlement of syntax—all this occurs in the very course of establishing the major works of Yiddish literature.

There is a constant straining among Yiddish poets, as among

Yiddish prose writers, to break past traditional limitations of subject matter. Individual poets rebel against the domination of the national-social theme—indeed, that is the main significance of the various groups that form, dissolve, and reform. They seek desperately to assert their own voices, their own temperaments and moods; they insist upon the right to shake off the burdens of the folk and the curse of history, so that they may sing or speak as solitaries. (That is one reason Whitman moves so many Yiddish writers.) And indeed, some of the major Yiddish poets convert this effort into the substance of their work. Yet the very need for reiterating their wish for individual sensibility testifies to the power and persistence of the burden of collective fate. In the end, the luxury of choice is denied them, and almost every poet, nationalist or aesthete, radical or believer, must turn back to the tragedy of our age.

Throughout Yiddish literature, and more explicitly in Yiddish literary criticism, there runs a steady concern, even obsession, with the idea of an immanent development of its premises, that is, with the fulfillment of Yiddish as *idea*. It seems almost as if there were a destined obligation to realize a platonic essence of *Yiddishkayt*, so that each writer had somehow to speak not only for himself but as part of a chosen few, entrusted with unfolding the complete word. Repeatedly, Yiddish writers are judged by critics not merely as individual talents, but also by the extent to which they fulfill the latent possibilities of Yiddish. The burdens thereby placed on the individual writer are heavy.

Yiddish poetry can never long turn its back on the folk. Its readers may diminish in numbers, and the sense of loneliness and entrapment come to seem overwhelming to the poets. Yet their experience is such that sooner or later they must turn back to readers who may not read, listeners who may not listen, fathers who warned against the temptations of the secular word. The idea of an autotelic or even autonomous poetry is sought after by group after group of Yiddish poets. Seemingly found, it proves to be a chimera, and no choice remains but to come back, with blessing or curse, to the themes of the fathers. Yiddish poets have absorbed tonalities from Heine and Pushkin, techniques from Blok, devices from Eliot; but it is the founding fathers of the literature—Mendele, Peretz, Sholem Aleichem, Reisen—who loom across every page written in Yiddish.

The external history of Yiddish poetry is that of a series of groups, almost all striving toward one or another version of modernism. Each group does reach part of the way, with innovation and experiment. But in the end all fail to enter fully or remain for long with modernism. That is one distinguishing fact that makes them Yiddish poets. For, if the external history of Yiddish poetry is one of repeated splits and ruptures, the inner history is one of tacit continuity. What makes Yiddish poets Yiddish is not that they happen to write in the language but that even as they seek and receive the impress of surrounding cultures, they cannot break past the visible and invisible boundaries of Yiddish.

The lazy poets never try to; the suicidal poets only try to; the wise poets move away and return, move away in order to return.

11 · ON TRANSLATING YIDDISH

About the usual and endlessly vexing problems of translation, and especially the problems that attend the translation of poetry, we shall here say very little. About the problems of translating from Yiddish into English we shall say a little more, mainly because they are different, sometimes in kind and sometimes degree, from those likely to be encountered in translating from French into English or German into French.

Translating from Yiddish is difficult not—as Jewish sentimentalists like to suppose—because the language is somehow "unique" or enjoys a special vivacity and richness of idiom. It is neither more nor less difficult to translate a Yiddish idiom than a French idiom: both are virtually impossible. Translating from Yiddish is difficult because Yiddish literature, especially in its "classical" phase, carries a weight of historical associations and cultural assumptions that is likely to be missed or misunderstood by a reader not familiar with the Yiddish tradition. See Glossary (p. 370), for Yiddish and Hebrew definitions.

Similar cultural difficulties arise, no doubt, in translating from any other language, but they seem particularly acute with regard to Yiddish, if only because the culture of *Yiddishkayt* has been both self-contained and at some considerable distance from the cultures of the West. Modern English, French, and Russian poetry may be packed with obscure allusions, but often these are no

more obscure in translation than in the original: their obscurity
derives neither from linguistic peculiarities nor historical partic-
ulars. By contrast, Yiddish contains allusions so deeply imbedded
in both the Jewish tradition and the local experience of *Yiddish-
kayt* that it seldom offers much guidance to the alien reader. So
remarkably close-grained and intimate is Yiddish culture that
the writer, at least until very recently, could assume his reader
was immediately prepared to grasp a Talmudic reference, a Ha-
sidic refrain, even the angle at which shoulders might be shrugged.
(The classical instance in Yiddish is Sholem Aleichem's marvelous
wordplay when he has Tevye the Dairyman mangle Biblical quota-
tions: to appreciate what is going on here one must know the
original sources.) A translator from Yiddish is therefore faced
with the temptation, usually a temptation to be resisted, of weav-
ing into his translation bits of commentary and gloss.

A large portion of Yiddish poetry, especially in its early stages,
is a poetry of song, and as W. H. Auden remarks, "when, as in
pure lyric, a poet 'sings' rather than 'speaks,' he is rarely, if ever,
translatable." Or, at the least, it is terribly hard to translate him.
The earlier Yiddish poets, most notably Reisen, are closer to folk
song than any other Western poets of this century; they are not
"sophisticated" in the sense that we often expect modern poets
to be; and they depend so much on musical effect and an inti-
mate tie between meaning and rhythm that in translation their
work can easily come to seem mere jingle.

The point holds, if less forcefully, in regard to those Yiddish
poets who are self-conscious modern artists. A relatively full-
throated and unashamed lyricism of a kind that is scorned by
"modernist" poetic schools has persisted in Yiddish with greater
strength than in most other contemporary poetries. This gener-
alization needs immediately to be qualified, however, lest it become
misleading: there is a sharp distinction to be made between the
lyricism of a poet like Reisen and the lyricism of later poets like
Mani Leib and Manger, who break away from the folk song while
still drawing heavily from it. In Yiddish poetry there has also been
a trend away from "singingness" altogether, a trend toward a
poetry of speech, as in Halpern's deliberate "anti-poetic" verse
and Glatstein's imprecations. Nevertheless, it remains true that

the lyric impulse is peculiarly strong in Yiddish, and usually a formidable barrier to the translator.

Much of Yiddish poetry is, in effect, bilingual—though even putting the matter this way can be erroneous, since it implies that a Yiddish poet who employs a Biblical phrase in Hebrew is consciously turning to another language. In fact he is usually not. He is merely sliding, by the most natural of linguistic inclines, into a usage that is just as much a part of his experience as the Yiddish he customarily employs. With certain writers, as for example Aaron Zeitlin and the narrative poet I. J. Schwartz, it is useful to think of their work as composed in a kind of Yiddish-Hebrew continuum. And in the work of some poets, such as those now living in Israel, there is likely to be a larger component of Hebraisms than is usual among Yiddish writers. For the translator, the likelihood of being able to render such linguistic shadings is rather small.

Yiddish reached whatever degree of stability in structure and usage a living language *can* reach a good deal later in its development than have most Western languages. Constantly invaded by alien vulgarism and constantly renewed by alien vitality—while often not quite certain which was vulgarism and which vitality —Yiddish has retained a greater freedom for verbal improvisation than has modern English. Or at the least: Yiddish poets in the twentieth century have been far more self-conscious about verbal importations and improvisations than have most poets in English. To the translator this presents still further problems—and we say nothing about such familiar difficulties, not at all unique to translating from Yiddish, as richness of idiom, frequent use of diminutives, differences in syntactical "fit," and the nuance of the reflective voice.

Finally, there are the problems that have arisen from the cultural distance between Yiddish and Western cultures, problems that after a time seem to take on an autonomous literary character. These we have discussed at some length in our Introduction to *A Treasury of Yiddish Stories* (Viking Press, 1954) and will not repeat here, except to remark that the criteria for estimating sentimentality differ sharply from culture to culture. What an American reader of poetry might immediately dismiss as sentimental need not seem so to an equally serious reader of Yiddish poetry. There is, for instance, far less inhibition among Yiddish writers in releasing strong feelings toward maternal and paternal figures than there is in English, while on the other hand Yiddish writers tend to be notably less free in writing about sexual experience.

Translation, remarks the Hebrew poet Bialik, is like kissing a bride through her veil. Most of the controversy about translation concerns the problem of whether one can ever reach the bride as long as she remains shielded by the veil. Being unanswerable, the question must be asked repeatedly.

In one of his pithy remarks, Robert Frost has said that "poetry is what disappears in translation." Empirically it is hard to fault him, since we all know how painfully high is the rate of failure in translating poetry. Yet Auden remarks that, while he does not know a word of modern Greek, he has been much influenced by the Greek poet Cavafy. Hence, he concludes, "there must be some elements in poetry which are separable from their original verbal expression." Among these Auden mentions certain "technical conventions and devices" of verse, the "imagery of similes and metaphors," and "something I can only call, most inadequately, a tone of voice, a personal speech" which has to do, one gathers, with the paraphrasable sense of the original. Auden continues:

> To the degree . . . that a poem is the product of a certain culture, it is difficult to translate into the terms of another culture, but to the degree that it is the expression of a unique human being, it is as easy, or as difficult, for a person from an alien culture to appreciate as for one of the cultural group to which the poet happens to belong.

In the actuality of translation these sharply varying premises lead to sharply different approaches. Vladimir Nabokov has amusingly shown how unfaithful, indeed shamefully disloyal, translation can be to the original text. As if to acquiesce in and perhaps respond to Nabokov's view that a faithful translation from verse into verse is all but impossible, while at the same time refusing to follow him into the sterilities of translating verse into prose, Robert Lowell has developed what he calls "imitations": at best semi-translations, loosely related to the originals, and sometimes new poems merely "suggested" by the original text in another language. The danger in this practice is that it may mislead people into supposing they have before them translations.

Another view has been advanced by the distinguished translator of Greek drama, Dudley Fitts:

> . . . Nabokov states strongly his regard for the thoroughly documented rendering. . . . The trouble is that such a translation, though it gives the prose "sense" of the original together with an explanation of whatever goes to lift the prose sense above itself and transmute it into a form of art, might also provide no evidence beyond the saying so that the art was art in the first place. . . . We need something at once less ambitious and more audacious: another poem.

Another poem! Our own predisposition, insofar as it has affected the translations in this volume, is toward the difficult view of Dudley Fitts. Difficult, because in saying that the translation should be "another poem" he does not yet specify the precise relationship to be sought between the original and the translation that is to stand as "another poem." So the problem remains: which elements of the original can be "duplicated" or "captured" in translation? And since choices and sacrifices are the common lot of all translators, which order of priorities is he to observe?

Ideally the translator should seek to render the paraphrasable sense of a poem, its distinctive tone, its metrical structure, its stanzaic scheme, its arrangement of imagery and allusion, its pattern of sound or musicality, and its rhymes. We have placed these items in a sequence indicating roughly what we take to be an appropriate order of priority. A translator concentrating on metrics and rhyme will have a difficult task in rendering the sense of the poem, as well as producing verse written in passable English, for the requirements of meter and rhyme will probably force him into usages threatening clear sense and pleasing diction. A dominant concern with sense, however, carries the opposite danger of losing what is "poetic" in the poetry, thereby reducing it to mere flat statement.

In preparing this anthology we have checked each translation line for line, both for sense and verbal faithfulness. This is not at all to claim that each line corresponds exactly to the equivalent lines in the original: it neither can nor should, given differences in linguistic structure and the need to create "another poem" in English. But, human frailties and errors apart, we have examined with care why at certain points a translator may have felt obliged to take a greater or lesser "liberty" with his text.*

The translations in this volume are meant to be poems in English reflecting as closely and suggestively as possible the Yiddish originals in both sense and structure, while also communicating something of the tone and quality of the originals. (The name of the translator appears at the bottom of each poem.) In regard to rhyme, we have allowed the translators a large degree of freedom, in some instances even suggesting that the effort to rhyme exacted too high a price in sense and diction and should therefore be abandoned. In other instances we have felt that the nature of the original Yiddish poem required that a strong effort be made to achieve at least some rhyme. Unavoidably—every translator, from every language, experiences this—there appeared clashes between the desire for faithfulness in sense and structure and the desire for rhyme. In most such instances, we acquiesced in the sacrifice of rhyme.

As we worked on this book month after month, it became perfectly clear to us that some of our poets lend themselves more readily to translation than others, and some of the translations are more successful than others. That is unavoidable in a venture of this kind. Bialik was right: translation remains a veil. The only question is whether in a given instance the veil is more or less appropriate, more or less pleasing, more or less transparent. Our hope is that, given the necessity of the veil, the bride too will appear.

---

* In a few instances where the translators of the poems in this volume lacked Yiddish wholly or in part, the editors supplied scrupulously literal English versions of the poems and then checked the translators' versions against the original texts.

I

PIONEERS

ABRAHAM REISEN
(1876–1953)

MANY A NIGHT

I wrote my songs through many a dark night,
Choosing my rhymes like jewels, rare and bright.
In all those nights they flamed upon the dark,
But on my life they never shed one spark.

John Hollander

THE WORLD AND I

If all the world were on the rocks
And I alone in clover,
I'd open wide my door and bid
The sorry world come over.

I'd comfort and caress the world
And ease it in its grieving,
Till all the world took heart again
And stood up straight, believing.

If all the world were full of cheer
And I alone in sorrow
I'd reach out for my share of joy
Before another morrow.

But since the world and I are lost
In wretchedness past knowing,
There's no place for the world to come
And nowhere for my going.

Marie Syrkin

HOUSEHOLD OF EIGHT

Household of eight.
Beds are two.
When it gets late,
What do they do?

Three with father,
Three with mother:
Limbs
Over each other.

When it's night
And they go to bed,
Mother begins
To wish she were dead.

A resting place
All her own.
Narrow—
But you sleep alone.

Nathan Halper

THE WORLD'S SORROW

In the quiet field I wandered where
All my troubles had driven me,
Till I stood waiting, silently,
And heard the whole world's sorrow there.

All was quiet; the air did ring
With sounds, and I could barely hear
Someone moving about somewhere,
The world, in silence, sorrowing.

The moon rose high then, as night fell;
From where, I could not tell, nor why:
It shivered there against the sky
And seemed to be sorrowing as well.

The sum of the world's suffering,
The sorrows of her years, past me
Rode along there, silently,
Fluttering by, and echoing.

John Hollander

A SONG

The sweetest melody
Your heart can sing
Keep for your autumn hour,
Not for the spring.

Glad is the blossom time
With its own tune and chime;
Ah, but the sunset day—
Sing it away.

Marie Syrkin

THE NEW WORLD

A new world being made—one hears
In childhood that it has begun;
Then comes the passage of the years—
Is it not yet fully done?

The new world being made—always,
From childhood on—and on the day
They finally set the door in place,
All the walls have turned to gray.

The roof is hung—but as they start,
The pillars gradually give out;
It all begins to fall apart,
And so, once more, they rush about,

Calling to build it up again
And work, a true, united folk!
A spark is struck nearby, and then
All the world goes up in smoke.

John Hollander

O QUICKLY, MESSIAH

O quickly, Messiah, come quickly at last,
The world is engirdled with serpents, in vast
Poisonous circles of famine and care,
Terror and torment, decay and despair;
The earth has denied men the nurture they need—
O Messiah, come now on your silvery steed.

O quickly, Messiah, come; we are yet bound
In slavery's chains, wrapped round and around;
Humanity's blood lies in rust on the sword,
With no room in the world for the blood that has poured
Out from under the knout, from the wounds that still bleed—
O Messiah, come now on your silvery steed.

John Hollander

YEHOASH
(1872–1927)

PEOPLE

Now fewer mighty ones and less of the many,
But see, the sky brighter and wider.
And still we go linked together, and closer,
Climbing up and up the steps to where
Each of us given his full height
Will push away the ladder
And stand alone, and share!

Raphael Rudnick and Joseph Singer

THE STRONGEST

I'll be the strongest amid you,
Not lightning, stream or mountain blue,
But dew that falling to the earth
    Gives birth.

I'll be the strongest in my hour,
And lofty tree and quiet flower
Will both drink gratefully
    From me.

I'll be the strongest in the land.
I'll be the word that heals, the hand
That unseen and still, as from above,
    Gives love.

Marie Syrkin

LYNCHING

"Father of my soul,
Where shall I find You?"

Defiler!
Look at your work—
A black body striped bloody,
Eyes rolled back white in the black face,
And gleaming teeth trying to eat
The swollen red tongue.

"Father of my soul,
And Lord of all bodies,
Where shall I find You?"

Profanity!
He who shudders
In the blue webs
Of your holy twilight,
He who sways in your lament at night
And your song by day,
He who trembles in the corners
Of your unborn desires,
He who calls you, craves you, tears at you—
Has become black meat
With thick lips and strange hair.

And you dug you
Dug nails into his ribs,
Knives into the heart.

Spitting on his agony,
You left him dangling
On the tree.

Raphael Rudnick

AN OLD SONG

In the blossom-land Japan,
Somewhere thus an old song ran:

Said a warrior to a smith,
"Hammer me a sword forthwith.
Make the blade
Light as wind on water laid.
Make it long
As the wheat at harvest song,
Supple, swift
As a snake. Without a rift
Full of lightnings, thousand-eyed!
Smooth as silken cloth and thin
As the web that spiders spin.
And merciless as pain, and cold!"

"On the hilt what shall be told?"

"On the sword's hilt, my good man,"
Said the warrior of Japan,
"Trace for me
A running lake, a flock of sheep,
A cottage with a cherry tree
And one who sings her child to sleep."

Marie Syrkin

KOSUMI, THE CARVER

When in Nippon land the year is young,
On the cherry trees white birds are hung;
Cherry blossoms fall on children playing,
The winds blow gently in their swaying
Through the mountains of the Ancient Men.
Fleeter speeds the rickshaw runner then,

And the geisha's foot more nimbly glances
In the teahouse, through the measured dances;
Velvet leaves within her small tread's whim,
And the cherry feast in every limb.

From the hills, night quietly comes down
In her sheer silk gown
And her obi blue.
Wreaths of white and gold
Her brows enfold.
Strings of fire sway
On each street and way,
So on all
The white joy of the white-blossom day may fall.

Comrades kneel before
Kosumi's frail door:
"Kosumi, come for your heart's delight;
Every street is black,
Every eye is bright
With the cherry's feast-day white.
Come and catch the white birds as they flutter
From the branches borne
Down into the white stars' sieve of silver,
Down into the gold nets of the morn!"

In his bamboo house
Kosumi shakes temples whiter
Than the cherry blossoms on the boughs:
"Leaves may die,
Leaves may fall,
Cherries call
Fuller than the beaker of a king,
Brighter than the eye
Of the daughter of a king.
All lips will be stained merry
With the blood of the ripe cherry.
In my basket I shall gather
Cherry pits for Kosumi, the carver,

Tiny Buddhas on the tiny pits
I shall carve.
Suki Manus full of goodness,
Suki Manus full of wisdom,
Kosumi wants only cherry pits!"

Marie Syrkin

YANG-ZE-FU

The Empress Yang-Ze-Fu
Has palaces fourscore.
A hundred rooms each palace has,
Each room, a golden door.
Black, giant slaves guard over all
With iron shields and lances tall.
To her mirror Yang-Ze-Fu
Laughs—"Who is as great as you?"

The Empress Yang-Ze-Fu
To the white stream goes nightly.
She grows smaller than a nut.
On the stream a leaf is put,
Wherein she sails lightly.
And the oars the Empress has
Are two dainty blades of grass.
To the water Yang-Ze-Fu
Laughs—"Who is as small as you?"

Marie Syrkin

MORRIS ROSENFELD
(1862–1922)

THE SWEATSHOP

Corner of Pain and Anguish, there's a worn old house:
tavern on the street floor, Bible room upstairs.
Scoundrels sit below, and all day long they souse.
On the floor above them, Jews sob out their prayers.

Higher, on the third floor, there's another room:
not a single window welcomes in the sun.
Seldom does it know the blessing of a broom.
Rottenness and filth are blended into one.

Toiling without letup in that sunless den:
nimble-fingered and (or so it seems) content,
sit some thirty blighted women, blighted men,
with their spirits broken, and their bodies spent.

Scurf-head struts among them: always with a frown,
acting like His Royal Highness in a play;
for the shop is his, and here he wears the crown,
and they must obey him, silently obey.

Aaron Kramer

MY PLACE

Look for me not where myrtles green!
Not there, my darling, shall I be.
Where lives are lost at the machine,
that's the only place for me.

Look for me not where robins sing!
Not there, my darling, shall I be.
I am a slave where fetters ring,
that's the only place for me.

Look for me not where fountains splash!
Not there, my darling, shall I be.
Where tears are shed, where teeth are gnashed,
that's the only place for me.

And if your love for me is true,
then at my side you'll always be,
and make my sad heart sing anew,
and make my place seem sweet to me.

Aaron Kramer

MY LITTLE SON

I have a son, a little son,
a youngster very fine!
and when I look at him I feel
that all the world is mine.

But seldom do I see him when
he's wide awake and bright.
I always find him sound asleep;
I see him late at night.

The time clock drags me off at dawn;
at night it lets me go.
I hardly know my flesh and blood;
his eyes I hardly know . . . .

I climb the staircase wearily:
a figure wrapped in shade.
Each night my haggard wife describes
how well the youngster played;

how sweetly he's begun to talk;
how cleverly he said,
"When will my daddy come and leave
a penny near my bed?"

I listen, and I rush inside—
it must—yes, it must be!
My father-love begins to burn:
my child must look at me! . . .

I stand beside the little bed
and watch my sleeping son,
when hush! a dream bestirs his mouth:
"Where has my daddy gone?"

I touch his eyelids with my lips.
The blue eyes open then:
they look at me! they look at me!
and quickly shut again.

"Your daddy's right beside you, dear.
Here, here's a penny, son!"
A dream bestirs his little mouth:
"Where has my daddy gone?"

I watch him, wounded and depressed
by thoughts I cannot bear:
"One morning, when you wake—my child—
you'll find that I'm not here."

Aaron Kramer

EARTH

O earth, you angry, filthy gluttonous
Ripped throat swallowing everything
And leaving pain alive
Torn to pieces in your great belly—

Only the tombstones say what you have devoured.
My rage and pain curse you, bitch—
But how can I curse you now
That my child sleeps in your black bosom?
Swallowed, O you have swallowed the sweet light
Of that clear-eyed look, my happiness!
It is not here now, and what it was is earth.

Raphael Rudnick and Joseph Singer

THE EAGLE

The emperor of birds soaring
Up where cloud giants race—
The great eagle flies
Above, in the highest place.

The slam of his beating wings
Makes the air that moves him move.
Lonely, alone, lonely
With only the sky to love.

When heavy from hard journeys
He rests, regaining might
At the edge of deep waters
On a high mountain of light.

Hooded eyes scorn the world below,
The great head nods from side to side,
Until force within him, hungry,
Throws him down in lost, fierce pride.

Raphael Rudnick and Joseph Singer

DAVID EINHORN
(1886–)

THE LAST TO SING

The last to sing before the Ark is dead.
Padlocks hang in the house of the Jews.
The windows are boarded, and shadows
huddle in shame in the pews.

Bereavement without end
creeps on the naked walls,
and blazoned crown and priestly hands
lie broken above the Scrolls.

The last to sing before the Law is dead.
There is no one now to go up to the Ark.
The eternal flame, alone in its nook,
struggles and sputters to dark.

And soundless on the steps of the Ark
the abandoned *Shekhina* rests,
her head bowed down in sorrow,
black as night her dress.

And her lips seem to shudder
a last hushed plea,
as if the Ark from its arras had spoken:
Too late, too late, O you who are faithful to Me!

Cynthia Ozick

AND ALL OF THEM
ARE GONE

And all of them are gone,
clean away, with no trail:
not one word left behind,
not one letter in the mail.
Phantoms transparent as the air,
a love scarcely tasted,
friends untried for wear.

And all the time before—
a wide waste reach,
no sign of how one lives and sins.
I have stopped at too many inns,
have lost someone at each.

Often I wheel my skull around
to view
that long lone ground.
Then somewhere I see
a grave; and the far stone
with a moan
beckons me:
he was alone,
and now
you.

Cynthia Ozick

A PRAYER

Vast God, what I crave
is not vast but small.
Give me a grave
tranquil and mild
and on it let fall
a tear of my child.

When death shuts my eye
I pray to see
a grandson stop by
my guardian tree
while summer's young.
Let him seek on my stone
in my father's tongue
a language his own,
still read and known.

The shade
I am doomed
to become
has need of no
heaven. Annul the creed,
let eternity go
and grant me grow
into earth's own niche.
Cruel to die in a ditch
on the road! Never to know
whose foot will tread
on the dreaming head,
on the last place where
the word
flies up into air
unheard.

Cynthia Ozick

II

DIE YUNGE AND THEIR CONTEMPO-RARIES

MANI LEIB
(1883–1953)

I AM

I am Mani Leib, whose name is sung—
In Brownsville, Yehupetz and farther, they know it:
Among cobblers, a splendid cobbler; among
Poetical circles, a splendid poet.

A boy straining over the cobbler's last
On moonlit nights ... like a command,
Some hymn struck at my heart, and fast
The awl fell from my trembling hand.

Gracious, the first Muse came to meet
The cobbler with a kiss, and, young,
I tasted the Word that comes in a sweet
Shuddering first to the speechless tongue.

And my tongue flowed like a limpid stream,
My song rose as from some other place;
My world's doors opened onto dream;
My labor, my bread, were sweet with grace.

And all of the others, the shoemaker boys
Thought that my singing was simply grand:
For their bitter hearts, my poems were joys.
Their source? They could never understand.

For despair in their working day's vacuity
They mocked me, spat at me a good deal,

And gave me the title, in perpetuity,
Of Purple Patchmaker, Poet and Heel.

Farewell then, brothers, I must depart:
Your cobbler's bench is not for me.
With songs in my breast, the Muse in my heart,
I went among poets, a poet to be.

When I came, then, among their company,
Newly fledged from out my shell,
They lauded and they laureled me,
Making me one of their number as well.

O Poets, inspired and pale, and free
As all the winged singers of the air,
We sang of beauties wild to see
Like happy beggars at a fair.

We sang, and the echoing world resounded.
From pole to pole chained hearts were hurled,
While we gagged on hunger, our sick chests pounded:
More than one of us left this world.

And God, who feedeth even the worm—
Was not quite lavish with his grace,
So I crept back, threadbare and infirm,
To sweat for bread at my working place.

But blessed be, Muse, for your bounties still,
Though your granaries will yield no bread—
At my bench, with a pure and lasting will,
I'll serve you solely until I am dead.

In Brownsville, Yehupetz, beyond them, even,
My name shall ever be known, O Muse.
And I'm not a cobbler who writes, thank Heaven,
But a poet, who makes shoes.

John Hollander

COME, SERENE PLAINNESS

Come, serene Plainness, with your bare blade cut
Through my soul's black entanglements until
My world, from heavy, sullen fetters freed,
Shines like a burst of sun upon my sill;

So all my eyes found blind, hidden and strange,
In murky darkness covered and remote,
Will suddenly grow clear like rainbow light,
Or like the linen whiteness of my coat.

And all of living, all not living things
Now severed and apart from me, bring near;
Make them transparent like pure water's flow,
Close like my hands' ten fingers and as dear.

Then from the tight cell of my narrow grief
The voice of all who suffer rising strong
Will cry to me like kin to kindred crying,
Will ring out cleansed, transmuted in my song.

Marie Syrkin

HUSH

Hush and hush—no sound be heard.
Bow in grief but say no word.
Black as pain and white as death,
Hush and hush and hold your breath.

Heard by none and seen by none
Out of the dark night will he,
Riding on a snow-white steed,
To our house come quietly.

From the radiance of his face,
From his dress of shining white
Joy will shimmer and enfold;
Over us will fall his light.

Quieter—no sound be heard!
Bow in grief but say no word.
Black as pain and white as death,
Hush and hush and hold your breath.

If we have been mocked by them,
If we have been fooled again
And the long and weary night
We have waited all in vain,

We will bend down very low
To the hard floor, and then will
Stand more quiet than before
Stiller, stiller and more still.

Marie Syrkin

SEVEN BROTHERS

Of seven brothers
with gray eyes
and with blue eyes
three are tall as
palm trees sinewy
and proud and upward-
looking and three
stand low as sugar
canes sweet-rooted
firm upon the
earth and I the
singer of this
song hang like a

green willow
between winds.

And now the father
of us all is dead:
our woe, our woe!
he dwindled like
a thin oak in a
receding landscape
and on that
sad and rainy day
his seven sons
arose from fog
and with hands
filled with rain
we covered our
father's eyelids
with the black
shards of death:
then all of us
helped shovel the
red clay of Long
Island over his
coffin.

And afterwards
the seven of us
put up a wooden
marker on his grave
and then like a clump
of trees caught
suddenly in an alarm
of wind our forest-
voices shook with
one lament, the single
prayer we sent up
for the dead:
yisgadal!

On the rainy day
our father died we
seven brothers with
gray and blue and sorrowing
eyes said our last
good-byes: we parted
on the outskirts
of New York
and each one of seven
went his solitary way
on one of seven
solitary avenues.

Miriam Waddington

INDIAN SUMMER

My Indian summer, like an offering,
Burns into gold and spirals of smoke.
With brown hand, I push my last
Starry ember through the ash.
Night and villages. On moonlit flutes
The crickets play a breaking music on my heart;
In white grass, by blue-washed pickets,
Gourds are yellow like the moon.
Trees—blue, waxen—in cool space shining.
Like candles, upright: men fearful before God.
Sharp in stillness, the fall of a spent leaf.
Even sharper—the worries in my step.

Nathan Halper

EAST BROADWAY

Of all rich streets, most dear to me
Is my shabby Jewish East Broadway.
Graying houses—two uneven rows:
Frail, restless and exhausted bodies:

The worry tinged with God's old fire—
It barely glows, yet it does not die.
And on the corners, seers and rebels
Who shout a nation's woe unto the sky.
And the poets. O rhapsodic brothers!
On the grime of each stone, you transmute
A nation's heart—finely—
Into the strains of a new hymnal.
Long after you, each stone will join
Your people in the prayer of your song.

Nathan Halper

TO A GENTILE POET

Heir of Shakespeare, knights and shepherds,
Gentile poet, you are fortunate.
Yours is the earth the fat pig walks on,
Giving pasture to him and to your Muse.
If you but pause on a branch, your twitter
Will gain replies from all the far places.
From the field, riches; the city, comfort.
Equanimity from sated spirits.
I—unneeded, a poet among Jews,
Growing, like wild grass, from a soil not ours,
My sires, wanderers with dusty beards,
Who feed on the grit of fairs and old tomes.
In an alien world I sing of the cares
Of men in a desert, beneath alien stars.

Nathan Halper

CHRISTMAS

The night awakes the copper of the bells.
The town is full of incense, torch and frost.
Their god arises peacefully from death
And, on high poles, the crowd is carrying

His image; and the blind and heavy tread
Bears hate; as in hushed and crowded quarters
Israel's children fearfully rely—
O compassionate God—upon Thy grace.
Beyond door and shutter sings the snow.
Frostily, the wide blue heavens glitter.
From its crown unto its loins, the night
Is hung with stars and rest. Only a cry
Beats against the wall of quiet—
The blood clamors in anguish at their knife.

Nathan Halper

BY THE THRESHOLD

That late night, a woman waited for him,
With all the windows shining to the stars,
With all the hot, sweet odors of desire
That, tenderly yet shyly, she had saved
For him alone. But, stubbornly, he stayed
Before a different window, watching
The strip of light behind the dark drapes,
For a second woman, who will bring him
Joy that she has stolen from another.
Soon she will lull the other man and child,
And come out, and lay around his neck
The other's shadow, the rope of her own noose—
Which he will tighten, there
By the threshold of bliss that he has left.

Nathan Halper

THE BARD

Let noisy steel, let gray stone
Replace green grass: the bang of hammer, tongs,
And rumble of wheel—the music of the bird.
Let crickets yield to whining saw:

The bard to trader. Yet, as in the first day,
The grass will thrust its blade through stone,
The cricket will arrive, above the sound of steel
A bird will fill the air with song.
So too the bard. Pious, away from shop,
The bustle of trade, the rush of steel,
With ink, parchment, pen he will move quietly,
To a holiness of word: to fashion
Prayer for Mankind: to bind the heart
To God: to unbind the heaviness on our lips.

Nathan Halper

SPARROWS

Snow in hair, winter in my bones,
The eyes weary, loyal, I greet
The sparrows like friends, this gang
That, in March, is already in my yard.
In a wide band, chirping, clamorous
They come and (hop!) are scattered
Like grain on the thawing snow:
Then call—and they are gone.
Longingly, the eyes follow. My heart wakens.
I recall my friends: my crowd
So noisy, like the sparrows in their dance.
They could not reach the joy of winter.
In summer, they left—before harvest,
The joy of their summer unable to sustain them.

Nathan Halper

INSCRIPTION ON
MY GRAVESTONE

Here lies Hirsh Itzi's son, the shards on his eyes,
Buried in a shroud, just like a seemly Jew.
To this world he came, as from a fantastic land
To a yearly fair on foot—there to

Sell the winds. A friendly, eager dealer, he would
Measure all he had into a pair of scales.
Then, as early stars had begun to draw the skies
Into the Sabbath kingdom, wearily
He would come home for the lighting of candles.
Here he lies. His grave, covered with green moss,
Is a dividing line between him and the gray week,
Between Sabbath peace and the hustle of the fair.
And, to his children, he has left in his will
A large remnant of the winds he did not sell.

Nathan Halper

ZISHE LANDAU
(1889–1937)

FOR ALL THAT EVER HAS BEEN OURS

Now, for our shattered Jewish life
I kneel, and pray to you for grace;
I weep for our old mother Vilna,
For Brod; for every holy place;

I weep for Warsaw, Kovno, Lemberg,
For every large and little town
Whereon the foe of old has fallen,
And which the foe will fall upon.

For every dirty Jewish alley,
Each dingy hole with goods for sale;
For every pawnshop, tavern, alehouse;
For our false measure, weight, and scale.

For every merry Jewish brothel,
That on a Gentile street seemed gay;
For all that ever has been ours
Now vanishing in smoke away.

There's goodness in whatever's Jewish;
Rebuild this poor life, Lord; restore
With words as yet unheard, unspoken,
Your people's needy souls once more.

Marie Syrkin

TONIGHT

An evening at home:
sitting in the house and looking
out the window.
The wife sits in her chair embroidering
and sewing maybe.
I turn around and look at her: she is just sitting there
not doing anything,
holding idle in her hands
the needle, the scissors, and the cloth,
thinking of our life together, day after day
each with its worries;
how when we have a talk, the important thing always goes unsaid,
and how you never can escape
the habitual and boring routine of daily life;
how every day gone is lost—
it will never come back, never,
and just like today, tomorrow will pass,
and whatever it was you lived for
has defeated you.

She is thinking like this
when hopefully, she looks at you
at the very moment you turn from the window
and look at her too; and in that glance
everything becomes absolutely clear.
So you get up,
go over to her, your own wife,
put a hand gently on her shoulder
and with the other smooth back her hair,
and want to say many loving things
but you can't.
You look out the window again,
the night dark, the stars bright,
and in your heart is peace.

Edward Field

PLEASURES OF THE SOUL

I'm not attracted to girls any more,
sixteen, eighteen, you know, teenagers,
dancing about, always on the go,
with eyes glowing at you
like motorcycle headlights,
wearing dainty little blouses
with the pink and blue ribbons of childhood,
and shorts with ruffled edges.

I don't even care for boys any more.

What gives me pleasure now
                         is:
Conversation in the evening
in a comfortable room, drinking hot tea,
talking over old times
and friends who are gone,
looking through photograph albums,
reading here and there in the classics;

                       and best:
women in their thirties or older
who have been through the mill
and know how to make love with a man.
They used to be active in the movement
but now begin to get heavy
and start squeezing themselves into corsets.
They don't always remember
to take precautions
and get caught sometimes
but their men know how to get it taken care of.

They have children,
set up nice, sunny apartments,
eat health foods,

read highbrow books,
and are bored.

Edward Field

ON THE EL

I hang on a strap in the El.
The train rushes on, hot and stuffy.
But I'm at home in the crowd
of women and advertisements.
So much to see. I look at the people,
at everything. My eye roams
back and forth, everywhere.
Like a dog, my nose
runs around sniffing:
It's greedy.
>   *And a whole part of myself*
>   *that I thought was surely dead within me*
>   *woke up then.*
The train races on, tenements passing.
Big blobs of women relax
with legs spread
and smile with a yielding sweetness,
their mouths chewing,
drowsy, tired, and lazy;
while others perch, thighs squeezed together,
lips pursed thin—
just like that: thighs squeezed
and lips thin.
You are groggy from the heat
and the train's rocking
from side to side;
but what fills you with sweet languor,
like drowsing in fresh-cut hay
yet alert for a child's cry in the night,
is the fragrance that comes from them.

Edward Field

AT THE SILENT MOVIES

"HOW ENDLESSLY FOOLISH WOMEN ARE."
REUBEN ICELAND

The pictures flicker on the screen.
They're hard to follow once you've seen
the girl with long hands and little feet
fidgeting for attention in the next seat.

You sneak an arm behind her chair:
Blissfully the minutes fly.
"I'd like to be a movie star."
You risk a hug, she doesn't mind.

Her body yielding as you squeeze,
she gazes softly in your eyes,
and on your face you feel her hair.
You whisper a line from a friend's poem,
How endlessly foolish women are.

Edward Field

MOISHE
LEIB HALPERN
(1886–1932)

THE TALE OF THE WORLD

I ordain the conquering of the world
—So the great king said,
And all the people were duly informed,
And all the mothers truly mourned
Their living sons as though dead.
But the plow in the field,
And the cobbler's leather sole,
And the mouse in his hole,
Laughed without sound
When the news was brought round,
The bad, black news.

Now the world has been conquered at last.
What's to be done with the thing?
The Royal Palace is far too small
—They forgot to measure the world at all
When designing the opening.
But the plow in the field,
And the cobbler's leather sole,
And the mouse in his hole,
Laughed till they cried,
Laughed so hard in their pride
That the king's crown was shaken.

The courtiers, meanwhile, hold that the world
Should be kept out there under guard.

But the king has turned a deathly gray,
Fearing the world will get wet some day
When the rain falls hard.
But the plow in the field,
And the cobbler's leather sole,
And the mouse in his hole,
Laugh till they cry,
Laugh till they nearly die.
The world's still there, outside.

John Hollander

MAN, THAT APE

Man, that ape, the first time in his life
He sees an elephant at night,
In all that darkness, the elephant's
Wearing, it seems, a pair of pants.
He broods about this for a while,
Then from some fig leaves, constructs a pair
Of pants, a pull-over, and underwear,
A shirt and shoes and then a hat,
And a skullcap for wearing under that.
Man, that ape.

That's nothing—the first time in his life
He sees the risen moon on high,
He locks his wife in an embrace
To singe the hair from off her face;
And after that, to make her gleam,
First he smears on a chalky cream,
Then sticks on all the gold he's got.
She doesn't emanate one beam.
He howls and bays and starts to scream.
Man, that ape.

That's nothing—the first time in his life
He sees the sun ascending where

The mountaintop and heaven meet,
He raises his right fist to swear
That he will follow it up there;
Since when, too short of time, he's run
From east to west, just like the sun.
The sun comes up, the sun descends:
He climbs, and falls—it never ends.
Man, that ape.

John Hollander

THE BIRD

So this bird comes, and under his wing is a crutch,
And he asks why I keep my door on the latch;
So I tell him that right outside the gate
Many robbers watch and wait
To get at the hidden bit of cheese,
Under my ass, behind my knees.

Then through the keyhole and the crack in the jamb
The bird bawls out he's my brother Sam,
And tells me I'll never begin to believe
How sorely he was made to grieve
On shipboard, where he had to ride
Out on deck, he says, from the other side.

So I get a whiff of what's in the air,
And leave the bird just standing there.
Meanwhile—because one never knows,
I mean—I'm keeping on my toes,
Further pushing my bit of cheese
Under my ass and toward my knees.

The bird bends his wing to shade his eyes
—Just like my brother Sam—and cries,
Through the keyhole, that *his* luck should shine
Maybe so blindingly as mine,

Because, he says, he's seen my bit
Of cheese, and he'll crack my skull for it.

It's not so nice here any more.
So I wiggle slowly toward the door,
Holding my chair and that bit of cheese
Under my ass, behind my knees,
Quietly. But then, as if I care,
I ask him whether it's cold out there.

They are frozen totally,
Both his poor ears, he answers me,
Declaring with a frightful moan
That, while he lay asleep alone
He ate up his leg—the one he's lost.
If I let him in, I can hear the rest.

When I hear the words "ate up," you can bet
That I'm terrified; I almost forget
To guard my bit of hidden cheese
Under my ass there, behind my knees.
But I reach below and, yes, it's still here,
So I haven't the slightest thing to fear.

Then I move that we should try a bout
Of waiting, to see which first gives out,
His patience, there, behind the door,
Or mine, in my own house. And more
And more I feel it's funny, what
A lot of patience I have got.

And that's the way it's stayed, although
That was some seven years ago.
I still call out "Hi, there!" through the door.
He screams back " 'Lo, there" as before.
"Let me out" I plead, "don't be a louse"
And he answers, "Let me in the house."

But I know what he wants. So I bide
My time and let him wait outside.

He inquires about the bit of cheese
Under my ass, behind my knees;
Scared, I reach down, but, yes, it's still here.
I haven't the slightest thing to fear.

John Hollander

LONG FOR HOME

Long for home and hate your homeland.
What can you be
But a tiny twig
Snapped from a withered tree?
An ashen speck
In a burning tower?
Little soul, raging on your day of woe,
When a man here goes astray
What can he aspire to
But insanity,
To rend himself and be alone?
Weep, then, for your passing years.
Like rain upon the ocean
Fall your tears.

Meyer Schapiro

SONG: WEEKEND'S OVER

There in the shadowy, dank hall
Right alongside the ground-floor stair—
A weeping girl, attended by
A grimy hand in the mussed-up hair.
——A little love in big Manhattan.

The hair—a whiff of some cheap rinse
The hand—hard, stiff and leathery
Two equal lovers, for whom this is

As good as it'll ever be.
——A little love in big Manhattan.

It's strange to listen to two people
Standing there in the dark, unheard;
Why doesn't Sammy say a word?
Why doesn't Bessie say a word?
——A little love in big Manhattan.

They may be talking, but it's all
Blanketed by the howl, instead,
From a million iron fire escapes
And all the dark ceilings overhead.
——A little love in big Manhattan.

Ceilings on ceilings and beds over beds;
Steamy air, wrapped in smoking shrouds;
From the top floor down, a chasm falls;
From above, acres open to the clouds.
——A little love in big Manhattan.

O huge night city, such grim strangeness
Wraps you up in the darkness here!
Man and wife sleep by the million
Like drunks all bloated up with beer.
——A little love in big Manhattan.

Like monkeys in the trees, the children
Hang in their fire escapes, asleep;
Soot drifts down from above their heads,
Dropped by the moon, a chimney sweep.
——A little love in big Manhattan.

And the girl Bessie knows "from nothing"
And Sammy, too, with his open mouth,
And Monday swims up before your eyes,
A desert of dead miles toward the south.
——A little love in big Manhattan.

And even Bessie's poor old mother
No longer asks, "Where is that kid?"
It doesn't matter that black hair
Has all been bleached to blonde and red.
——A little love in big Manhattan.

It isn't that he's ill, the sad one
Who contemplates these things at night;
But sick of his own sadness only,
He lies and broods, his pipe alight.
——A little love in big Manhattan.

John Hollander

THE LAST

Evening sun.
And, in evening cold, all the flies
In the corners of the panes are numb,
If not already dead.
On the rim of a water glass, the last
Is alone in the whole house.
I speak:
"Dear fly,
Sing something of your far-off land."
I hear her weep— She answers:
May her right leg wither
If she plucks a harp
By strange waters,
Or forgets the dear dung heap
That had once been her homeland.

Nathan Halper

MY HOME, ZLOCHEV

Zlochev, O my home, my town,
With a steeple, *shul* and bath,
Wives who sit in the market place
And little Jews who scramble like dogs
Around the peasant who's coming down
With a basket of eggs from the hill—
How life in the spring wakens in me
My poor little bit of yearning for thee—
My home, Zlochev.

But when I begin to recall
Rich Rappaport, as he goes
With his fat belly to *shul*,
And Shyeh Hillel, the pious man,
Who would sell the sun and its shine
As he would a pig in a poke—
It is enough to darken in me
Like a candle, my longing for thee—
My home, Zlochev.

How does it go, the tale of a fop:
Once, in the twilight, he looked so long
At the angels around the sun
Till a drunken *goy* with an ax
Gave him such a blow in the vest
That it almost finished him off—
The drunken *goy* is hate in me
For my grandfather and therefore thee—
My home, Zlochev.

You are my witness. It really was so.
When grandfather, helped by the police,
Put my mother out of the house,
My grandmother, on widespread feet,
Simpered almost as honey-sweet
As a peasant girl with two soldiers—

Cursed be that hatred in me
Which reminds me of her and of thee—
My home, Zlochev.

They stood in a ring, like naked Jews
Around a scalded man in the bath,
Shaking their heads, stroking beards,
At the thrown-out packs
The rags and tatters in sacks
And the broken remains of a bed—
My mother still is crying in me,
As that time, under heaven, in thee—
My home, Zlochev.

Yet the world is a wonderful thing.
With horse and wagon over a field
We dragged ourselves to a train
That flies like a demon over the land
Till it reaches a steerage that goes
To downtown New York—
This is the only solace to me:
That I won't be buried in thee—
My home, Zlochev.

Nathan Halper

PAIN OF THE WORLD

The city begins not far from my house.
On a stone, outside in the night,
An old god sits and weeps
For all the doors have been closed to him.

Near to my house, between night and smoke,
The watchmen laugh so loud and wild—
As if, by hitting iron on gold,
They would still their own fright.

In a stable, not far from my house,
Sit three ancients with hoary beard
And crowns of light on head and hands,
Holy men from eastern lands.

And, on hard straw, the wife,
Also naked, old and gray,
Moans, a thin tree in the wind,
And rocks herself as you rock a child.

Over us—the pain of the world.
It cries through the windows and curses
The star which had been awaited
And, with light, deceived us once more.

Nathan Halper

POEM

I'll sit there with that beard, my green one,
Across from the empty, golden tray;
A herring's head of mother-of-pearl
In my black lapel will gleam away.

And she'll come in then, in her gray dress,
Like something carved in ivory,
And I'll lower my eyes to the empty tray
And only think about getting free.

She'll weep, then, like a wounded bird
With bleeding wings, facing me there
As a star slides down from heaven
To hang above her in the air.

And like a great king, then, I'll tug
At my long, downward-curved mustache,
Then vanish with my head sunk low,
To golden spurs' resounding crash.

I'll hear a rustling sound behind me
Like a heart stretching out each hand;
I'll slowly turn around once more,
Confronting her then: there I'll stand.

Still looking as if made of wax—
I shall take pleasure in the sight.
But meanwhile all her lovely hair
Will turn quite silver-gray with fright.

Standing this way, and motionless,
Without a flutter, I may die,
And my beard, green moon of sorrow,
May seem longer to my eye.

So in the vast, glassy palace
Heavy stillness grows yet more still:
White-shrouded corpses, a thousand years,
Peer in past every window sill.

Until, outside, their whiteness plays
On harp strings as the night wind nears;
She will see that my blood is a flying cloud,
Is starlight that weeps and disappears.

John Hollander

THE WILL

So this is how I did myself in:
No sooner did the sun begin
To shine, than I was up and away,
Gathering goat shit for my tune
—The one I wrote just yesterday
About the moonlight and the moon—
And then I put with these also
Some poems from my portfolio
In re the Bible's sanctity

(Just thinking of them sickens me)
And these I wrapped up in my rag
Of an old coat, packed up like a bag,
After which, I took the whole shebang,
Put up a nail, and let it hang
Outside my window, on a tray.
Adults and children passed my way
And asked what that mess up there could be,
So I answered them, on bended knee:
These are all my years; I think
They went all rotten with infection
By wisdom, and its ancient stink,
From my precious book collection.
But when my son, the little boy,
(In my sea of sorrow and cup of joy
He's just turned four) strained his eyes to see
Those summits of sublimity,
Well—I put him on my knee
And spake thus: Harken thou to me,
My son and heir, I swear that, just
As none disturb the dead in their rest,
So, when you have finally grown,
I'll leave you thoroughly alone.
Want to be a loan shark, a bagel-lifter?
Be one, my child.
Want to murder, set fires, or be a grifter?
Be one, my child.
Want to change off girls with the speed that those
Same girls keep changing their own clothes?
Change away, my child.
But one thing, child, I have to say:
If once ambition leads you to try
To make some kind of big display
Of yourself with what's hanging up there in the sky;
If you dare (but may that time not come soon!)
To write about moonlight and the moon,
Or some poem of the Bible, poisoning the world,
Then, my dear,
If I'm worth something then by way of any

Money, so much as a single penny,
I'll make my will, leaving everything
To my *landsman,* the future Polish King.
Though we've both stopped calling each other "thou,"
I'll chop up, like a miser shredding
Cake for beggars at a wedding,
All the ties that bind us now:
Poppa-chopper   Son-schmon
And so   help me   God in   Heaven
This
Will
Be
Done.

John Hollander

POEM

Judging by the desolation
And the harsh animal roar
I would have thought it's a desert out there,
With an old lion creeping
Round a boulder, because he is sick
And needs a place to die.
But in truth it was a dreary city
Where a lunatic on hands and feet
Circled a fallen house
Dragging after him a skull on a string
Tied to his belt.

Irving Howe

REUBEN ICELAND
(1884–1955)

STILL LIFES—I

Like cool ample breasts
hiding a secret ardor,
the heavy grapes lie near
the brown virile pears.
Consumed by redness,
two apples with brazen femininity
nestle close to a glistening,
ripe-with-wisdom orange.
A pair of bananas gape like clumsy yokels.
Eagerly,
like a girl after her first kiss,
a cherry breaks away from its red stem.

Etta Blum

STILL LIFES—II

The cold black vase—
a slim youth waiting for a command,
who raises high
a thin bright stem with tender bells.
About the stem
fully blossomed lilac like an evening cloud.
Doomed to perpetual confinement,
the submissive flowers
curve over the rim.

Etta Blum

STILL LIFES—III

Bread and cheese and honey on the rustic table.
From two slight glasses
tea beckons goldenly.
Veiled with dew,
the carafe winks coolly green.
In one corner a woman's handkerchief.
Close by, the small discreet hand
on a slim book of poems
bound in wine-colored silk.

Etta Blum

AT THE PORT

You strangers with the large veined hands,
bowlegs, and faces tough like hides,
from whom emanate odors of sea and tar
and rust of heavy anchor chains:
O you, to whom all races and languages are unknown,
yet who carry about with you
the dust and mold of all lands
together with nostalgia of remote skies:
O you, from whose shoulders defiance sprouts,
welcome me!

Etta Blum

WILLIAM BLAKE

Tiriel! Tiriel!
Wrathful warrior and scoffer!
Revered and jeered one,
More sober in drunkenness,
saintlier in sin.

You, eternal child
with the seer's eyes,
cat's claws and
wings of an eagle!

Etta Blum

H. LEIVICK
(1888–1962)

ON THE ROADS OF SIBERIA

Even now
on the roads of Siberia
you can find
a button,
a shred of one of my shoelaces,
a belt,
a bit of broken cup,
a leaf of Scripture.

Even now
on the rivers of Siberia
you can find
some trace:
a scrap of one of my tattered shoes;
in the woods
a bloodied swatch dried stiff;
some frozen footprints
over the snow.

Cynthia Ozick

THE NIGHT IS DARK

The night is dark
And I am blind,
From my hand the stick
Is torn by the wind.

Bare is my sack,
Empty my heart,
A burden are both,
A useless load.

I hear the touch
Of someone's hand:
I pray you allow me
To carry your load.

Together we go,
The world is black:
I carry the sack
And he . . . my heart.

Meyer Schapiro

LAMENT AT NIGHT

At midnight I would hear my father rise
And chant the threnody for Zion's fall.
I envy him his prayer—for fifty years
That cry pursues me, mourning over all.

And yet I do the things my father did;
I mourn for ruin and the guiltless dead;
Like him I bite my lip and grit my teeth,
But this I lack—his beard of flaming red.

In fifty years, I wonder, will my sons
Long after me with the same love and pain?
Will they start up at night trembling and awed,
Some line I wrote upon their lips again?

Should that be so—then hear me, Lord of Time,
And show this mercy to these sons of mine:
Erase, wipe clean, as chalk is wiped from slate
My nights, my dreadful nights, of nineteen thirty-nine.

Marie Syrkin

HERE LIVES THE
JEWISH PEOPLE

The imprisoned life of the prison city
burns with a white blaze.
In the streets of the Jewish East Side
white fires burn still whiter.

I love to wander in the fieriness of the Jewish East Side,
to shove in and out of the cramped stalls and pushcarts,
breathing the smell and saltiness
of a feverish stripped life.
And always when, gazing, I see creep up through the whiteness
Jews bearded and from head to toe hung with
Ladies' and girls' dresses dragging them down,
and Jewish men, or women, with sick little birds
that for a penny pick out a fortune card and turn yearning and
  pleading eyes on the buyer,
and Jews pushing themselves along on two-wheeled platforms,
  blind cripples, who sit sunk down deep
in their shoulders and can see with their shoulders
the color and size of every thrown coin—
then I am roused by a buried longing, a boyhood longing
to be transformed into the lame beggar
who used to hop from street to street of our town
(Luria was his name)
and clatter with his crutch over sidewalks and thresholds.

Who knows if sometimes I see the same beggar sitting on that
  barrow,
the beggar my boyhood craved? His blindness sees my staring.
Once the world was not imprisoned as now,
though white as now,
fiery and white.

Hour by hour I walk the streets of the Jewish East Side,
and in the fiery whiteness my eyes paint fantastic turrets,
elongated columns soaring up over the ruined stalls,

up to the emptied sky of New York.
Turrets hung all over their parapets with signs flashing and
glowing:
Here Lives the Jewish People.

The imprisoned life of the prison city
slips into yellow-gray shadows
and in the streets of the Jewish East Side
the yellow-gray deepens.
Step by step come the Jews dragging dresses for sale,
for ladies, for girls—they vanish around some corner;
the woman is carrying the cage with its sick little bird,
and the box still full of fortunes.
The blind cripple is trundling home
through streets cleared of pushcarts and stalls.
My longing grows. I let myself follow
the hard jutting shoulders of the cripple.
(Luria was his name.)
I am enticed by his progress, his nest-seeking.
Until suddenly I am knifed by a look,
the look of an eye sprung open in the middle of his back.

Stillness. Midnight.
Once the world was not as now,
dark and shadowed.

And in the darkness the turrets loom in earnest,
they that in the white flame of day were a dream;
they reveal themselves in all their vastness and roundness,
like the thick towers of fortresses.
Turrets hung all over their parapets with red warning signs:
Here Sleeps the Jewish People.

Stillness. Midnight.
The years of my childhood cry in me, the longing.

Cynthia Ozick

SANITORIUM

Gate, open;
door sill, creep near.
Room, I'm here;
back to the cell.

Fire in my flesh,
snow on my skull.
My shoulder heaves
a sack of grief.

Good-bye. Good-bye.
Hand. Eye.
Burning lip
charred by good-bye.

Parted from whom?
From whom fled?
Let the riddle slip
unsaid.

The circling plain
is fire and flame:
fiery snow
on the hills.

Look—this open door
and gate. Guess.
Hospital? Prison?
some monkish place?

Colorado! I throw
my sack of despair
on your fiery floor
of snow.

Cynthia Ozick

GROWN FOLKS

Lay your head upon my knee—
Sweet to lie so, easefully.
Children fall asleep alone,
Lullabies are for the grown.
Children have their toys for play
When they will or when they may.
Grown folks play with one another.
Grown folks must play on forever.

Marie Syrkin

GOD, A BOY

Night and fireflies,
a zigzag lane.
I wish I had a song
that could explain.

Words can only stare
and ebb away:
the newborn earth has lived
one day.

In the aftermath of storm
the Milky Way is spun.
God's sweet scent
still rides around the sun.

Fresh up from the abyss,
flung toward purposes,
everything's without a name.
Smile, Enigma, play your game.

The moon's a cotton toy
of bells and flickerings.

God's a little boy
at play with childish things.

How queer to see my head
peering from a well!
The moonlight spreads
where my reflection fell.

I stand and gaze with fear:
how is it he comes here—
ancient gray-haired man—
on an earth that just began?

Night and fireflies,
a crooked trail.
Hark; wake, look up.
See my song sail.

Cynthia Ozick

A VOICE

A voice calls out: "You must!"
Must what? O voice, explain!
Instead of an answer I hear
That call again.

I peer behind the door,
I dash at every wall;
I search, though no one strange
Has sent that call.

I've known them all my life,
The caller and his call,
Yet it seems to me I hear
What I never heard at all.

It cries: "You must! you must!"
And only God can tell
Whether *must* is my redemption,
Or *must* will be my hell.

Cynthia Ozick

CAIN AND ABEL

Abel lies in the field,
killed. Cain eats
with his snout in the pot,
a bear after sweets.

Noon, the sun is afire.
A dry waste field—
only a patch is tilled,
and no sower.

Face up, the killer lies
gorged.
His steely body swells
as he snores.

His fingers are tangles
of thorns.
Red hairs on his temples
whorl like horns.

Beasts come.
Weak and numb
they turn and creep
from that fearful sleep.

They crawl to the other,
who never stirs
face down in the furrow
on all fours.

Abel lies still, earth
in his mouth:
over him at evening
the lion's mane dangling.

Over Abel's head the lion roars
for marrow and meat.
Sweating Cain snores
and grinds his teeth.

The lion bides his time
till Cain's grunts wane
and stars gleam
on the pot's rim.

He sinks into Abel's limbs,
his hatred foams.
Abel with his mouth down
keeps kissing the ground.

Cain rouses and yawns—
the lion runs. Cain
wants his brother's love again:
sparse are his remains.

A head. A foot. Bits of rib.
Cain howls into his pot.
The head in the evening light
smiles—face up.

Cynthia Ozick

THE BOOK OF JOB

SECTION FIVE

(Job is lying as if immersed in a mound of ashes, invisible to a side view. He is in great pain: his face and body are sore and swollen. Though he can occasionally move his hands, he cannot

move his body. His hair and his long gray beard are wildly di-
sheveled. A tent rises above him. A clay oil lamp set on a bit of
stone is barely flickering. It is late at night. Job's wife, desperately
angry, stands before him. To one side, his three friends—Eliphaz,
Bildad and Zophar—sit on the ground. Job is complaining in a
high-pitched, grieving voice that breaks from time to time, an
indication that his cries have been going on for a long time and
are beginning to weary him. He has been lamenting in this fash-
ion for a day and a night. As he recounts his grief, his voice is
now stormy, now diminished to a weary groan, as if he were in
his final agony. Sometimes he is tempestuous, giving no sign that
he has wept; sometimes his voice is hushed, prayerful, almost
unheard.)

JOB: *Let the day perish wherein I was born,*
And the night in which it was said,
There is a man-child conceived.

Let that day be darkness;
Let not God regard it from above,
Neither let the light shine upon it.

WIFE: Cursing again. Still cursing yourself. The same words
Since yesterday.

JOB: You, at least, could stop tormenting me.

WIFE: It's that voice of yours that offends me.
Curse God—not yourself.

JOB: O to hear such things.

WIFE: It's the coward in you speaking.
If God wants you to die a death
As guiltless and unnecessary
As that of our children,
Then curse *Him*—and die.

ELIPHAZ: Woe to all of us who hear such words.

BILDAD: She must be out of her mind.

WIFE: I tell you, dear friends, go away.
            You punish him with pious chatter.
            And my coward does the same.
            Instead of raising a fist against God
            He keeps busy cursing himself.
            Ever since last night
            He repeats the same complaints,
            The same questions.

            You say I'm out of my mind!
            Yes. I watch his torment,
            Unable to help him
            And I'm going mad.

JOB: I beg you, from the depths of my sorrows,
            Wife, don't say such things.

WIFE: If you haven't the courage to raise a hand
            Against the tyrant God,
            Then I will do it.
            I'll throw sharp rocks at Him—
            Let Him throw them back to kill me.
            A curse . . . and finished.
            I'll go where my children lie . . .
            Into the black fire that destroyed them.

            (She goes off.)

ELIPHAZ: Woe. Woe.

JOB: Did she say death? To be finished?
            That's my desire as well.
            That's my desire—to die.
            How much better death
            Than this disintegration of my bones.

               I do complain, but that's not blasphemy.
               Mine is a righteous cry:
               I'm innocent.

ELIPHAZ: Don't reject what we have to say.

JOB: You've talked the whole night through,
               Overwhelmed me with sharp, punishing words.
               Why won't you hear what I have to say?
               Can't you see that my innards are bursting?
               That my skin is erupting?

BILDAD: But you've talked more than we have
               Since last night.

ZOPHAR: To our smallest word
               You replied with seven.

ELIPHAZ: And we received them with respect.
               We will receive your sorrows
               No less respectfully.

JOB: To this moment, you are filled with impatience
               To fling at me the poisoned arrows
               Of reproach. But what more can you say,
               Or what more bitterly
               Than you have already said.

               That I have too much pride?
               That I don't understand God's secret ways?
               That I'm stubborn and stiff-necked?
               I've heard all that from you.

BILDAD: Even now you speak with too much pride.

JOB: Would you like me to speak humbly to you?

BILDAD: O Job, good friend.
               Don't let your pain
               Darken your understanding.

JOB: Let me ask you again:
           Do you really think you know
           Something that I do not?

           What if I complain?
           My complaint is to God,
           To the almighty; to Him, and not to you.
           I have cried out, nor will I stop complaining.
           O earth. You shall not cover up my blood.

           (Outside, responsive voices are heard.)

VOICES: We won't allow your blood to be covered.
           We won't allow. We won't.

ELIPHAZ: Those are strange, wild cries, Job.

JOB: Let my voice go everywhere . . .
           To everyone.

VOICES: It carries everywhere
           It reaches us everywhere.
           Cry louder. Louder still.
           Nor stop your lamentation for an instant.

JOB: Are those really living men that answer me?
           Or are they feverish imaginings?

ELIPHAZ: The gathering of an ugly mob—
           The blind, the leprous, the diseased.

BILDAD: It is your outcry that has brought them here.

ZOPHAR: Put off your bitterness,
           At least for a little while.

JOB: I beg you, take those tongues of yours away.
           I want to be alone. Leave me.

ELIPHAZ: How can we do that?

JOB: No matter what I say, it displeases you.
What I say is bitter, because true
And you are false consolers—even your salves
Are worthless smearings. I don't need them.
Let me, rather, have hard shards again
With which to scratch and tear my wounds.

ELIPHAZ: You shame and insult us.
But you don't know whether one day
You will not be ashamed
Of your present lamentations.

ZOPHAR: If this is how it's going to be, then I too will unloose
My bitterness after all we've said to you
Over these tedious hours.

You have destroyed the entire order
Of the universe. Because of your cries
A wild spirit has entered into man,
As well as into beasts and cattle.

BILDAD: And into vineyards; into wells.
And birds gather into huge flocks
And cover the fields like locusts.
And animals have begun to speak like people.
Even sheep open their huge mouths . . .
Even the dead, they say, rise and complain.

ZOPHAR: And the worst of all horrors is the horror
Of self-deceit and false visions:
People turned into snakes,
Or wolves, or donkeys, or black goats.

ELIPHAZ: And most terrifying of all is this ingathering
Of the dregs of humanity here, in your fields.

You will be held especially to account for them.
Because they all lie there
Expecting something of you
And the anger of your lamentation.

JOB: (In a new access of grief)

My marrow is burning
My bones fall away in the heat.

(He lifts his hands above his head.)

O Lord, again, I call you to judgment.
I have been calling since last night.
Come down, and let us openly come to judgment.

ALL THE FRIENDS: Woe, woe. The same blasphemy.

THE OUTSIDE VOICES: Blessed be the afflicted man

Who calls God himself to judgment.

(The voices approach the tent.)

ELIPHAZ: They're pressing closer. Don't allow it.

(All three friends hurry outside. There is the sound of
confusion, now near, and now receding. A lull. Job
gradually lowers his arms. His voice is almost inau-
dible.)

JOB: I call on You, and You don't answer.
I ask: In what way have I deserved my griefs?
Why do you drag out my pain
Instead of cutting off my breath at once?

(His voice breaks. He lies in a faint. Satan limps in . . .
a beggar on crutches. He approaches Job, looks down
at him, observes that he has fainted. Tenderly, he asks)

SATAN: Asleep, my Lord?

(Job does not reply. Satan withdraws to one side, musing.)

His breathing is a bit unsteady. A bit. Good.
He's not asleep. He's fainted. Good.

(Again, he approaches, studies Job and withdraws once more.)

At least until a real sleep overtakes him,
A sleep with neither pain nor grief,
Let him content himself with confused guilt.
In the midst of his assertion of his innocence
He may begin to recognize his shame,
And stumble on disgust for his own outcry.
Then even God might notice
That Godhead too can use humility.
That God Himself, not merely all his creatures,
Ought now and then to be immersed
In an abyss of loathing.

(Again, he approaches Job and speaks gently.)

Asleep, my good Lord?

(Job does not reply. Satan, satisfied, moves back.)

I tell you, God, if this man is guilty—
And, in substance, that is your desire:
That man should be inferior with guilt. . . .

Are you not just as guilty—even more?
Since you put him in the presence of temptation,
(Isn't that your usual intent?)
Why should not man put *you* to temptation?

My first playful idea is already disappearing
In the presence of the twisted earnestness
In the faces of the ugly mob that's gathered here.
They give me insight into entirely new temptations.

And in that crowd lies your defeat, Job.
In them and not in God, because their grief
Is more than all your woes and lamentations.
In their presence you are lower than in God's.

It's well that this idea has come,
Teasing my brain with its full sharpness,
Bringing its light along.

Just now another shining insight comes to me:
That these crowds turn turbulent
And caught up in the stream of justice
Only when they are a crowd.
Alone each one thinks of himself
And each is harsh and petty to the other,
There is in none of them that innermost
Fusion of pain that I have glimpsed
In your innocence—your sacrifice.

(Again he approaches Job.)

The sufferer, I see, is dissolved in his suffering.
Does it mean that he is then dissolved in God?

(He bends over Job.)

Asleep, my good Lord?

(Job still does not reply. Satan moves back.)

He still lies helpless. May dreams
From time to time embrace him
As at intervals
Grief did before. Now he lies still.

His earlier grief, no matter what,
Will follow him forever, like an echo,
And therefore I can now
Ease his pain a little.

(He moves to Job's head and stands, making circular movements with his hand above him. He steps back toward the exit. Job opens his eyes. His suffering has somewhat abated.)

JOB: Is anyone here?

(Satan, moving toward the exit, is silent.)

I ask . . . is anyone here?

(Satan does not reply. Goes off.)

I thought I heard a voice that asked
If I had been dissolved in God?
Why are you silent, God? Why don't you say
"Yes: I am dissolved in you."

(Isaac steals in, trembling and silent. He does not dare to approach Job's resting place.)

I do hear steps; I do hear someone breathing.

ISAAC: (In a fearful voice)
My Lord. O . . . don't be angry with me.

JOB: Have I the strength for anger . . . I
Who can hardly lift a hand?
Come here . . . to me . . . so I can see you.
Stranger, come here, whoever you may be.

ISAAC: (Comes near and covers his face with both hands.)

JOB: Am I so frightful?

ISAAC: Forgive me, my Lord.

JOB: But . . . haven't I seen you before?

ISAAC: You saw me last night, my Lord. When I arrived.

JOB: Is it night now?

ISAAC: Long past midnight.

JOB: Did you tell me your name yesterday?

ISAAC: Yes, my Lord, and who I was.
And even who my father is.
I'm Isaac and my father's name is Abraham.

JOB: My mind is weakened. I have a vague
Impression that you told me of a sacrifice.

ISAAC: Yes, it was I.

JOB: Is it you . . . the one who was the sacrifice?

ISAAC: Indeed, my Lord.

JOB: Don't call me Lord. Say . . . "Grandfather"
Because I feel a nearness and a warmth in you.

ISAAC: If I find favor in your eyes—

JOB: Please, bend closer.
You see how my body is decaying;
That I am edging toward my end.
That I am dying.

ISAAC: (Bending over him)
Oh, no, not that.

JOB: Why have you come to me?

ISAAC: Grandfather, your cry of pain
Brought me here
As it brought that crowd outside.

JOB: Is it really true that crowds have come?
Has my lamentation really

Reached so far? It seems to me you said
You're from Bar-Sheba.

ISAAC: Your grieving cry went farther still.
Grandfather, I'm sure that you'll prevail.

JOB: How do I know that you are not
One of those easy consolers
Like those prattling friends of mine.

ISAAC: Oh no! Since I myself have come
To be consoled.

JOB: (With a wan smile)

To me, for consolation? To me
Who has one foot already in the grave.
It's true that my suffering has eased a little ...
I can breathe a bit more easily.
But what does that mean? My body,
My poor body will decline
No matter what. Have you been as
Tormented as I have?

ISAAC: I have.

JOB: You are young. I am old.
You hear me groaning.

ISAAC: That groan will shatter the pillars
Of the world.

JOB: What do you know about pillars, my son?

ISAAC: I want to know more. That's why I've come.

JOB: Is it really true that your old father
Laid you on an altar to be sacrificed?

Isaac: It was what God commanded.

Job: Must an altar be of stone only,
Or will ashes do as well?

Isaac: One may not ask such a thing.

Job: Why not?

Isaac: I'm afraid I'll see it again.

Job: Then you think I *am* on an altar.

Isaac: I'm afraid to think of it.

Job: Don't be afraid. Were you bound?

Isaac: Hand and foot.

Job: Cried out?

Isaac: No.

Job: In your heart? No outcry there?

Isaac: Perhaps. Yes.

Job: A cry to God?

Isaac: To my father's outstretched arm.

Job: But wasn't he God's messenger?

Isaac: He was.

Job: Did you curse when you cried out?

Isaac: (Almost inaudible)

No.

JOB: (In an access of rage, he lifts his hands and waves them frantically)

You lay there like a sheep, with no outcry.
Like a sheep. Go away . . . away. Out of my sight.

(In his great excitement, he lifts his head violently, then lets it fall again. His hands, however, remain outstretched and tense. Isaac, frightened, makes as if to retreat from the tent. Job calls him back.)

Don't go away. Stay. Come near me.

(Isaac approaches. He is silent.)

Why are you mute? Say something.

ISAAC: If my words bring only sorrow. . . .

JOB: Forgive me. Speak. Tell me a little more
About your altar.

ISAAC: My going to the altar was a temptation.

JOB: How do you know? Who told you?

ISAAC: I understood later . . . after I heard
Some trembling words of my father's and—
Because of the sudden death of my mother Sarah
Whom I mourn sadly to this day,
And because God's wing touched my cheek.
It is more likely that even your sorrows
And your thrashing in the dust
Are temptations from the Lord.

JOB: (His voice heated once more)

Temptation! To be tested. Just like that!
Without crime or sin on my side.
That consolation leaves me unconsoled.

If I am to suffer, I want clearly to know why.
After all, you were tied by a father's hand
While I am bound by the hand of God Himself.

(A long pause. Isaac moves off. A grief rises in him
which he cannot contain. It escapes him in spasms.
Job says gently)

I hear you weeping . . . so quietly.

ISAAC: Grandfather, I want to share your suffering.
            Your pains . . . to take them on myself,
            Even a part of them.

JOB: (Again with excitement)

            Then make an outcry with my voice,
            And not with a lamentation no one hears.
            You want to share with me?
            Lie in the ashes, as I do, and tear the flesh
            From your body, though it is whole
            And feels no pain.
            As long as there's a man in torment,
            Call on God though *you've* no need to call.
            Call God to justice for another's pain,
            Though your own heart is tranquil.
            And wail just when your lips desire to smile,
            Wail just when your throat desires to sing.

ISAAC: Forgive me for my helpless grief.
            I don't know what to do with myself,
            And know much less how to console you.

JOB: The consolation that comes when all is ending,
            When life is at its ebb, can only wake
            A sharper pain.

            Where was it . . . this comfort of yours . . .
            At the beginning? What's the good
            In your coming here today

If yesterday you did not come?
Or can't you see that I'm at my last gasp?

ISAAC: I see, clearly, that my words displease you.
Then why won't you let me go away?

JOB: (In a muted tone)

Don't contend with me, my unknown son.
Tell me, rather, something of yourself
And forget me. Forget.
In any case, your being here does soothe
My pain a little. You say that you are troubled
By your mother's death. Are you in any
Way to blame for it?

ISAAC: O! How can you think such a thought.
I, to blame for her death? I?
She stands before me to this moment.
Three full years have passed and still
I carry her last breath in me.

JOB: Tell on. There's something in you
That revives me, though you lay
On your altar like a sheep;
It's your behaving like a sheep that I cannot stand.

ISAAC: But that's exactly why you heard me cry:
Because I hoped my tears might wash away
The very sheep in me.
I was a sheep only at the beginning.
Later, a real sheep took my place
To be the sacrifice. But a wicked
Rumor brought my mother ambiguous news
Mixing up my death with my survival
And her heart broke
Just as I arrived from Mount Morea.

JOB: Go on.

Isaac:　She was still stammering something
And her eyes glittered at sight of me
The instant that I crossed the threshold
Of her tent. Ah, Grandfather,
Dear unknown Grandfather. Her gaze
Trembling with pitying affection
Still flickers in my memory;
And I see her writhing lips
Flecked with foam . . . endeavoring
To speak . . . and saying nothing.

I fall beside her, my lips against hers.
I comfort her: "Mother," I say. "See.
I am alive. My throat is whole.
My body is unburned.
The good Lord was merely testing me . . .
After that a sheep became the sacrifice—"
I urged her in this way, and tried
To revive her, but she never did return
To life. Her breathing became shallow,
A final smile rose to her lips
And she said softly, "O, my own dear Isaac.
A sheep took your place? When?
At the very end? But before that?
Before the end? It was you who was the sheep?
You who lay there, waiting for the knife?"

And before I had the time for a reply,
It was too late. Do you hear me, Grandfather?

(Job does not reply. Isaac asks again)

Do you hear me, Grandfather?

(Isaac, perplexed)

Good heavens. Is he asleep, or is there something
wrong?

(He bends over Job, then steps back.)

Yes. He's really asleep. A miracle.
He breathes so peacefully.

(He stands, transfixed, as in a dream. Out of the
shadows the tent makes, a huge sheep with a shaggy
coat emerges and makes its way to his feet.)

SHEEP: And my throat. May *it* be cut?

ISAAC: (Shuddering, calls to Job.)

Help, Grandfather!

(Job, sunk in his stupor, does not answer.)

Am I dreaming?

SHEEP: No. It's all reality.
You remember well how I took your place.
You've just finished telling the story
In which you mentioned me.

Let me ask you: Why did I deserve it?

ISAAC: It wasn't all my doing.

SHEEP: But what had I done to deserve the knife?

ISAAC: Have I said that you deserved it?

SHEEP: But weren't you glad when your father's blade
Descended on me, instead of you?

ISAAC: (Is silent.)

SHEEP: I'm asking you to tell me: Weren't you glad?

ISAAC: Perhaps . . . yes.

SHEEP: What do you mean—perhaps? Say, "Certainly."
          How frequently have I heard you
          Complaining of those moments when you lay
          And waited with your throat against the knife?
          How often have I heard you grumble
          Against lying on the altar like a sheep.
          And now—silence.

          (To Job)

          And what about you, old sufferer.
          Suddenly your mouth is shut. Why?

          (Again speaking to Isaac)

          Take a good look. See how deeply
          My throat has been carved. Was not
          Your father's knife your knife as well?
          Or is the blood of a sheep not really blood?
          Perhaps I am an incarnation of yourself,
          A living prophecy regarding you;
          The first inkling of the razor edge
          That must inevitably cut your throat . . .
          If not now, then later . . . later.
          What if the knife on Mount Morea missed you?
          Has not its sharpness revealed the slaughter
          Being readied for you generations hence
          By knives as long as the long night?

ISAAC: But now—what is it you want of me?

SHEEP: I want nothing from you now. Only to ask
          Why did you leap so lightly from the altar
          And thrust me on it with such violence?
          Why? One victim dragging the other to
          His death. Why are you dumb? Speak.
          Forget that I'm a sheep. Tonight's
          The kind of night when even a sheep
          No less than man is privileged to speak;
          To murmur against death and call
          For justice. Even a slaughtered sheep.

And you. Consider yourself well.
Touch yourself with care—has not
Your father somehow slaughtered you?
Touch your throat and every limb with care.

ISAAC: Away. Vanish, insanity!

SHEEP: Maybe it's you who ought to disappear
As well as this exhausted grieving man.
Fling him across your shoulder. Go away.
Make your escape with him. To Sheol.
To a chasm. Go. God can do
Without you both. He turns from you.

He is with me and my carved, drained throat
With me and my seared flesh,
And you are Cains, both of you, both.
Though you lament with the grief
Of Abel, to be the veritable Abel
Is beyond you, for Abel waits, like me
Murdered and cast aside, for someone
To make an outcry for his death.
But he waits in vain. He's been
Forgotten—long ago. See where he lies.
Go and see.

(He goes off. Abel appears in his place.)

Leonard Wolf

I. J. SCHWARTZ
(1885–   )

THE LIGHT OF SUMMER'S END

The heart sings plaintively, the tired heart,
In the clear light of summer's end.
The charm and woe of fading hovers,
Spreading through the park, on grass and tree.
The skies are blue, deep-blue,
The sun shines brightly in blue radiance.
With eyes half-closed, my face turned
Toward the sun, I sit and drink
The caressing warmth. Ceaselessly
Trees rain upon the grasses
Their yellow leaves. Bees softly buzz,
Birds twitter from the boughs.
Within the quiet of the luminous day
That glides by with tranquility and repose,
There hums from depths of mind and heart
(As though a dove were cooing from a ruin)
An old song that once I knew
And long forgot, and only now recall:

> *I walk about in a strange wood.*
> *The sun is shining, yet I am cold.*
> *There's nothing left to do but sing—*
> *Though nowhere do the echoes ring.*

Oh, lucid radiance of autumn days,
For forty years now I have seen your splendors

And there is no end to heart's delight!
The eye can scarcely sate itself
With the largesse of tints and colors
And the mild light that streams
In full serenity.

      The raspberries,
Like coral clusters, illumine
The chartreuse branches of the trees,
And columns of white smoke ascend
From smoldering raked leaves.
And when the gentle breeze blows through,
There reaches me on my sheltered bench
The acrid odor of burned leaves,
Smelling of wine and bitter juices
And yellowed grasses, parched, in flame.
And through the curtain of white smoke
The din and clamor of children at play
Reach noisily to me as from another world.
The acrid smoke makes drunk my senses
And in my heart there trembles and rings:

> *I walk about in a strange wood.*
> *The sun is shining, yet I am cold.*
> *There's nothing left to do but sing—*
> *Though nowhere do the echoes ring.*

A half-hour's walk from the hill on which I sit
Lies stretched the field of spacious rest,
Shaded by trees and covered with grasses:
And in the elegiac light of day
The time comes back, of building and of brawn
In the strange new world—a massive forest,
A green uproarious forest in ascendance
With birds and song. That era is engraved
In my heart with charity and grace:
I remember the old bard, Eliakhum,
As he would sit outside his printing shop
On East Broadway in the hot summer days

And slumber on his stool. (I here confess
I did not read his poems myself,
But recollect them from my mother's lips.)
And I recall Yehoash from nineteen-hundred-seven,
Who radiated subtle distinction
With his mature wisdom and young faith;
And Rosenfeld from nineteen-hundred-nine,
In Claremont Park in the Bronx, under a tree,
As one infuriated, shattered by life;
And Lyessin, man of combat and song,
His Jewish stubbornness and consecration;
His rebel's cry to a hostile and unfeeling world.
A great strong generation, rooted
In earth soaked through with our blood,
And with heads uplifted to the skies.
Soon there came to swell the chorus
A multitude of youth. With the great stream
That flowed here from the countless ships
Carrying refugees to our free shores,
Each ship, together with its poverty,
From the old home brought abundant tribute
To our Yiddish song. These, as the former,
Did not search for gold or pleasures—
They wanted nought and sought for nought
Except the song that burned upon their lips
And flamed within their eyes and hearts.
Each with his own countenance, this generation
Like wild young grass in an old field,
Grew up overnight with clamor,
Branches rustling and rich with fruits.
Some fell by the harsh roadside
In their most blossoming years: Moishe-Leib—
I see him now as in that youthful time
Before his head became ash-gray:
A lad a loafer, with a ruddy face
Amply sprinkled with summer freckles;
Our street drummer in the land, who
Clapped the cymbals to the moment of his death.
And Landau's princely image from that time:

A tender, graceful sprout, sprung up
"From a kingdom not of this world"
With his blue eyes and blond locks
Of wheaten gold—"the man of song."
All now lie on the field of spacious rest
Where all the generations seem as one,
Shaded by trees and covered with grasses
A half-hour's walk from the hill where now I sit.

Etta Blum

IN THE APPLE ORCHARD

To the North American autumn I sing this praise,
O loveliest, most blessed time of year!
Translucent are the days, and clear
In fervid, gentle blue. The joyful landscape
Glows replete, within your apple orchard.
The vast, broad valley—verdant emerald,
Breathing with warmth and spraying gold,
Gleams iridescent in your light and shade.

O time of ripeness, bursting with abundant force
That lies imprisoned in the solid fruit—
Sealed tense and stubbornly within red globes
That dew and sun have filled to brim with juice.
The apple's side that's opposite the sun is rose;
The other, curved in leaf moisture to stem,
Is pale and gently green. A tree in flame—
From copious summit down to green grass!

Bowed by their great burden, the branches
Bend in tautened arc, apple to apple
In thick heavy plaits. Long apple chains
Strung red and green, gladden the eye.
And on the ground, inside the tree's full sweep,
The apple fall lies crowded on the grass.

All's good and still. The buzz of a plump bee
Cuts through the silence, hovering back and forth;
Wing-flutter of a small bird: *pe-ek, pe-ek.*
It dances on the carpet, in the red of green—
A *pe-ek* here, another there. Whitely, smoke
From heaps of burning leaves coils in the air
And mingles with the tender apple smell,
Carrying to me its sharp and acrid breath.

O great strong earth of North America,
In your ripe autumn's blessed plenitude,
My heart is filled with song and praise to you!
God grant your rapt serenity be not disturbed
For ever and for ever. Nor shall I tire
Of singing your large splendor and satiety.
One prayer do I carry in my heart, one plea:
May your apples bear the fragrance of my song!

Etta Blum

J. I. SEGAL
(1896–1954)

AT MY WEDDING

At my wedding
a red-haired madman fiddled
on the smallest gentlest little fiddle;
he played his sweet lament
and fabled song
while other fiddlers watched in dumb amazement.

Where did he learn it,
this red-haired simpleton?
When you consider that he lived and worked
in backward villages,
and played only at drunken gentile brawls;
if you can picture it, he could hardly
scratch together a handful of holy words—
not even to save himself.
As for sleeping, he bedded on a wooden bench,
and if a servant
gave him radishes from the master's garden,
he was fed.

It was at my wedding this poor devil played,
no one could stand still, yet all were rooted,
ears in the air like pointed spears,
while the little fiddle tenderly caressed
and fiercely scored the people,

tore them to bits, flayed them and drew blood
to all their veins
until strung as taut as violin strings
the old folk, doddering, cried out for mercy.

Miriam Waddington

OLD MONTREAL

There's an old back street in Montreal
That was once the center of town,
Now the stone walls are yellow and burnt out,
And there's a broken-down church which God forsook

When he moved away to a new cathedral;
Yet whenever I walk that way
I imagine I hear ghostly bells ringing
Behind those ash-gray walls.

A little way down is an oblong cemetery
With small headstones, and smack in the middle
Stands a tall stained marble column
Keeping its long watch.

Not far away is the harbor market
With high buildings, wooden and blind,
And you can see a dirty red flag
Hung out for no reason at all, teasing the wind.

Between these narrow streets and glimpsing walls
The chimney of a dockside ship pokes out,
And a midday thread of smoke goes curling up
As from some cosy winter house.

Miriam Waddington

LATE AUTUMN IN MONTREAL

The worm goes back to the earth
the wind glitters and sharpens his sword;
where did all the colored leaves fly
to, anyway? The branches are all locked
in a vise of sleep; the skies aspire
to climb higher, their clear-blue
washes over the rooftops and stillness
assures us that all is well.
Our churchy city becomes even more pious
on Sundays, the golden crosses shine and gleam
while the big bells ring with loud
hallelujahs and the little bells answer
their low amens; the tidy peaceful streets
lie dreaming in broad daylight murmuring
endearments to me who am such a Yiddish Jew
that even in my footsteps they must hear
how the music of my Yiddish song sounds
through the rhythm of my Hebrew prayer.

Miriam Waddington

RHYMES

Two respectable rhymes
skipped out of their pages
like two proud roosters
from golden cages;

They walked many a mile
in search of a home,
but could find no space
for themselves in a poem.

They grew tired and sad
but wherever they went

nobody advertised
poems for rent.

People whispered and said:
haven't you heard
that a rhyming word
is considered absurd?

In modern times
who needs rhymes?
Those high-flying words
went out with the birds.

At last one night
all weary and worn
they came to a house
in a field of corn;

and there lived a man
who still wrote lines
according to rules
from olden times.

So he took them in
with doubles and pairs,
and set them to music,
and gave them new airs.

Now they ring again
their bells and chimes,
and the children all sing
those respectable rhymes,

with one rhyme inside
and another one out:
the rhymes were befriended
and my poem is ended.

Miriam Waddington

TEACHING YIDDISH

The children from my neighborhood
all come to me to learn Yiddish:
I tell them not to open their books,
I want to look at them and read
their faces as if they were pages
in a book; I want to know and be known,
so this is how I talk to them
without ever saying a word.

Dear boys and girls, Yiddish sons
and daughters, I want to teach you
what you've come to study but first
I have to learn how to read you I
have to write you and describe you
as you are and I don't really want
to be your teacher but an older
brother; so what shall we do?

First I think I'll read a story
by Sholem Aleichêm just to see how much
you know about Yiddish laughter.
If you can laugh with real Yiddish flavor
at one of Sholem Aleichem's stories
I won't need further proof;
you'll do well with *chumish* in Yiddish
and even with *gemorah* in Yiddish,
and with literature naturally—
in what but Yiddish?

But you're laughing already
even before we get to Sholem Aleichem's
Motl Paisie the Cantor's son:
so today we're having our first lesson
in Yiddish laughter and all around me
shine your open faces and your lively eyes;
so let's tackle Sholem Aleichem head on
and go into a huddle of laughter.

Miriam Waddington

A JEW

My comrades are all such travelers
buzzing around in planes,
with one look they take the measure
of the wide bend of the sky.

If they have breakfast in Montreal
they drink coffee in New York,
of course that's all very grand,
even wonderful—but also queer.

Theirs are pleasures I renounce
especially on rainy days
when I can sit down beside the window
and think about an old wayside inn;

And how a cart full of Hasidim
drove up there late one night
and changed the simple little inn
to a beautiful palace;

And how the small band of faithful
sat around the wooden table
as radiant as if they were gathered
in the corridors of heaven.

Later I couldn't even remember
the Torahs and Haggadahs
but my heart is still full
of sweet worshipful longing.

It's no use my turning east
and it's no use my praying west,
I'm forever on the road, in transit,
dragging my baggage of exile.

That world is all gone now,
there's no monument to mark it,
and the only leaf left from the deluge
is a page in a Yiddish book.

So what is the leaf's green message
what stories does it bring?
only that a tree stood on the road
lighted by a single star.

The tree is still standing there
with the little star on its branch,
and it shines so strangely on the road
and the tree too has grown strange;

But it survives, my Jewish tree,
like a talisman of homecoming
and it longs to gather all us Jews
from our spaceless boundaries of loss.

Miriam Waddington

AUNT DVORAH

Our only aunt called Dvorah
Has gone and left us too,
And on her grave is carved a small Menorah
And on each side a slender stalk of wheat.

That is how the stonecutter Reb Nachem
Worked it out, and in between, her name;
We stand and gaze into religious silence
As from our lips there falls a last amen.

No member of her family survived her,
Her comely daughters, Esther and Hadassah,
Were lost in the great burning
Beyond the ghetto walls, in some side street.

And when they brought them home to her,
Their bodies raped and spoiled, well do I recall
How Dvorah clamped her mouth in iron silence
And sat, held in its bitter vise for days.

Widening her sorrow by their narrow graves
Our auntie used to sit, and in the evenings take
Her children's clothes and thoughtfully caress
Their measure; then shivering and bleak

She'd close the trunk and draw over her face
A darkness deeper than cavernous wastes
Of empty cupboards and more desolate
Than all those hangers peeled and bare.

Miriam Waddington

SCENARIO

The enemy returns
home to his German village,
and the white blossom on the tree
waves to him, bends to him,
smiles to him, "Welcome!"

His dog jumps up to meet him
and trembles with recognition,
and all around him lie his fields
as fresh and frank as summer.

In the doorway of his house
waits the housewife, pale and dear.
Lost in the joyous pulse of dream
she stands rooted and still as a bird.

He runs toward her
and she falls into his arms;
all is husband and wife between them,
together they enter their warm house.

But I, whom the German enemy destroyed
in seed and root, in branch and bud,
whose last living child he has killed,
and whose native city he has bent
from its ancient Polish pride—
I am the one who in my rags,
my ribbons, and my pure bright hate,
remain outside, and like a beaten cur
I must watch and see

How these German trees still celebrate
the summer's whiteness, and German fields
submit their earth to the sharpened plow,
while in the barn German horses

Bear German colts, silky and fair,
which German lads will mount and ride
possessing July and the burning sun
between fertile forests of wheat and rye.

And Jewish children? Sealed within winds
and their quenched ashes and desolate crumbs;
and only the emptiness of street
will remember and miss them, and only
the echoing cobblestones will weep.

I know they will not ever be transformed
to innocence, they will never be
angels astride on palominos
in a blossoming heaven; they will never be such
as tumble through fields and gamboling, shout,
"Welcome!" around the feet of God.

Miriam Waddington

RASHELLE VEPRINSKI
(1895-)

WIDOWS

Widows—gray grass in autumn
bowed to the earth.
Eyes among shadows
seek buried summers.

Naked, their grief weeps, and they shame
to lift their eyes:
bowed
and bearing a dead name.

And the womb is difficult to bear
pinched to silence;
faces erased
are hid beneath lashes cast down.

They are lost on every path,
and God has quieted desire;
they pick, from life's abundant fields,
stalks of wheat left behind.

David Goldberg

LET US

Let us meet again:
it's October,
when leaves must part
and winds cry.
Then let winds cry,
I have no more tears,
and let skies mourn,
I am empty of mourning.

Let us meet again:
two gravestones
standing
with wind
between.

David Goldberg

ANNA MARGOLIN
(1887–1952)

YEARS

Women much loved, who never had enough,
going through life with laughter and anger,
their eyes brilliant as fires or agates—
that's how the years were.

And they were actors playing Hamlet,
muttering disdainfully with half a mouth;
arrogant tyrants of a rebellious state
dashing the rebels down.

Yet see how dispirited they are now,
my God! dumb as a smashed keyboard
they quiver at every threat or jeer,
searching for you, in whom they don't believe.

Adrienne Rich

A CITY BY THE SEA

When did it all happen? I can't remember.
It hangs in the air like a ghostly song:
a seaside town, nocturnes of Chopin,
iron lilies of balconies.

Night. Two sisters dreamily touching
with their slender fingers the dim stream

of memories in an old-fashioned album.
Slowly the old photographs grow young.

Through the half-open door, among the ferns,
trancelike, intoxicated figures fold
in a last waltz. O dead youth!
The dancers swim and fade like shadows.

It was—it was—I can't remember.

Adrienne Rich

JOSEPH ROLNICK
(1879–1955)

EVENING GOLD

On a scorching August Friday eve
The men, their bodies covered with sweat,
Run to the pond near the bridge to bathe.
They strip without the slightest shame
And getting only a finger wet
Give the evening water a try,
And stand stretched out
As if to decide:
Is it worth it to dive?
And the household women,
Old and young,
Who must pass to and fro,
Turn away their eyes, appalled
At the sight of the men who stand there sprawled.
But the evening sun
Laughs at everyone.
She has gilded the shabby windowpanes
And rewarded with gold
The masculine frames.

Lucy S. Dawidowicz and Florence Victor

BREAD FROM OUR POCKETS

Sabbath, after dinner, when you go out,
The road is like a desert, sandy and hot.
But the first small bridge is straight ahead.
And though the bare ground burns like blazing coals—

The water is cool on the turf of the walls,
And smooth as newly poured-out lead.
And little fish, their backs to the sun,
Turn themselves around
And circle the pound.
From our pockets we throw them pieces of bread.
They swallow them and—continue ahead,
And show us not a sign of fright.
The grownups see in this the Creator's might.
But we make it into a game—
All of us are the same.
And when we've reached the very last crumb
We turn our pockets inside out
To show there is nothing more to come.

Lucy S. Dawidowicz and Florence Victor

THE TWIG

A man plants a stick,
Pats the dirt
And says, Mine.
Now he is committed,
Let him pray for the sun and rain.
Each night he covers miles
For the sake of that naked twig,
And in the morning
Runs to it as fast.
He is worn out with worry
And waits for his last days.
But how that stick
Branches in his mind—
A mighty tree,
Full of shade,
Where years later he can sit
In the middle of the day
As the sun grows warm.

Harvey Shapiro

AT HOME

I needn't dispossess a soul
And no one can say: "Pay me
To move out." Windows and walls
All mine and mine the key.
It takes only a wish from me
And the house is open as it used to be.
The sounds of one's feet
As on cool concrete
Echo and fade.
From one's own loam
The floor was laid,
I am at home.
I'll stay for a day here alone
And count up all that I own.

Lucy S. Dawidowicz and Florence Victor

RIVERSIDE DRIVE

Pulling myself out of bed
I leave the house.
The blueness caresses me,
The wind pushes my hair.
A whole world of quiet
I fill with my steps
On the sidewalk,
And in the street
The milkman's horse.
Somewhere, on a higher floor,
Along a dark corridor,
The milkman makes his shining rows.
Running, the papers
Under my arm,
I don't look at numbers.
I know the way

Like the horse.
The sun is already up
On the east side of the city.
Its flames, its grace
Spill, whole canfuls, on the cliffs
Of the Jersey shore.
At 310 Riverside Drive
A man on a low balcony,
Young but with mustache and beard—
His appearance not of here—
Stretches a hand toward
The west and shouts
Something like, See there!
And I stand like him
With my papers raised
Like an offering
To the light—
The two of us
Come for the first time
To this place,
To the red cliffs
Of this morning.

Harvey Shapiro

C E L I A   D R O P K I N
(1888–1956)

POEM

You sowed in me, not a child
but yourself.
So it's you growing in me daily,
greater and more distinct.
There's no room left inside me
for myself
and my soul lies like a dog at your feet
growing fainter and fainter.
But, dying into you,
I still, even now, can make you songs.

Adrienne Rich

POEM

I haven't yet seen you
asleep.
I'd like to see
how you sleep,
when you've lost your power
over yourself, over me.
I'd like to see you
helpless, strung-out, dumb.
I'd like to see you

with your eyes shut,
breathless.
I'd like to see you
dead.

Adrienne Rich

III

YIDDISH POETS
IN THE
SOVIET UNION

III

DAVID HOFSTEIN
(1899–1952)

POEM

On Russian fields, in the twilights of winter!
Where can one be lonelier, where can one be lonelier?

The doddering horse, the squeaking sleigh,
the path under snow—that is my way.

Below, in a corner of the pale horizon,
still dying, the stripes of a sad fallen sun.

There, in the distance, a white wilderness,
where houses lie scattered, ten or less,
and—there—sleeps a shack, sunk deep in the snows.

A house like the others—but larger, its windows . . .
And in that house, to which many roads run,
I am the eldest of all of the children. . . .

And my world is narrow, my circle is small:
in two weeks I've gone once into town—if at all.

To long in the silence of space and of fields,
of pathways and byways that snow has concealed. . . .

To carry the hidden sorrowing
of seeds that wait and wait for planting. . . .

On Russian fields, in the twilights of winter!
Where can one be lonelier, where can one be lonelier?

Allen Mandelbaum

SABBATH IS GONE

Sabbath is gone.
On the far-off snow,
A big someone
Pours gray ash.
In the little store,
Already waiting—
A sallow girl
With a black flask.

The whip is rested.
Beside the oven,
Idle—leaning
Into the dark.
On the ledge,
A half-seen napkin—
Softly hiding
The Sabbath bread.

The meal is eaten.
In the dimness,
My father melts
Into the board.
Between my sisters,
In tired shadow,
A thread of voices
Whispers, weaves.

My mother, by the window,
Searches for a distant star.
Does not find it.
Sits in thought.
I shrink into sadness,

Trying not to think
That the cow is waiting
For me, hay, and night.

Nathan Halper

PARADE

We move with you, in your advancing ranks,
marching mankind,
the proud and the courageous, the seething and the chill—
step by step!
Held high on poles of shame, swaying, swaying there—
the old God.
Its tatters patched with air, there flutters still and flutters—
the old red banner—
no step back!
And sleepless drumsticks pour their pellets on stiff hides,
and cymbals clash—their sharpness hones the pliant air—
and flinging high its cry,
the gleaming trumpet . . .
Today I, too, am a piece of clanging brass—
I leap across
quiet velvet places,
I wake the weary,
I cover the sigh of the exhausted
with raucous laughter—
no step back!

Allen Mandelbaum

SONG OF MY INDIFFERENCE

For some the now is good enough—
and that is fine for them!
But what shall I do
when I always
see before me

phosphorescent questions flashing:
Where?
Where to?

I am already tired
of hovering,
of flickering,
of swimming,
of soaking in strange seas.
Would that my own could tempt me!

Well, once upon my land,
in a green,
a valley corner,
in Galilee—
there was a Jewish mother
who had a child,
and from that child
there grew a man with sheepish, trusting eyes . . .
Whose business is it?

How long,
against the hollow of heaven,
above the cloistered steeples,
will golden stripes crisscross?

How long
will fugitive eyes
flash before me
at each of my weary,
each of my bloody steps?

And there was
a second man,
a darker man
who jingled—
within the blind,
within the hungry bosom—
thirty pieces of silver . . .
Now be cursed,
all you who exploit!

Chase
and scatter yourselves,
each against the other,
all of you who whisper
about eternal
brimstone hail,
about eternal wandering.

Learn
to lift your heads!
See:
from the dust
of worldly markets
there is made
a mountain.

In a broad northern land,
within the capital
(for years they trembled,
fenced in by the thorns
of a Jewish shop)
in Moscow,
beside the believing Kremlin,
that lion-like bust—
Marx!

Listen!
From the breast
wrapped up in ancient fear,
from shivering, chattering, Jewish teeth,
is torn a voice, a tempest—
it speaks
across the broad Russian land—
Leib Bronstein. . . .

My great indifference!
There's nothing here for you,
nothing for anyone!
There's no one here who knows
my hatred, my hot hatred.

My love, my pure love!
One call I've always heeded—
mute, I've carried it
a thousand days:
above the gray head
of my people,
to be
a youthful radiance!

The gray head
of my people!
Like all heads, a head
that has its share of lice.

My great indifference,
there's nothing here for you,
and no one knows
my hatred, my hot hatred,
my love, my pure love!

And where?
And who—
are the people?
Shopkeepers?
What do they handle?
All the same!
A devil take your father's father
with his rags or linens.

Ah, the earnest
shopkeepers
who once
had given the world
Heinrich Heine!

No!
This is the way it goes—
fanatic,
stubborn pedants—

great-grandfathers
of Albert Einstein!
Farther there,
deeper there,
out of the black rubble of excommunication,
blooms at times
in white, in gleaming garments
striped with roses,
the polisher of limpid lenses,
Baruch Spinoza!

You secure peoples
of masters and hangmen,
I am already sick—
remembering
the way you guard
my far, lost steps
upon your silent, gilded cemeteries,
in cities of the dead,
in dead cities!

Fugitives,
disgraced,
with quivering bodies,
with children and with women,
rip away the last borders,
the last chains.

With old, with longing arms,
I've gathered up myself
in all your crevices,
in layers of dust, for you—I dig graves . . .
together with the sharp, the heartfelt gaze
of Lev Shestov,
prepare yourselves—all of you—
for the blade of the slaughter,
the radiant
end!

Allen Mandelbaum

PERETZ MARKISH
(1895–1952)

POEM

I don't know whether I'm at home
or homeless.
            I'm running, my shirt
unbuttons, no bounds, nobody
holds me, no beginning,
no end

my body is foam
smelling of wind

                        Now
is my name. I spread my arms, my hands
pierce the extremes
of what is. I'm letting my eyes roam around
and do their drinking from the foundations
of the world

eyes wild, shirt ballooning,
my hands separated by the world, I don't know
if I have a home
or have a homelessness,
or am a beginning or an end

Armand Schwerner

POEM

the last color of dusk fades, a soft
black wraps the head of the world

night surrounds him
from under the earth, sky, distance
quietly under its loosened black shirt
hides him

man and horse listen and keep quiet but the wind
moves around talking
to the walls
the windmill motions to the sky

Armand Schwerner

POEM

I won't put on a light all night
the wall disappears in tears and quiet
from the blue dovecot of my prayed-out face

ripped out of my eyes, the dove,
by itself, and gone.
           A rope
circles my head. My head is the shame
under a rope. And my hands, my cheated hands . . .

loneliness, I'll make up a bed for us
on the threshold. Would you
caress me? if you would caress me, caress
me

will the dove come back in the morning?
she will. I'll kiss you, world, your fingers,
and close my eyes

and splash out
your blue secret.
                Thank you, God.

the wild dove ripped itself
from my eyes. It flew. Somewhere my walls
walked quietly off.
and where did you hide your hands?

I won't put on a light all night
in the blue dovecot of my mourned-out face

                                 Armand Schwerner

POEM

the winds dry the bloated fences, my feet
clot the black dirt
tell me today swollen earth
answer me this time unkempt and carefree wind
I think I see you
the first time
             I've got you
in my three-year-old eyes

the red cows, the valley
of mud, the dirty asses and filled up teats,
pleasure hits me quietly: morning warm, the dried hay
from last year, naked horses

I would embrace all the cows
and stretch out with them on the earth
and howl together

                                 Armand Schwerner

POEM

I dress myself in darkness
                    over my head
over my feet, my hands . . .
I walk about as in a great black prayer shawl
(edges torn on all sides)
and grapple with black walls . . .

dark creatures trail me endlessly
congealed with distances . . .
vast emptiness lies open
                    before me
where I step on the feet
of dark straying girls . . .

I march about—crowned!
darkness grows out of me
darkness stretches itself
into my remoteness . . .
the earth turns from me
                    dark
and from everywhere
black horses leap upon me . . .

Etta Blum

POEM

Hey, what're you trading in—sorrow?
What're you selling—despair?
I'm a buyer and do business
and I barter and I wander
where it happens, as it goes,
day and night, at odd moments—
on a scale of joy I weigh it.

First I buy and then I sell
at fairs, markets, crossroads,
with whom I chance to meet,
and whomever I greet.
I pay cash!

I'm a buyer and do business,
and I barter and I wander . . .

What do you buy—corpses? rags?
Dead fathers?
Hey, you!
(So I lost a customer—)
Die and be reborn . . .

                                        Etta Blum

POEM

on their horns cows bear
the bleating of herds

    in our great land of woe
    sorrow ripens on the trees . . .

I'll hone no ax on them
nor fix myself a hedge

    from the sky's bright fabric
    my mother sews me a shirt

on deserted depots my destiny
unseeing, awaits a train

                everywhere
sorrow on your bosom
inexpressibly
great Land of Terror

so what if the throat
lies stretched across the rails—
on Sunday there'll be a carousel,
despair will caper . . .

Etta Blum

1917

Got a bit of heart? Forget it!
Want a little peace? Choke on a bone!
Somewhere strum the balalaikas
Bursting wildly on a stone.

Got yourself a pain? Spit on it!
Salt your eye and have a souse.
Somewhere cats will drink *l'chayim*
In a corner with a mouse.

I too am now a welcome guest,
Tear the rags off till you hurt.
For a kopeck buy my head,
Strip your pants and rip your shirt.

Catch a dog, pull him closer,
Pitch your faith into his ear,
Somewhere lunatics are dancing
Round a circle made of cheer.

Got a bit of heart? Forget it!
Want a little peace? Choke on a bone!
Somewhere strum the balalaikas
Bursting wildly on a stone.

Irving Howe

SAMUEL HALKIN
(1899–1960)

OUT OF THE PAST

Father's lips move as though about to bless someone,
Eyes turned toward the night that comes on sharp and green.
At the window he draws aside the stone-cold curtain,
His fingers wiping clear the dripping windowpane.

Two stars appear—two needle points stuck in the sky.
Frogs are muddying the silvery pools' white shine.
Oh, don't spread out the weekday tablecloth—
Let some afterglow of Sabbath linger on.

Edwin Honig

RUSSIA—1923

Russia, if not for my deep faith in you,
I'd argue with you differently.
I'd say that you misled us, you
Bewitched us like a gypsy.

Each blow of your hand is precious to us,
And painfully hard to bear—
But however great the misfortune or shame,
We turn to you and implore:

What is the promise that lies overseas?
What lands and what countries?

Here on Russia's happy streets,
We'll gladly live out our lives.

Till now you weren't fated to see us
Snuffed out by our wild birthright,
And now we go harnessed,
Now from your kisses we die.

Edwin Honig

POET

They say that Homer had been blind awhile,
And then occurred this splendid miracle:
The closer he got to us each century,
The greater seer he appeared to be.

But miracles on earth are rare enough . . .
And so, if we are found unworthy of
Any, at least let no one leave behind
The word that while still living we were blind.

Edwin Honig

POEM—1959

Shall I bless the day that I was born?
Let others decide—they know better.
Only that great moment when they set me free
From barbed-wire fences and the lightless prisons,
That moment suddenly arrived, unguarded,
With early March's glittering frost, and heaven
Lit up with stars at noon, and on my lips
The blessing not said since childhood suddenly
Recalled as if it were but yesterday—
I make myself believe: to every lover
Of mankind that day will be a holiday,
Arriving without asking to come in.

Edwin Honig

ITZIK FEFFER
(1900–1952)

I'VE NEVER BEEN LOST

In all my short, happy life, I've never
Been lost, nor forgotten the way I came.
I laugh to myself when I remember
That I carry some famous rabbi's name.

The name that my grandfather wanted for me
Was the Holy Reb Itzikel of Skvira's,
That I might lay *tefillin* and wear a *tallis*
And do my singing of prayers and *zmires,*

That I might be the richest man in town,
And my wife's housekeeping be the best,
So days and nights gave way to each other,
And each year came to follow the rest.

The sun has blessedly bronzed my body,
My life is all battles and songs of fame;
It really breaks me up to remember
That I carry some famous rabbi's name.

John Hollander

SO WHAT IF I'VE
BEEN CIRCUMCISED?

So what if I've been circumcised
With rituals, as among the Jews?
Field winds have tanned my middle-sized,
Pale, dreaming feet to darker hues.

Some Jews long for *tsimmis* yet—
We toughs, for smoke, and flame in motion;
Eight years' embattled meadows, set
Underneath the sky's blue ocean.

I'm a quiet guy and hardly a villain;
My honesty has no great appeal;
I'm never known to put on *tefillin*,
I'm never known to wheel and deal.

So what if I've been circumcised
With rituals, as among the Jews?
Field winds have tanned my middle-sized,
Pale, dreaming feet to darker hues.

John Hollander

SABBATH NIGHT

Sabbath night; time for *Havdalah,* but must
That be it? See, the moon has bloomed;
Moon-filled alleys smolder with dust,
Sprayed with girls impeccably groomed.

Sheerest of girls in the sheerest of hose,
Imported coats, English shoes—I see
They've read Blok, Mayakovsky, and all of those,
But they don't know Aaron or Izzy or me.

Tomorrow is Sunday, let papas prepare,
For girls and Blok on the village mud,
When the whole village turns out for the fair,
Moon-filled alleys dustily trod.

John Hollander

IZZI CHARIK
(1898–1937)

POEM

Who cares if eternity won't know me,
if no one ever watches my footsteps—
but now, right now, when hearts are burning,
I come with fists in my song.

Of course I'd like to sing myself away,
to cry out all my hurting with the wind—
but, though I would not find that hard, I cannot,
when life bears down too much on everyone.

The stars are not—till now—my enemies,
and I can keep my peace with all the winds,
but when I am ablaze I must not listen
to the air that, rustling, lingers over me.

Who cares if eternity won't know me,
if no one ever watches my footsteps—
but now, right now, when hearts are burning,
I must come with my song!

Allen Mandelbaum

LEIB KVITKO
(1890–1952)

I AM TIED

I am tied to a great today.
Its big tree, my friend,
Has perfumed me from its roots.
I am tied to a great today.

The plow is sharp,
My friend, the soft earth moist;
Whether there's sun or not,
The cows' smell strengthens me in the courtyard.

With my feet solid
And my strong hand,
I could wrench the head
Of a young ox.

Martin Robbins

TO ODESSA

Mama, let me, Mama,
Go to Odessa.
I too want to hear how the Marseillaise is sung,
See how the workers stand on the barricades,
How hopes beat back
This dark century.

A child there, Mama—
No one will step on him—
A child can also help
To drag the planks.

And Mama, don't you know?
The whole world
Is made of workers;
It's all poor people,
Brothers to us,
We are storming as one.

Mama, let me, Mama,
Go to Odessa.
Revolution stands on tall barrels.
Big and small:
Get up!
Come on!
Let's go!

Martin Robbins

JACOB STERNBERG
(1890–)

DAWN

Dawn glorifies the yards,
Glorifies a pig's head . . .
Sweet quietness. Wheel screech
With a quiet tread.

Summer night rides off
On a wagon piled with straw—
A wagon drawn by two oxen—
Going home with some *goy* once more.

Like a calf dipping under an udder,
Pails nuzzle well water in play.
A barefoot old *goye* comes running:
Day!

John Hollander

NIGHTS OF CRISIS

Nights of crisis,
Of bare, analytic devices.
Nights of bitterness. Poisoned nights.

When, as every evening in the butcher's window, lights
Reveal the dripping, hung meat to your eyes; the under places,

Soft and red, deliberately exhibited and faces
Of all the slaughtered cows, hung up there with one thing in mind.
Spic and span. No butchers, shoppers. No, nor any kind
Of knives, meat axes, cleavers. Tidied up sadistically.
And a lock on the door so there is no way to get free.

Nights of crisis,
Of bare, analytic devices,
When bloodied meat, offended by knives, lies in reverie.

John Hollander

MY FATHER

I stare at the fire in the way that my father
Would sit through the winter nights, endless and hard,
Musing and brooding and watching the burning
Brands.

The beard in his teeth: he would chew it and chew it,
Then his mouth would suddenly lose it again—
There'd be shuddering. Twisting. A clapping of bony
Hands.

The crackle and flash of burning logs blended in
A presence of Something, a wave of sun,
And soft emanations extended throughout the
Room.

In that mirror—the family's fate and heirloom—
That stands in the darkness, a light appeared.
My ghost with a candle meanders amidst the
Gloom.

And the fire—a girlish and naked body,
A salamander bandits once found in the house
Where a landowner tossed in his crazy bed, old and
Weird.

I stare at the fire in the way that my father
Would sit through the winter nights, endless and hard,
Musing and brooding, and chewing, late, on his
Beard.

John Hollander

WITH THE MOON'S AX

With the moon's ax
On my back, like a Roman legionnaire,
I dream, going everywhere.

Do soldiers cry? And does an ax?

A tear tracks
Down my cheek . . . Is it mine? Or the moon's?
I can't tell. The moon is an ax,

Over my shoulder it goes.
Shall I smash my bright idols of hatred?
Hurl shining ax into red flesh of foes?

With the moon's ax
On my back, like a Roman legionnaire,
I dream, going everywhere.

Do soldiers dream? And does an ax?

John Hollander

IT'S COOL

It's cool . . . Around the hall, the windowpanes autumnal, chill,
A ring of boys from a street gang sleep like pigeons, who stand still
Waiting for the market's opening all night.

Bareheaded, ragged, showing a frail, froglike nakedness,
The city sleeps, the fire of its eye put out, in glass
Of gleaming bulbs and twinkling lamps and crystal bright.

Pale, transparent still, the vandals of the future sleep.
Will they awaken, then? The gentle night makes them drink deep,
From its blue saucer, some of the moon's poisoned light.

John Hollander

IV

MODERN
YIDDISH
POETRY
IN EUROPE

MELECH RAWITCH
(1893–)

A TOLSTOYAN IDYLL, 1917

because it was quiet in the world and was quiet in the fields
and at all the crossroads—crosses of wood
and on every cross the king with the crown of thorns
and pictures of mary on every tenth tree
and people from everywhere meeting and greeting each other
in jesus' sweet name
amen—forever king jesus

and because the plague was creeping in from all over
over muddy as well as still-wild roads
where it crept in like an alligator creeping out of its nest
and people from everywhere meeting and greeting each other
in jesus' sweet name
amen—forever king jesus

and because the war crossed all the borders like waves
and the country's best boys died knee-deep in blood
and because the country's own blood fell on them like a river
and people came from everywhere meeting and greeting each
    other
in jesus' sweet name
amen—forever king jesus

and because everyone's eyes are now blue
and their faces are plowed under and their hands are like bark—
    and raw

only the blood doesn't seethe any more and the blood doesn't cry
and hands in the villages close around hats
when a cross passes by or a picture of mary
and their lips are trembling and their hearts are silenced
praised be king jesus—
forever—
amen

Jerome Rothenberg

THE FAMILY POEM

and know that you were young
and were my mother
though wondering still that you should be my mother
you and not some other woman
and why it should cost me so much pain
remembering you—
and remembering those sleepless nights
the pain of childbirth thrust itself into your body
and how the cry ran through all those well-lit rooms
where the family waited sleepless and in terror
half the town up and three doctors
and Shaindel too your ninety-year-old grandmother
and at dawn our rabbi sent a wire to the Belzer Rabbi:
Hindeh, child of Blumeh, labors: beg for mercy!

there were tears by then and no end of it
you in childbed with a third brother coming—
Mazel Tov!
but who can measure a newborn's luck
luck of a sunflower out in the sun
exposed to all winds and all nights?
now we're grown—
three brothers—
luck's gone different ways—
above ground or under it

mother
there's white in your hair now
each hair a token
of a night's waiting in pain
for a white dawn to come to your window—
now it's night again
and I see you—
you're standing silent at a window—
the pain of it beats on the glass like a bird—
asian frost melts on the windowpane—
like a beaten dog
from the chimneys of burned-out houses
the *shtetl* wind's howling

father's old, he's tired, he says:
go to sleep, Hindzeleh, you'll be getting up early
then goes to check if the doors are shut
and turns down the light—
and there's only a torn piece of tin beating on the roof
every couple of minutes—
fear in that sound
like the stroke of the great clock that beats for the world—
and the wildness of my father's first, tired snoring
breaks through the room

and your sons, all grown
adrift now in this monster of a world
above ground or under it

Jerome Rothenberg

KADDISH

When he was dead, when mourning was over,
Our mother got up from the mourner's bench
To write letters to her sons: one north, one south,
One to the other world.

All began the same way:
How our sick father called to her in the night,
Put his head on her shoulder
And, like a fallen bird, silently closed his black eyes.

She lifted his head from her shoulder
And put it back on the pillow. His skin was warm.
The hair she had always loved—it was not yet entirely gray—
Was curly, fine as silk, even after he was dead.

The letters ended in a different way.
The living—north, south—
Were told to cherish his name.
The one in the other world: Greet him in proper fashion!

That is how our mother wrote three letters to her sons.
One north, one south,
One in the real world.

The sons received them,
They bowed their heads,
And in the night, thought of their beloved father.

Nathan Halper

M. KULBAK
(1896–1940)

FROM "CHILDE HAROLD"*

I

A train. A window. Beaming face.
A pipe is held between stiff lips.
A young man goes into the world.
All he has is sturdy ribs.
In his pocket, he has poems,
A pack of cigarettes, a shirt.
(His father left his native land
With a prayer book in his hand.)
The wheels make a clatter.
Frontiers swoop, kingdoms change—
O it is a stirring thing!
To battle is to be alive.

II

In the car—gabble of a nation.
Biedermeier ladies, brainy glasses,
Stripe of a general below his cape,
Long, Polish mustache—honor and will—
And every eye is blank like a lorgnette,
Forever frozen in this moment.
Each has the likeness of a human shape,

* This sequence of poems was published in 1933; it deals with the author's
experiences in Germany during the years 1920–1928.

Only all humanity has fled—
The bourgeoisie climbs into trains.
It hurries wordlessly to Russia's gate.
And he stood there—smoking.
A nomad. Passenger with Pipe.

III

Autumn. Bare. A calf by a well.
Moist distance painted with blue of trees.
The ghost of a train drags itself to the border,
Dying anew at every stop.
A ruined station. Quiet. Late.
Rain washes down the telegraph wire.
Yet—past windows, a shadow marches.
A bayonet drifts. It's a Bolshevik.
Cigarette in his teeth.
Looking cross-eyed, he stands guard.
And in that train only the Pipe is able
To listen calmly to his step.

IV

For nineteen years the gallant Pipe
Has been reading poems and romances,
Till the world became a novel
Where Civil War is one of the components.
It will be a treat to hear
The slogans sound, banners flutter.
A dialogue of little guns—
A thriller of Ned Pinkerton's.
An aged cannon thuds in the street.
A German helmet rolls in the gutter.
The Pipe is ecstatic. Though he's sheltered,
He feels like a character in Sabatini.

V

Suddenly, he's on a train. He will study
In Europe. To each his own. A bird will sing,

A Bolshevik make revolutions. So he
Has to study. Daylight ebbs. Steely color.
The hot eyes ingest the vista.
White Russian fir in a valley. A bridge.
A muddy pond sweeping by.
Telegraph poles chase backwards.
Homeland ends— If something calls or makes demands,
Be quiet, friend. All in this train are quiet.
Just as, on the white horizon,
Three silver pines are quiet—lonely, without any arms.

VII

Summer eve. There is a pushing
In the station. A rushing from the subway,
The noisy el, the tram—
Bonnet, hat and fresh-trimmed beard.
Autos bark. Electric ads
Write themselves into the sky. A radio yells
Into the heat of Berlin's July,
"Youth! Prosperity! All right!"
The cabaret is lighting up.
The clock is counting nine.
His first manic day,
He studied in the Berlin way.

VIII

Childe Harolds rarely eat.
This one does it less than many.
He is dark, slim and bony.
Clean, if poorly shaven.
In his face, the wear and tear
Of generations of needy tailors—
The Pipe has a room on Bellevue.
He washes dishes in a beanery.
In Berlin's hot evening blue,
He seems a European chap.
To fill the bill—he has to get
A dog, pajamas and a dose of clap.

XIII

He has friends. Two weary cavaliers
Of art. Two hungry knights:
Yusuf Abu and Eric Dern—
Restless figures of a run-down time.
Abu is a dreaming Arab,
A sculptor, soft, with moon-like hands,
A short, fumbling lad,
Who yearns in plaster for the Orient.
Dern—a Man of Sorrow.
A quiet German, who speaks only to himself.
European, much refined,
With quicksilver in his spine.

XV

Berlin nights. The floor is jumping.
He is near the jazz band.
Berlin nights. The girlies topless.
What could be more cultural?
Wizards of the surplus market:
Sharpened skull, hanging cheek,
Black lapel and spacious chin.
Neck and nape, lavishly creased.
Each is a fleshy service
From which come most delicate symphonies of drink—
The jazz band cries. Voices from the colonies,
Black fires of the Negro dance.

XVII

Sammy Pipe applies himself—
Burning. Burning. Burning.
Abu has reflective hands,
But Dern has the keys to life.
"O do not be involved. Take what is ready-made.
Get a sheep dog, friend.
Let him be the escort of your world.

No books—they are not healthy!
To undo what has been done
Is possible—in cards.
Be a gentleman *par excellence.*
Do not laugh when all are laughing."

XIX

It is a confusing age.
Uneasy voices clamor.
An aging middle class in cap and bells.
Noises in the arts and drama.
A wicked Granach bleeds
On an arid stage. Moissi croons
Like a swooning, pale ballerina.
Unburied—poetry stinks.
Deathbed of a distant vigor.
It's the ugly that is sweet.
Expressionism on red feet.
Dada—with an open fly.

XXI

So Childe Harold tried
To taste experience, enjoying all:
To nibble each aspect of the world,
Licking himself at every morsel.
A dark mixture started to ferment—
Mendele and Lomonosov.
It's a vibrant Europe, new
To a small-town philosopher.
Only once, late at night,
He said into his pillow,
"I am like an air balloon
That has escaped its tether."

XXII

By the shore, a lantern burning
Its last hour in the pallid sky,

Abu introduced him to her—
A little blonde dove from Tientsin Strasse,
In a short, white cape of fur
And narrow little shoes from Vienna—
And she never ceased to laugh
And babble in a dozen tongues.
And he looked at her with eyebrows raised.
He didn't know, or understand.
And she whispered to the Pipe,
"I love you . . . Je vous aime!"

XXXIII

He was in love. On a secluded bench
In the Tiergarten he made his moan,
"What is the reason for my rosy thought?
Of my lovely pain—the reason?
Yet, like the lion, drowsy in the cage,
Like these decent, stinky bears,
I will make a hidden fig
To my dream and desires.
As ever I'll stay true
To the large clan of tailors . . .
You blonde little lark of Tientsin Strasse!
You little girl of Dresden china!"

XXXIV

The gloomy pelican, homesick in his cage,
Sorrowfully hides below his beak.
Our Berlin lad, however,
Is modish even in nostalgia.
Pipe smoking in a small-boned hand.
Dark eyes liquid.
And, above him, a white spray
Of jasmine, drooping. Gallantly he pines,
Like Conrad Veidt. In this rare day of June,
He is European—very.

To fill the bill, he has to get
A skinny English bulldog.

XLIII

"I am ailing, Mademoiselle.
Like the century, I'm ailing.
I who once made an amazing
Leap from my father's threshold.
Daring, young rage, impudence,
Bits of Blok, Schopenhauer,
Cabbala, Peretz, Spinoza,
Rootlessness and sorrow, sorrow.
You wait away the years
For your world to catch the lightning.
Till your youth has driven by you.
You sit there—left with nothing."

XLIV

"I have spoken." Gently smiling,
He wipes cold sweat from his forehead.
"Smelling salts!"
A rush of tears.
Just as, after showers, a willow by the water.
Negative. Apathetic.
Wanly sitting by the fire,
Childe Harold has a nice cry.
The landlady peers through her lorgnette.
The irate bird begins to trill,
"Ye gods! Has a knave of hearts
Begun to sing of his loneliness?"

XLV

Midnight. House is sleeping—
Dreaming. Moonlight glances off the walls.
Disheveled, confused, oppressed,
The Pipe ran down the steps.

Disturbed, he guzzled with friends
Till he was ready to collapse.
With burglars he slept in a den.
With servant girls in the park.
And Dern, spouting epigrams,
Gives the pro and con of self-immolation
To his students. But, by this time,
They are peacefully lying in the cell.

XLVI

Viva Europe! Bread and
Circus. Bluff and high-grade bluffers.
The worker, restless in his bed,
Listless by a mug of lager.
In a cheerless factory yard
A blue ax sounds. The platform rises.
Pugilists will break their necks,
While the people belch.
O what swank! The stairway decked
With tapestry. The path is swept.
Tapers flare. Nostrils wide,
The masses catch the spoor of their foe.

XLVIII

K.O. Round the arena,
A spellbound circle of heads
Hears the fists punching
Melody on a keyboard of flesh.
Suddenly— Bang! A chill.
A fall. A sigh. Silent
Is the assemblage. Someone in tails is feeling
The pulse of the attractive victim.
Tapers flicker. White lights
Wander, desolate—
Childe Harold hollered with the masses.
He was a . . . socialist.

L

The alleys are still.
You hear no whisper. No rustle or stir.
Only the breathing of classes.
A searchlight beams by your door—
A steel eye, whose glances
Uncover strips of the night.
They post the last placard
Or are changing the guard.
Between the beams that are striping
The places round and about—
A worker sits with a whistle
On an overturned tram.

LI

Battle. In Nettlebach Strasse
The Security Police. The lorry dazzles—
A grimy mass in the shadow:
Rifles, orders and hands.
A lieutenant with binoculars
Leads Death in his Citroën.
"All—quiet!" Night shivers.
"Colleague! Nothing is happening.
The bums are not willing to die."
"Colleague! Aren't those footsteps?"
And sometimes—a flowerpot flies
And opens the skull of some louse.

LIV

Morning. Wedding,* fearfully dawning,
Bleeding in the gray beginning,
Like an animal bleeding by the edges
Of a forest. Dreams run off

* A Berlin suburb.

Like waters. Young men sprawling.
Injured paw is in their mouth.
The present is terror.
The past—deceit.
Morning. Through roseate dust
Weak color is seeping.
On the doors, a thin orange.
Blue—where a windowpane's left.

LV

Then, sunlight was washing
Horror off the gray faces.
Youth, hands in the pockets,
Cigarettes in the mouth,
Laughed in squares
And committees.
"We will sweep the manure
Out of Germany's cities!"
Flags, ribbons and ties
Flowing—and red.
In the yards, they were chanting
Of the struggle of the classes.

LVI

Day. Angry singing
From cellar, garret and roof.
Only steps, only motion.
A million flood from their crannies.
Red, waving. Flag after flag.
Winding through places and streets.
Only breath. Hostility. Eyes.
A cold, gray million.
Doors—barred. Empty
The yards. A wind is curling.
A million gather in Wedding—
A coarse and clenched fist.

LVIII

Suddenly, a hush that verges on fear.
In the gleam of the lifted ax,
Wrath lies on its hairy belly.
The city has been stilled.
A savage beauty. A woods
That a tempest has torn open.
Bolt after bolt, gnashing,
Writing in a script of phosphorus. Each grimace
Is fixed—a Laocoön.
The stony spring of an animal.
A cold, gray million.

LXI

No velvet, no silken suits.
Denims and corduroys surge.
From each band comes the snarl
Of hot, undisciplined brass.
The drum, like a bear in a cave.
Tones of a clamorous hate—
And, slowly and clearly,
The enmity of the bass.
Then, suddenly—a hush that verges on horror.
A salvo. A command. Men lie on the ground.
Blood streaming from the mouth . . .
Death! A million is silent.

LXII

Night. A tavern in Wedding.
In bow tie and jacket,
Four thin silhouettes
Sit on the oaken benches.
"Comrades"—Harold is speaking.
"Man is always good.
He has shed,

And he will shed blood.
What is left is—drinking.
Softly be it said,
'Man begins his stinking
Even before he's dead.' "

LXIII

Night. On squares and corners
Four make a demonstration.
"Europe, Europe,
Our sword is for you.
Aged Sodom—you are sinning
On an unmade bed.
Down with Beethoven and Goethe
And the Dome of Cologne!
Because the skies are graying
We are turning gray.
We—the last wolves howling
In the ruins of a world."

Nathan Halper

VILNA

I

Someone in a *tallis* is walking in your streets.
Only he is stirring in the city by night.
He listens. Old gray veins quicken—sound
Through courtyard and synagogue like a hoarse, dusty heart.
You are a psalm, spelled in clay and in iron.
Each stone a prayer; a hymn every wall,
As the moon, rippling into ancient lanes,
Glints in a naked and ugly-cold splendor.
Your joy is sadness—joy of deep basses
In chorus. The feasts are funerals.
Your consolation is poverty: clear, translucent—

Like summer mist on the edges of the city.
You are a dark amulet set in Lithuania.
Old gray writing—mossy, peeling.
Each stone a book; parchment every wall.
Pages turn, secretly open in the night,
As, on the old synagogue, a frozen water carrier,
Small beard tilted, stands counting the stars.

II

Only I am stirring in the city by night.
No sound. Houses are rigid—bales of rag.
A tallow candle flutters, dripping,
Where a cabalist sits, tangled into his garret,
Like a spider, drawing the gray thread of his life.
"Is there anyone in the cold emptiness?
In our deafness—can we hear the lost cries?"
Raziel is standing before him; he gleams in the darkness.
The wings an old, faded parchment.
The eyes—pits filled with sand and with cobweb.
"There is no one. Only sorrow is left."
The candle drips. Stupefied, the weak man listens.
He suckles the darkness out of the angel's sockets.
The garrets breathe—lungs of
The hunchbacked creature who is drowsing in the hills.
O city! You are the dream of a cabalist,
Gray, drifting in the universe—cobweb in the early autumn.

III

You are a psalm, spelled in clay and in iron.
The letters fading. They wander—stray.
Stiff men are like sticks; women, like loaves of bread.
The shoulders pressed. Cold, secretive beards.
Long eyes that rock, like rowboats on a lake—
At night, late, over a silver herring,
They beat their breasts. "God, we are sinful . . . sinful."
The moon's white eye, bulging through the tiny panes,
Silvers the rags that hang on the line,

Children in beds—yellow, slippery worms,
Girls half-undressed, their bodies like boards—
These gloomy men are narrow like your streets.
The brow mute—a rigid wall of a synagogue yard.
The eyebrows mossy: like a roof above your ruins.
You are a psalm inscribed upon the fields.
A raven, I sing to you by the flow of the moon.
No sun has ever risen in Lithuania.

IV

Your joy is sorrow—joy of deep basses
In chorus. The quiet Maytime is somber.
Saplings grow from the mortar. Grasses push from the wall.
Sluggishly, a gray blossom crawls out of the old tree.
The cold nettle has risen through mud.
Dung and rigid walls are steeping in their damp.
It may happen by night. A breeze moves a dry pebble on a roof.
A vision, moonbeam and drops of water,
Flows through the silver, tremulously dreaming streets.
It is the Viliya, cool, mistily arising,
Fresh and baby-naked, with long, river-like hands,
Who has come into the town. Blind windows are grimacing.
Arching bridges are crooked on their walls.
No door will open. No head will move
To meet the Viliya in her skinny, blue nakedness.
The bearded walls marvel—the hills around you.
And silence. Silence.

V

You are a dark amulet set in Lithuania.
Figures smolder faintly in the restless stone.
Lucid, white sages of a distant radiance,
Small, hard bones that were polished by toil.
The red tunic of the steely bundist.
The blue student who listens to gray Bergelson—
Yiddish is the homely crown of the oak leaf
Over the gates, sacred and profane, into the city.

Gray Yiddish is the light that twinkles in the window.
Like a wayfarer who breaks his journey beside an old well,
I sit and listen to the rough voice of Yiddish.
Is that the reason why my blood is so turbulent?
I am the city: the thousand narrow doors into the universe,
Roof over roof, to the muddy-cold blue.
I am the black flame, hungry, licking at these walls—
That glows in the eyes of the Litvak in an alien land.
I am the grayness! I am the black flame! I am the city!

VI

And, on the old synagogue, a frozen water carrier,
Small beard tilted, stands counting the stars.

Nathan Halpei

CHAIM GRADE
(1910–)

MY MOTHER

The cheeks collapsed and the eyes half-shut,
My mother listens as her knees sigh:
The whole morning under the winter sky
She ran about to every market.
So let us now at the gate of the wall
Sleep through the night . . .
And her hand cries:
A bird too gets exhausted from fluttering about
As its wings rise and fall . . .
And her head sinks down—
But my mother flicks the daydream off,
Like a tree shaking off the rain.

Her face smolders, a fire pot,
Her hands measure, weigh;
She pleads, she calls,
Till again she dozes with eyes half-shut;
Her hand taps at the freezing air
And stays there, stretched-out.

Just like
A shadow on the snow,
She sways back and forth the whole day long,
Until late at night;
She rocks herself like the pointer of her scale,
To the left, to the right.
Hunched-up, one large hump,

She rots in the snow flurries,
Like the apples in her basket—
And sleeps . . .

Her cheeks glow like coals,
Her neck is whipped by the sleet.
Wrapped up in wind and snow
My mother sleeps standing on her feet.
And when the market snores like a grisly black hound,
She gathers her baskets,
Like a beggar his pennies,
And the market's red eye is put out.
But right at the threshold her steps start to weep:
Wasted hope!
Worn out, she stumbles through the hut
And sleeps.

The lantern hiccups in her hand,
Choking with smoky tears.
She rocks at the wall
As in front of a grave,
And sleeps.

The ax lurks in her hand,
Above her twisted fingers,
And the fiery tongues of the little stove
Menace her wrinkled cheeks—
And she sleeps.
She forgets to take out her hands:
They are freezing in the kneading bowl.
Her thin shoulder shakes,
She washes, she trembles with eyes cast down,
And she sleeps.

When at last she takes the pot between her knees,
The spoon to her mouth,
Again her hand falls down,
Exhausted and slow
She falls asleep—
My mother sleeps . . .

Florence Victor

LAZER WOLF
(1910–1943)

WHY

Why does a dog bay at the moon?
Because he thinks it a piece of meat.
Why do stars fall?
It's gloomy being with God.

Why does teacher beat his pupils?
They are slow at A B C's.
Why do we chop trees?
So the beasts may come to the city.

Nathan Halper

NO CHILD WITH HONEY HEART

I have never been mild.
My heart is wild
Pulling, like a tiger at a chain,
Pushing like a darkling sea
To a sand
Where sunny, singing days
Are making jubilee.

I have always been sinful.
No child with honey heart—
Like a willful horse

I have broken bit and stall
And bathed only in the coldest waterfall.

I have always yearned for fame.
I may as well be blind
If the cosmos will not be in bondage to my call,
If I do not take all space into my embrace,
If I do not get to gourmandise the farthest star—
If I never grow
Into the forever.

Nathan Halper

SONGS

It is a while
Since I was foolish or wise,
But I have guile
Like an experienced snake.

I am absurd
Like an actor who,
At ninety,
Keeps playing Richard the Third.

My loves are old, cold,
Like portions of ice cream in a cool cellar.
Yet, within them,
They have something older
Colder
That goes back to Cain.

My love for you is transparent—
Like a silken gown.
It is obvious.
Two plus two equals four.
Your love for me is unclear—
Like a pointless joke:
A piece of herring paper in a little store that sells kasha.

Nathan Halper

A MURDER

Night is brown
Like Pushkin's face.
The moon, a red ace.
Two robbers, walking,
Are talking of murder.

Waves are silvery.
The scene is saintly—
Like Leo Tolstoy's beard.
Two robbers, walking,
Are talking of murder.

One says: Let it sink
All the way into the heart.
The other smells of drink
And keeps asking questions.
They slink into the village.

A peasant sleeps in the barn,
His little bag around his neck.
They strike a fire,
Throwing a light upon his face.

The peasant's breath is low.
He does not foresee his death.
Two blades go into his throat.
Blood flares like fire.

His two small coins
Disappear into their hands.
They run. Moon smiles,
Pale—like Yesenin's hair.

                                        Nathan Halper

ISRAEL STERN
(1894–1942)

MEN WHO HUNGER

Their eyes are different, also their voices.
The sky is a head with its hair fallen out.
The days stand in white rows like hospital beds
While the odor of chloroform flows through the streets.

Their eyes are different (as are their voices)
And burn like a lamp with lowered wick.
Why then is their speech like a sharpened awl
Since they seem well—like water and like bread?

Their eyes are different, also their voices.
When they say *man*, the world breaks into a rage—
As though the sun's golden hair were clipped off.
And when they say *branch*, the woods start ailing—
As though the birds had lost their song.
And when they say *hay*, a fire is kindled in the stacks—
Because alien, alien, alien are their voices, their eyes:
Because the hungry can be strict and hard like bone,
Telling themselves a tale of horror deep in the night
That the stars in the sky are small white heads
Come to ripeness from inflamed boils . . .

So they go off on desolate roads,
Searching for a long spear with which to stab the skies
And free the pus
That will flood the world.

Etta Blum

TWILIGHTS

Twilights are children discovered behind fences,
Twilights are the aged who cannot achieve death,
Twilights are lamps—the wicks already burning.
Twilights are the eyes of inarticulate madmen,
Twilights are letters written and torn up;
something is easing, something perishing . . .
Twilights are rings on axed-off fingers:
blood on gold, gold on blood.
Twilights are arms of beautiful beggar girls,
Twilights are flags in lost battles.
Twilights are fiddlers, while devils
snatch the brides from our homes . . .
Twilights are windows of abandoned synagogues,
the panes lamenting in color . . .

                                                            Etta Blum

NAHUM BOMZE
(1906–1954)

A WEDDING AT HARVEST TIME

It was such a night as this—
I looked out through the window
and saw:
wagons standing before the terrace,
father and mother in front,
my brother in his white waistcoat,
and all the neighbors and guests.

Afterward I heard
the horses neighing from afar.
That night in my trundle bed
a dream with dark wing
brought them back again:

They are riding through woods, lakes, mills,
and old jesters are playing
sleepy and weary
the song of the bridal canopy.
They rush on, rush on,
toward the bride in the city,
but a jester has loosened a wheel
of the wagon.

And though they all lie now in the ground
(even Meyer Pudding and his horse),
I thought of them today.

Because it was such a night as this,
I looked out through the window
and saw:
leaves dancing in the wind,
and I alone in the house—a child
in terror.
They have all gone away to the wedding,
all night I have waited for them,
but they have all deceived me.

Jacob Sloan

SOMETIMES I DREAM

Sometimes I dream: I am a child,
My white shirt is flapping wild
And all the grownups laugh.

I run ashamed through streets I do not know,
The wind picks my shirt up from below
And all the grownups laugh.

They lead me all around the town,
The shouting inside me dies down
And all the grownups laugh.

They strip the shirt off my back,
My bareness burns on their eyes' rack
And all the grownups laugh.

And suddenly I see: a wondrous sight—
I am old—my beard is white—
And all the children laugh.

They lead me through a tangled maze,
My dead parents come to meet me on the way
And all the children laugh.

I stand alone in the blue night
With my tears and my cry
And all the children laugh.

Jacob Sloan

RAJZEL
ZYCHLINSKA
(1910–   )

POOR PEOPLE

Being poor has one color
Everywhere.
Poor people walk over the earth silently
Speaking to the worms.
From beneath all the rocks
Death looks at them
And calls.

Lucy S. Dawidowicz and Florence Victor

THE BED SHEET
AND THE STRANGER

A person slept here
A night,
A bed sheet laments him.
The walls are indifferent,
The door has already forgotten him,
Only the sheet is afraid
And longs for the stranger.

Lucy S. Dawidowicz and Florence Victor

OF ALL THE FACES

Of all the faces that tossed me about
All through the day,
One face is left
To which I am anchored.

Of all the voices
That outshouted me,
One voice is left
In which I tremble.

Of all the paths that led me
Astray,
A town emerged,
With its streets,
Squares
And tunnels.

Lucy S. Dawidowicz and Florence Victor

EVERYTHING WILL REMEMBER

Everything will remember
That I was here.
The ships will be the color
Of my clothing,
The birds will use my voice for singing,
The fisherman on the rock
Will ponder my poem,
The river
Will follow my footprints.

Lucy S. Dawidowicz and Florence Victor

ELIEZER STEINBERG
(1880–1932)

THE SACRIFICIAL KNIFE AND THE SIMPLE SAW

So happens a slaughterer would
sometimes have to saw off a piece of wood.
One day
Brother Knife sees Brother Saw across the way
and lets his tongue cut loose.

Hey there, he says, look at that dumb goose
flashing his pearly-whites! Lord, what a show!
You want to know something, that sure is a set
all full of, you bet
scratches and
patches
a whole banged-up row!
That saw looks unkosher from head to toe!
And see what he's wearing—them poor wooden threads!
When I take a look at some deadheads
I thank my old father in the sky for making things sweet and
    ugly too.
I'm doing great! Just a lucky old Jew!
Not a spot
of rot
on my kosher steel!
Not a blot on my ideal!
No wonder Reb Elkonoh's saintly hand can close

around me with holiness and repose
while he prays, watching heaven along the line of his nose!

True, says Brother Simple Saw (can he be *that* naive?)
I do really believe
Reb Elkonoh shouldn't say a blessing over *me*.
No, some stuff would not go down,
people would laugh both of us out of town.
I'm just an honest worker, plain to see,
I don't sparkle not one spark,
just stand in a corner where it's dark,
keep in my place and don't try to appear too good.
Lord knows I'm only fit for cutting wood.
But you—no joking matter—you cut throats!

> Let's give a twist to the tale and add some moral notes:
> Brother Saw's still an honest worker, plain to see
> a black spot on his family tree,
> while Brother Knife is playing a sharper game—
> he kills and blessings are said over him just the same.

Jerome Rothenberg

THE HORSE AND THE WHIP

"O may a great disaster
Fall on your noble master,
Mr. Wagon Driver Feitel
(To give him his proper title)
And on you, too, of course,"
(Says the horse
To the whip)
"It's a gyp,
To be clobbered like this with no fault on my part;
Do you think that it's fun to keep dragging this cart?
And you've no sense at all of how I might need
A few oats for a feed,

Before starting out for the day.
—Anyway,
Try talking with whips, they've got nothing to say!
If, like me, you were all cut up
You'd give up whipping,
Slashing and ripping.
What, again? I'll yell blue murder—"   "Shut up!"
(The whip cracks now, like a sharp tongue)
"I know very well that dragging
A cart like this with your stomach nagging
Means nearly emptying each lung.
Let me give you a tip—
You keep getting the whip
Not for not pulling; but you're due for
Being converted into glue for
Not getting the point, for letting yourself, you ass,
Be harnessed up and brought to such a pass!"

John Hollander

THE BRUSH AND THE SHOE

Whish! Whush!
—That's the dance, on a shoe, of a brush.
The swifter that the dance will get,
The shoe will be the shinier yet:
Just to watch them is a delight!
But the shoe is quite a haughty sight;
He lives on the foot of the rich Mr. Green
And feels (not the man—it's the shoe I mean)
Put off—look who has the nerve to dance
Before his shining countenance!
Reddening with outrage, and torn
By anger he cries out in scorn
"These dreadful brushes! It never ceases—
He leaps at my face, the boorish clown!
I'd dearly like to knock him down
And break him into several pieces!"

"Please be calm, Mr. Shoe," says the brush,
"Why all this outcry, fuss and rush?
You'd be quite dull without me, true?
Well, so I get to dance on you."

John Hollander

DVORAH FOGEL
(1902–1942)

BILLBOARDS IN THE RAIN

Today the rain coats gray houses
with another coat
of gray,

You, far away.

Everyone away,
there's no one to be with.

I lean
against a wall of billboards
pasted with posters of lemon and orange.

Today the rain dissolved
the vermilion letters
announcing the film
of the red ballerina.

Red lines, caressing,
and other hands heavily moving
across hot yellow figures.

In a row of ten gray houses
a red and yellow wall of boards,
the only sign of life.

And one can lean against it
as against a human body
now far off,
out of reach.

Adrienne Rich

WAITING POEM

How long, waiting by the window,
walking yellow streets, blue, gray,
till you make the three-hour journey
to my city from yours?

I can wait a year.
Every day, live till eleven o'clock.
But you don't come.
Not the first week, not the second.
Every week dies seven times
of waiting. For you.

I've worn out the streets with looking.
The yellow street of twelve o'clock
where everything is already lost,
the street of three in the afternoon
where everything is the way
it has to be forever.

In the glassy night street
where a yellow-papered fence
turns into a body with gestures.
First, second, third street.

I came home by all the streets
where I met twenty bodies, fifty bodies.
Only not yours.
Where is it, then?

Adrienne Rich

OUT OF LONGING

Today I bought yellow cherries
smelling wetly of loneliness.

Cherries never grow old.
Just sixteen, seventeen years old.

Today I'm a yellow cherry,
I taste emptily of drifting
through night streets, city streets.
Yellow lamps.

Every night something should happen in the world.
Something should come
of all the walks
one takes in a day.

But last year
and again two and three years ago

Only the watery taste
of loneliness.

Adrienne Rich

JOSEPH RUBINSTEIN
(1904–)

MOSCOW MORNING

In the morning Moscow gets up drowsy, its eyes
Crooked windows, feverish at sunrise.
The night howls in the street smelling of prison.
In fear the yellow street light is left on.

The streets wake up aching, swollen.
Sleepless women fight for a place in line.
Crowds rush by. Near the walls of the secret police
You cross the street in terror, run past in silence.

Stanley Moss

TO YESENIN

To my Yiddish prayers your springtime does not listen.
Your Russian wind does not hear my Yiddish songs.
Can your words calm the tears of a Jew, O Yesenin?
Is there comfort to Jewish sorrows in your songs?

Like you, I am a poet. I write as an alien guest,
A Polish Jew not properly addressed.
Like you I have dried my shirts on Russian fences,
And my tears wash down the path of your sadness.

Stanley Moss

THE OTHER LOOKS AT ME

Flags fly on the night of victory.
Above the Kremlin, lights play on the head of Stalin.
Held up by balloons he swings with the wind.
His face stares down at me.

Berlin's on fire, Hitler dead.
Fear burns my flesh to ashes.
He burned my mother, Hitler is dead.
And now the other eyes me in the darkness.

Stanley Moss

MY SHADOW

My shadow stands and prays to an unknown God,
Who has no heaven and no name.
My shadow wanders through the city
Searching the walls for his night-like face.
After dark in his house of darkness—silence.
Something on the floor catches my eye, I see
My shadow in prayer beneath the sofa,
I hear the sighing of my shoes,
The groan of my bookcase on rusty hooks.
I spring to my feet and switch on the light,
Move to the middle of the room, away from things.
Over there swinging on the wall
My shadow rocks restlessly, disheveled:
He prays to himself with outstretched hand,
A pious Jew, his tears storm against his house.

Stanley Moss

THE BLIND WALL

Does the blind wall understand it is blind?
Does the warped door know its crooked shape?
It is likely summer's fragrant wind
Does not know the flower or the grape.

The clear day brings forth sun and light.
The night comes shadow-like, a blur.
Does the day know its own face is bright?
Or the night see its own dark figure?

A star has led me to the shoreline.
Galaxies wake my wish for infinity;
Perhaps the star looks for a new design,
The constellation, like me, has lost its way.

Stanley Moss

V

MODERN
YIDDISH
POETRY
IN AMERICA

JACOB GLATSTEIN
(1896–1991)

FROM "KLEINE NACHTMUSIK"

Trust me from here to there
And a few steps more.
I won't fool you; I come alone.
I bring my open face
That you may fathom every why.
I'm saddened through and through with books,
Heavy with old wine,
Phlegmatic as a cat whose bowl is filled.
See how I come back
To the wonder of my first word.
Close the window, friend,
Shield me from the smallest wind.
In the dark there are two of us;
What could be less?
I am the hearty patron
Of all the hungry tasters.
Let us saddle sleep
And ride off in our private park.
The mays will kiss
The must-nots in the dark.

Chana Faerstein

MY FATHER ISAAC

As Isaac in his old age was led to the sacrifice,
he lifted his clouded eyes to heaven
and said in a tired voice:
"I know I'll be your choice."
No good angel came flying;
the flames burned more brightly and higher.
"The blade has been sharpened for my throat."
Isaac, old, was not deceived
as when he'd been that lad from Genesis;
he knew that there would be no lamb.
And as they bound him to the altar,
and as he smelled the searing fumes,
he spoke his mind thus:
"God will not interrupt this slaughter!"
He called out in a tired voice:
"Here I am—prepared to be your ram."

Etta Blum

RABBI YUSSEL
LUKSH OF CHELM*

I

Who can bear
The wail of a young orphan?
Or the tears of a needy widow?
Who can endure
The loneliness—like a stone's—
Of a woman who is barren?
Or the shame of an ugly wife
Whom a husband has deserted?

* Chelm is the name of a legendary Jewish town in Eastern Europe, composed
of fools whose foolishness was not always foolish.

Worst of all is the dumb misery
Of a beaten horse.
The whip crackles
On the pelt.
The heavy head bends lower
Without reproach; without opposition
Or resistance.
Such anguish should come before God's Majesty
And there make its plaint.
"Master!
Master of this Universe—
Why?"

Yussel Luksh cannot bear it.
He would gladly get in the shafts.
Giddy-up, giddy-up,
He would run, year after year.
Taking those blows—
Like bracing lashes, stinging besoms—
Like
An atonement.

The wan fields seem greener now
After the wash of rain.
A rusty plow comes up singing.
Their heads washed,
Peach, currant, gooseberry,
Greet him.
And here, a dressed-up cherry tree
Looks over the orchard's fence. . . .
This is God's grace.
This—and more—have been made for man's enjoyment.
Nonetheless, Yussel—do not be misled!
No matter how beautiful this tree,
How beautiful the plow—
The quiet glitter of the steel,
The supple branch, the rocking bough—
Beauty is only for the eye!
Let Him really show a miracle.

Let Him hand out justice—
Evenly.
One deal
To poor and rich.
One measure
For the high and the humble.

If—for the sake of my sires
I had good will
In Heaven,
I would straighten my back,
And—in friendly fashion—
Have it out with the Almighty.
Only one
Could presume this—
Only one—Reb Levi Yitzkhok.
He had a knack. He could talk to Him
Like a crony—
Button to button.
He could get down to brass tacks.
"How may one be a glutton,
While another
Lacks?"
He'd ask the score.
How come? What for?
"Why does one man have the fat?
Grabbing the best
In his fists—
While another man is gaunt,
In want of a spoon of food?"

Strong, his words.
Wide his stand.
"I—Reb Levi Yitzkhok—command!
To Your system
To Your set-up—I say, 'No!
No!—with a capital N.
No!—in a Turkish overcoat!' "

I? Yussel Luksh?
What weight, what substance,
Have I—Mud, the son of Mire?
A snotling—
I—should I aspire—?
One-two- and I am squelched!
"Mannerless fellow—
Learn your place. . . .
So the way that I manage
Does not meet
Your full approval?
Smart aleck—
Could you run it better?
So many who want,
So many who claim,
So many who praise, so many who blame,
So many demands,
So many mouths, so many hands. . . .
Some are spared, and some are speared. . . .
Yet it's all—all the same.
Their voices rise. And their cries,
Their cries—they are not to be borne!
You are lucky. You have your solution.
Get in the harness. Draw the cart.
Giddy-up here, *giddy-up* there. . . .
You acquit your debts with a tear.
I am *No*—but you are *Yes*.
I—I am the harsh judge.
You—you are the heart. . . ."

II

Do not put
The fur cap on me!
Do not call me Rabbi Yussel!
My piety. . . . My virtue. . . .
Their like grows on any dunghill.
Why do you crown me?
I am not worthy.

How may I lead you?
I myself am astray.
How do I get
To deal with your questions?
I have no replies.
My head is buzzing
With little birds who ask me
Their silly puzzles:
"Who is right? The driver? The horse?
Or—is it
The whip?"

Men—no fooling—
Do you not see the hitch?
Pretend that I am the judge.
You come to me for my ruling—
Who won? Who lost?
What's what? Which is which?
Who gets what wages?
Who pays how much cost?
Folks—I tell you—I am a fool,
A tomfool—
With a little goatee.
Imps—on broomsticks—in a ring—
Dance around me; and they sing,
"Yussel Luksh. He's sublime.
He is the wise man of our time!"

"Eloquent," the people call it.
"A head for you—
No harm befall it!"
"You hear, Reb Itze!"
"I heard it—Reb Pitze!"
"I saw the wisdom on his brow.
Heard the Law—as from Sinai.
Saw how he unlocks
The very Temple!"
"The depth of brain." "The flash of mind."
"Who is right? The driver? The horse?
Or is it the whip?"

"What a quip!"
    A goblin leers.
    Shows his tongue—and disappears.
    Crownèd goose!
    Anointed booby!
    We chant your praises to the realm—
    A piece of glass becomes a ruby.
    Yussel—
    Yussel Luksh of Chelm!

III

Shnyim ohzin:
To hold
A prayer shawl. . . .
Once there's two, there's a brawl.
They are not able
To share God's legacy.
Over a deal. Over a trade.
Over a coin. Over a maid.
Chelm's preoccupations. . . .
Shnyim ohzin. . . . Two hold
One chattel.
If there's two—you have a battle!

Therefore the sages—
(Silver and gold!)—
"Divide"—they say. . . .
A precious thought.
A world of wisdom in one word.
Wiser than Hillel—yet,
To the comprehension of a child.
You may learn it even as
You stand
On one foot.
Quick . . . as a gazelle. Or quicker—
As a gesture. . . .
A lightning flash. . . .
Divide. Why bicker?

Gather ye on a market day,
With your crusts of trouble,
Your crumbs of joy. . . .
Your penny bags of noble thought. . . .
With your pretty wives, your servants,
With your horses, with your mules,
Your capons, the fatted quail,
The fragrant spices, the rich drinks—
And—
Divide!

Consider it. . . . Here's a glut.
Here—a shrunken gut. . . .
Why rancor? Why do people hanker
For this man's wife, for that man's kine?
Because Simon has a lot
And Reuben has an empty pot. . . .
So the wise
Did devise
One word—a precious word.
Divide! Let it all be shared!

IV

To the world, it is a little tent.
To itself, Chelm is a town.
With an icon. A God.
A church. A hill.
A market place. A Jewish quarter.
Crooked houses—brick and mortar.

Ancient gates.
Alleys, lanes. Broken panes.
Tatters, rags. Moneybags.
Women pure. Women prudish.
Women—
Loose and lewdish.

It's a town. . . .

Jewish men in wadded coats.
Wives
Over charcoal pots.
Onion rolls. Honey cakes.
Horse beans.
Herring barrels.
Kerosene. Healing salves. . . .
Peasants in their homespun. . . . Calves.
Ducks. Ganders.
Butchers' apprentices.
Thieves. Priests.
Tumblers. Buffoons.
Holy men. Loons. Dreamy kids. . . .
Dead. Demons.
Ghosts and ghouls. . . .
Fools?
Not a one.
I will give you a prize at once
If you find me a single dunce.
Not here.
Absent.

He is shrewd. He is shrewder.
He's the shrewdest of the shrewds.
Chelm is a scene of feuds.
Carnage.
Raps. Slaps. . . .
Palms are like boards!
They row over isms, over schisms.
Over things that are eternal.
Or an article in a journal.
Till they come to Yussel Luksh.
"Rabbi. You settle it.
Who is wise? Who is wiser?
You are the fellow with the upper story.
Why—of course—you are one of us.
Which party is correct?"

Yussel feels he is slaughtered.
His throat is cut—
Without a knife.
Each side threatens.
His bit of poverty is at stake. . . .
His world. His comforts.
His here-and-now. His nibble of bread.
His dribble of kasha. . . .
All lie in the scales
Of his masters. . . .
Each bunch comes
With its cross-purposes.
His chores
Weigh on his shoulders like a hunch.

v

God has a job in this world.
Yussel, a job in Chelm.
But he is ready to keel over.
A humpbacked hovel.
An asthmatic chimney.
And the spouse that they have gotten him.
Not a woman, but a sword.
The eyes no eyes.
They are peepers. The breasts no breasts.
They are dried-out figs.
A mouth having no silence.
The words—
They are hot coals. . . .

Yussel Luksh—
Provider mine!
Just listen to his line:
>   He is right. He is right.
>   No blame. All are right.
>   Zionists.
>   Socialists.
>   Anarchists. Anti- Semites.

Tatatatars. And the Christs. . . .
Ain't no Yes. Ain't no No.
No Stop. No Go.
No black. No white . . . no day.
    No night.
No blame.
All are right.

He furtively puts on his torn cape.
Takes a clean shirt
And sneaks off to the bath.
Having washed away the dirt,
Yussel sits on the grass.

VI

The west is seamed with pieces of gold
And with pieces of fire.
A painter has begun
To lay his stencils on the sky.
All is still—
The stillness of wonder.
Ah, a pleasure. . . .
No one sees him. No one hears.
God alone hearkens
How a man weeps.
Chelm's rabbi sobs.
He moans.
Life is short.
A day. A night.
I—the silliest fool—
A leader of fools—
Am tired.

I do not, Lord—
I do not understand Your Chelm.
But it is a pity—
A pity on each blade of grass.
The ant. The horse.

The water carrier.
On the boor and the learned man.
The poor man.
The rich.
They know all. All of it.
A little?
God forbid!
Each man owns the key to Your granary. . . .
And they want.
They shout.
Compete . . . fight. . . .
They hate. They love.
They strive.
They live.
A day—a night. . . .
Oh, a pity
On Your Chelm!

He is right. *He* is right.
I am right. You are right.
There is no black. Is no white.
No guilt.
All
Are right.

Nathan Halper

A. GLANZ–LEYELES
(1889–1966)

ISAIAH AND HOMER

Homer's grace is unparalleled: it is *Homer's!*
    The dignity, the full, childlike desire;
The manly power, and the sublime heroics—
    But even more rare is Isaiah!

Homer—a wide pool, flowing and yet profound:
    He bathes Aegean shores in the sun's high fire,
Or strokes the ear with moonlight's silver vespers.
    But the water of life is Isaiah.

Homer—a field of brightness, a forest of fragrance;
    Royal stags roam there; gently, birds rise higher;
Young lambs leap to the singing of green earth;
    But heaven's own eye is Isaiah.

Homer danced on the hillsides with laughing nymphs;
    His splendid creature, Man, plucked bow and lyre.
But "Purge thyself of the buck's darkness, the deer's"
    So man must declare in Isaiah.

Homer left Hector to the savage dogs,
    Had Achilles rob him of his funeral pyre.
Inferring the Fallen State from the infant's tear,
    The bitter words rushed from Isaiah.

How wonderful bearded Homer's gold and green,
    His rare blue universe, crystal entire!
But the world will only glow for the stranger among you
    When victory comes to Isaiah.

John Hollander

THE PENGUIN AND I

It occurred to a penguin, his opened beak aimed sunward,
    To blow a toy trumpet monotone; I heard
An unsilvery sound, neither rare, nor triumphant,
    But it blared forth the secret joy of being bird.

His appearance, that of an earnest little professor
    Wearing a white shirt and a black frock coat;
Which, of course, made it all the more surprising
    When he blasted out a brazen trumpet note.

All this occurred on a frosty Sabbath in March:
    I had fled from town to the far, sequestered zoo,
Seeking my day of rest in the marvelous garden
    Filled with many kids, mothers and grandparents too.

Penguins love the bright cold, glistening in sunlight.
    In announcing their passions, intimate and profound,
What matter to them if a musical theoretician
    Turn up his nose at the tune, and their voices' sound?

Hearing a penguin, then, wind his sudden bugle
    (With a certain kind of joy, I must confess),
I saw green trees, and a distant swing, and in it
    Was swinging, free, a girl in a crimson dress.

Swinging toward danger, the girl rose ever higher,
    Singing a strange and passionate song, and then
Her loose dress bared, like an opening red fan,
    Two thighs that braved both God and the world of men.

Somewhere beneath my well-worn path lies buried
    Sun, storm and the worries of half a hundred years,
But still that girlish, high-bouncing rebellion
    Replenishes my eyes and floods my ears.

Professor Comedian of the rich, feathery kingdoms,
    Penguin in cold, bright daylight of early spring—
Little girl, tossing away the heavy baggage
    Of generations with each wild, high swing—

You turn me, both, toward my wastes and my desperations:
    Have I not, through a maze of language, run
All my life after your deep, animal outcry
    Which flowed free on the wind, and toward the sun?
                       John Hollander

N. B. MINKOFF
(1893–1958)

LANDSCAPE

From behind white mists
I'll bring you to your rest.
I will awaken the slumbering waters
that dream of your last poems.
Silver pitchers, blue-fired,
I'll present to you.
Consider the sadness of flame.
Draw breath with my regrets.
Let my bow pass over your strings,
may the gold of your voice crimson . . .

Etta Blum

A STAR BLOOMS

Bread and water—the quiet blessing,
That is all we possess.
A star blooms in the empty stable,
disappears with the coming of day.

The threshold's ready. The candlesticks.
The bit of straw. The door is open.
Bring in the coverlet, hush-sh . . .
let the psalm Jew sleep on.

The bones no longer awaken.
From dusk the eyes become blind.
An entire world dims and dissolves,
and all is veiled with silence.

Bread and water—the quiet blessing,
That is all we possess.
A star blooms in the empty stable
and fades quietly at dawn.

Etta Blum

AT EVENING

Like the sky you are shut.
I cannot comprehend you.

The hours go toward you
while my life becomes more
and more empty.

Figures of the long-since dead
come and go before me
bringing radiance from you.

I long for your human visage,
I want to comprehend you.

My heart has become gray.
Death sleeps on my fingers.

Etta Blum

ELIEZER BLUM–ALQUIT

(1896–1963)

FOUR POEMS

I

I no longer had anything,
So I lay in the night and waited.
I no longer had thought for my possessions.
Such an abundance of weakness
stored up within so few days!
So I waited for the dawn to come
and give me back the walls of our room,
the writing table, the mirror that,
as in the hands of a jongleur,
showed me a straw of the sun
before the sun itself could be seen.
Over everything rested that early gray.
And when the light, finally,
put each thing in its proper place
and everything was back again, again
you came into the room and said *Good Morning*—
and God once more created the world.

II

I drew you out of that particular night
that spoke in half-words,
I wanted to see you in daylight.

And, believe me, even in its childish spots,
your clarity is as the wholeness of language—
sufficiently halved and so incomprehensible
as to make me beside myself.
So why the need to divide it again?
You sit here in the shade of a tree,
studying a July afternoon.
Summer birds, like golden letters,
flutter about you, about me.
I sit down beside you.
What could be simpler?
Yet where does the road lead to?
Back to that particular night
with its half-words?

     III

Is there a darkness then which was not once light?
And is there a light which becomes lost forever?
I am old enough to be my agèd father.
So I speak to you and ask:
If Einstein had faith,
then what do you have to lose?
Sky, stammer, earth and roots—
weeping twigs in the earth.
From the least worm to the highest leaf
all was under the seal of that particular night
with its sunken treasures, everything,
each white dot under lock and key.
And you with all your meanings came to plead
and to sorrow yourself into a word,
into a poem, to reconcile yourself
in a silent Jew who retreats and returns again—
who emerges from the night
as the sun emerges from coal
when we gaze at the fire,
when we love each other
and gaze at the fire.

IV

Since I scarcely know what to do with you—
Dress you in colors that no one else can see?
Carve you into wood?
Catch you in my eye
And then shut it?
Taste you with my fingers?
Give you existence in clay?
Love you into words?
Shall I wrap you about in letters
So that, like Hanina,*
When he burned inside the parchment,
I can see you in your ascension?
You, descendant of the *Lamed Vov,*†
Beloved,
Should live by the touch
Of my eyes, my hands.

Etta Blum

* The legend is that Hanina, a Jewish martyr in the time of Hadrian, wrapped himself in the sacred parchment; and, as he was burning, the letters flew of themselves up to heaven.
† The *Lamed Vov* refers to the Thirty-six Just, the spiritual pillars of the world, according to Jewish tradition.

A. LUTZKY

(1894–1957)

A BEARD WISHES
TO ESCAPE

A white beard
Wishes to escape from an old Jew
In the wintry street—
Waves like a flag on high.
His hat keeps blowing off
Under the trembling fingers
Of his left hand
And peals of laughter
Enter his right ear.

Meyer Liben

A PAPER SUICIDE

A scrap of paper is weary of life,
Falls onto a railroad track
And awaits the approaching train.
When the train bore down
He was terrified of its power,
Struggled from the earth
And flew off in a fearful joy.

Meyer Liben

A GIRL CAUGHT
IN A STORM

A bitter wind
Has swept up a girl
Painted on a tin sign
In front of a tailor's house.
The storm is spinning her 'round—
She fights off the elements
And in a tiny voice cries:
    Tailor!
    Take me in!

Meyer Liben

EVENING

Do you think only you are sad and lonely at evening time?
All things on the lonely earth
Become lonely in the evening.

Look at the staring houses,

The frightened signs,

The very twigs under your feet.

The blades of grass tremble like small children
In the dark fields.

Even the whirr of the far-off wagons
At the boundaries of the world . . .

Can you hear?

Meyer Liben

STORY OF THE PENNIES

Pennies are chummy mostly with poor people,
With beggars.
Their pockets are hangouts
This is their saloon.
Now and then they meet up with cronies
Rub up against acquaintances,
Maybe a relative

Sometimes a penny scorched in a fire
Sometimes an old cent dug up from a well
Sometimes an old-style penny, the size of a dollar
Sometimes a penny returned from the other world.

At night
When the beggar goes home,
The pennies trade stories.

One penny said:
"A child warmed me in his mouth
What a pleasure!"

A second penny said:
"Once I was rolling in a house.
A cat chased me
Thinking I was one of those . . .

"So I lay down
And let myself be sniffed.
She looked at me angrily.

"She sprang up
Eyed me from a distance
I lay still . . .

"She ran over
Snarled at me
Tried to scare me
I lay still . . .

"She began to tickle me with her paw
I stiffened out of fear
So her tail stood up.

"She thought
That I was crying.
In fact I was laughing,
To create attention—
Soon enough a stranger heard
And picked me up."

A third penny said:
"Once
In a pocket
I was scared of a key
Thought it was a saw
That wanted to cut me in two.

"The key started up a conversation.
He turned out to be some key,
He himself is scared of a hatchet.

"We are all scared!"

Meyer Liben

ABA STOLZENBERG
(1905–1941)

BOLSHEVIKS

They came on ponies, barefoot,
brandishing guns that had no bullets;
wore ladies' hats backwards; their leaders
with the look of deacons; and packs
of ox-men, heads wrapped in sacks.

They came in early autumn, shook down
the pears they could not pick by hand;
sprawled across sidewalks and church steps
and felt themselves masters of the land.

The motorcycles spring out of nowhere.
A blast from the roaring White Guards!
Of Trotsky's soldiers nothing remains here
but some sad little mounds near the woods.

Stanley Kunitz

I KNOW NEITHER
ENGLISH NOR FRENCH

I know neither English nor French, scorning these tongues.
—God, let me grasp the language of things.

I beg for words to speak the wound
of boys and girls whose time comes round.

Of a stricken man in his stony hour,
or a humiliated one: to catch his half-tear.

Stanley Kunitz

REASON

Reason, you solve all riddles with your edge,
Prove everything and make it mirror-clear,
Black on white, like an official seal.
Eternal gardener with your pruning shear,
You block us from misfortune with an iron wall.

Lenore Marshall

WHAT AM I IN
TIME AND SPACE?

What am I in time and space?
A weeping willow,
A field not tilled.
A bush that flickers.
A creature grasping life's joke,
An ox harnessed in God's yoke.

Lenore Marshall

A. TABACHNICK
(1901–)

IN THE BEGINNING
WAS THE WORD

In the beginning was the word
And then the word spread thin.
God was present in every place
But we did not come in.

God was there, the word was there,
Stranded, where were we?
Left with a blurred shadow,
A yellowed family tree.

Lenore Marshall

AND WHOEVER BRINGS

And whoever brings the song should buckle on a sword,
And whoever carries the word should also carry a spear,
And whoever comes with God—he should come as a lord
And sweep the earth like fire.

Lenore Marshall

ITZIK MANGER

(1901–1969)

LIKE A MURDERER

Like a murderer, with knife in hand
Ambushing his victim late at night,
I listen for your steps, O Lord, I wait;
I, from whom you hide your smiling light;
I, the grandson of Iscariot.

I'm ready to do penance with my blood—
Your prophets' blood still burns my fingertips . . .
Although a shepherd, in the midst of spring,
Is fluting silver magic with his lips
And no one calls me to account for anything.

To see you! Just to see you once.
To know with certainty there is a You;
To know you really crown a saint with light;
To know with certainty your sky is blue . . .
And then, to hide forever from your sight.

I'll fling the thirty silver coins
To be confounded with a careless wind;
And, barefoot, Lord, I'll make my way to you
To weep before you, like a child returned
Whose head is heavy with the crown of sin.

Like a murderer, with knife in hand
Ambushing his victim late at night,

I listen for your steps, O Lord, I wait;
I, from whom you hide your smiling light;
I, the grandson of Iscariot.

Leonard Wolf

SATAN'S PRAYER

So many eons have I fought
Against Thee, O great Lord of Light.
Now, with my scorched wings, I stand
Before Thy blazing sight.

So be it—there, my kingdom lies
Shattered underneath Thy feet;
While every nerve in Thee declares
The joy of victory is sweet.

So be it—my black crown burns out
Into a thousand sickly stars.
Lilith, meanwhile, crucifies
Herself, upon her tears.

Accept the grief of one who ran
With crimson torches through the night
And shook her tresses to the wind
Like serpents— O Thou Lord of Light.

Accept the grief of one who could
Blaspheme and yet believe in Thee;
Who in the sisterhood of Hell
Looked up toward Thee, longingly.

I bow before Thee, Lord of Light;
But she, my wild one, may not bow.
O quench the sorrows of her hair
And rest Thy smile upon her now.

Kindle pleasure in her eyes—
Those eyes that darkly, darkly grieve;
A boon—a boon. Grant me thy boon:
And for my wild one, give Thy love.

O Lord of Light, from Thy great realm
Whence holy icons shine upon us,
Set your crown of Song of Songs
On her, most sinful of Madonnas.

Leonard Wolf

ABRAHAM SCOLDS LOT

Lot—it's disgusting—it's got to be said—
You and your nightly carouse—
Yesterday, in the "Golden Hart"—
What a terrible scandal that was.

Manger, the tailor, can do such things,
But it simply won't do for you.
You've a couple of daughters to raise, knock wood,
And besides, you're a wealthy Jew.

You've cattle and sheep and flocks of goat—
Take my advice—fear God.
Already, a swilling gentile is said
To be "As drunk as Lot."

I know how it is, on a Friday night,
To drink a cup or so
Of wine with fish, while the Sabbath light
Sheds a holy glow.

But how can one go on drinking
Day in, day out—like you.
It's all right for Havrillah, the Sabbath *goy*
But certainly not for a Jew.

Consider what will be said one day—
That the Patriarch Abraham's kin
Was worse than a convert—steeped in wine
And other kinds of sin.

They're saying already— Listen to me!
My God, don't you care what they think?
And you're a father . . . the matchmaker
Avoids your threshold like a stink.

Even the humblest tailor's lad
Considers himself too fine
To marry a daughter of yours—their braids
Turn gray—all for the sake of wine.

Lot—it's disgusting—it's got to be said—
You and your nightly carouse—
Yesterday, in the "Golden Hart" —
What a terrible scandal that was.

Manger, the tailor, can do such things,
But it simply won't do for you.
You've a couple of daughters to raise, you're rich,
Knock wood—and besides, you're a Jew.

Leonard Wolf

ABRAHAM TAKES ISAAC TO THE SACRIFICE

The gray light of the dawning
Touches the earth with dawn.
Eliezer, the loyal servant, puts
The black team's harness on.

Taking the child in his arms,
Old Abraham shuts the door.
Over his ancient roof, there gleams
A blue and pious star.

"Up, Eliezer"—the whip rings out,
The road has a silvery look.
"Sad and lovely," the poet says
"Are the roads of the Holy Book."

The graying willows on the way
Run to the house again
To see if his mother weeps beside
The cradle of her son.

"Daddy, where are we going now?"
"To Lashkev—to the Fair."
"Daddy, what are you going to buy
At Lashkev—at the Fair?"

"A soldier made of porcelain,
A trumpet and a drum;
A piece of satin to make a dress
For mother who waits at home."

Abraham feels his eyes grow moist
And the steel knife pressing, where
It scalds the flesh beneath his shirt . . .
"It's going to be some Fair."

"Eliezer, stop at the water mill.
Stop for a while and wait.
Isaac, my son, and I will go
Alone from there on foot."

Eliezer sits on the driver's seat
And casts an anxious look.
"Sad and lovely," the poet says
"Are the roads of the Holy Book."

Leonard Wolf

HAGAR'S LAST NIGHT
IN ABRAHAM'S HOUSE

Hagar, the servant, sits in the kitchen,
A smoking oil lamp spills
The shapes of shadowy cats and dogs
To flicker on the walls.

She weeps because her master
Fired her today.
"Beat it, you bitch," he told her;
"Can't you let me be?"

It was Sarah who egged him on—
That proper deaconess,
Saying, "Either get rid of the girl
Or give me a divorce."

Hagar takes out of her trunk
A summer hat of straw;
She takes her green silk apron
And her blood-red beads of coral.

These were the gifts he gave her
Once upon a day
When they strolled the meadow
By the railroad right-of-way.

"How like the smoke of a chimney,
How like the smoke of a train
Is the love of a man, dear mother,
The love of any man.

God knows where we shall run to,
Myself and his bastard child,
Unless in some alien kitchen
We are allowed to hide."

She takes the kitchen broom,
She sweeps the kitchen floor.
Under her blouse something still says
She loves him—and sweeps some more.

Again, she does the dishes,
And scours the copper pan.
"How like the smoke from a chimney
Is the love of any man."

Leonard Wolf

KING DAVID

Even in the king's window, the sun dies.
The king is old; he is as white as snow.
Still to his harp, his wandering glances go.
Even in the king's window, the sun dies.

Death, his echo, waits behind his back,
A smiling Lord of Lords. Upon his head
He wears a crown that is suffused with red;
He stands enfolded in a gold-trimmed cloak.

The king leans on his harp and starts to doze.
Death gently murmurs, "Now, I will enclose
The king within his final nightly grief . . .

This king . . . who was believing as a child,
Sinful as gods, and like the wind, as wild,
And fair, as dreams are fair—past all belief."

Leonard Wolf

CAIN AND ABEL

Dost thou sleep, my brother Abel,
That thou art so wonderfully fair?
Never have I seen thee
As beautiful before.

Does the beauty lie in my ax,
Or is it, perhaps, in thee?
Before the day is done,
Speak—answer me.

Thou art still, my brother Abel,
As the heavens and the earth.
Such pensive silence, until now,
In thee I never heard.

Does the stillness lie in my ax,
Or is it, perhaps, in thee?
Before the day is done,
Speak—answer me.

I stand beside thee, here,
And thou art so alone.
Never before hast thou been
So strangely alien.

Does the strangeness lie in my ax,
Or is it, perhaps, in thee?
Before the day is done,
Speak—answer me.

Come, mother Eve, see how
My brother Abel lies still.
He never slept, so bemused,
In his cradle, for all of thy skill.

Does the stillness lie in my ax,
Or is it, perhaps, in thee?
Before the day is done,
Speak—answer me.

Come, father Adam, and look
At the scarlet ribbon of blood
That wriggles along the earth
And smells so sad and good.

Does the grief lie in my ax,
Or is it, perhaps, in thee?
Before the day is done,
Speak—answer me.

Leonard Wolf

REB LEVI YITZKHOK

Reb Levi Yitzkhok in prayer shawl and *tefillin*
Is rooted where he stands
Before the altar, with prayer book open,
But will not utter a sound.

He sees the ghetto like so many pictures
Of agony, trouble and pain.
Silent and stubborn, the old man quarrels
With his old God again.

Leonard Wolf

MEYER STIKER
(1905–)

YIDDISH POETS IN NEW YORK

They came from small and from large towns,
In coats bulky, coarse, and shoes with patches,
Their eyes wide open and their lips in prayer
That their separated fathers might recognize them.

In rooms like hovels on Reed and on Pitt streets,
In meager parks with hardly any grass or trees,
They moved at first with halting, bashful steps,
Clinging to the seam of their dreams, dreams that

Had followed them from home, dazzling them
Like snow or rustling branches in bloom.
Now in dark alleys of granite and of brick
They have sown the kernels of a poem
Thereby to cover up old patches—and again
Their fathers do not recognize them.

Arthur Gregor

A DREAM

A dream climbs up smooth walls,
A picture hanging upside down,
A wind gone wild, insane,
A watery surface is in flames,

A smokestack lies stretched out behind a wall,
A cripple is galloping.
And where are you?
I ask in vain!

Arthur Gregor

PHOENIX

How much can it hold, this paw?
Some copper, gold or silver bits?
It is none of these I want, but this:
That amid the ashes of my estate
The bird with steel-blue eyes
Break into song once more.

Arthur Gregor

ROME

A city of nuns, icons, madonnas,
Priests in black broad-rimmed hats,
In long, faded robes;
City of rowdy boys, of Michelangelo
In that darkening, that ominous hour
Of here and not of here.

Everything that lives is on paintings and on stone.
Touch them and you feel flesh, bone,
Eyes, lips, jaws and hair—
Except that it's old linen and marble you're touching there.

From corners everywhere: smells of antiquity,
From all sides: patricians and celibates,
And—Michelangelo in that darkening, ominous hour
Whose deep and heavy blue now seeps
More and more into my sadness.
Still the fly in Titus' ear buzzes, buzzes.

Arthur Gregor

TO A GUIDE IN JERUSALEM

Don't lead me. I can find my way.
I'm at home here, keep that in mind.
I won't get lost, won't need to seek.
My nose is led by the reeking dark,
My head used to hard resting places,
My eye to these ancient dusks
And to the corkscrew *payes*
On lean Natura Karta faces.

Arthur Gregor

KADIA MOLODOWSKY
(1894–   )

conv w/ god

WOMEN SONGS

I

The faces of women long dead, of our family,
come back in the night, come in dreams to me saying:
We have kept our blood pure through long generations,
we brought it to you like a sacred wine
from the kosher cellars of our hearts.
And one of them whispers:
I remained deserted, when my two rosy apples
still hung on the tree
and I gritted away the long nights of waking between my white
    teeth.

I will go meet the grandmothers, saying:
Your sighs were the whips that lashed me
and drove my young life to the threshold
to escape from your kosher beds.
But wherever the street grows dark you pursue me—
wherever a shadow falls.

Your whimperings race like the autumn wind past me,
and your words are the silken cord
still binding my thoughts,
My life is a page ripped out of a holy book
and part of the first line is missing.

II

There are such spring-like nights here,
when a blade of grass pushes up through the soil
and the fresh dawn is a green pillow
under the skeleton of a dead horse.
And all the limbs of a woman plead for the ache of birth.
And women come down to lie like sick sheep
by the wells—to heal their bodies,
their faces blackened with year-long thirst for a child's cry.

There are such spring-like nights here
when lightning pierces the black soil with silver knives
and pregnant women approach the white tables of the hospital
with quiet steps
and smile at the unborn child
and perhaps at death.

There are such spring-like nights here
when a blade of grass pushes up through the soil.

Adrienne Rich

SONG OF THE SABBATH

I quarreled with kings till the Sabbath,
I fought with the six kings
of the six days of the week.

Sunday they took away my sleep.
Monday they scattered my salt.
And on the third day, my God,
they threw out my bread: whips flashed
across my face. The fourth day
they caught my dove, my flying dove,
and slaughtered it.
It was like that till Friday morning.

This is my whole week,
the dove's flight dying.

At nightfall Friday
I lit four candles,
and the queen of the Sabbath came to me.
Her face lit up the whole world,
and made it all a Sabbath.
My scattered salt
shone in its little bowl,
and my dove, my flying dove,
clapped its wings together,
and licked its throat.
The Sabbath queen blessed my candles,
and they burned with a pure, clean flame.
The light put out the days of the week
and my quarreling with the six kings.

The greenness of the mountains
is the greenness of the Sabbath.
The silver of the lake
is the silver of the Sabbath.
The singing of the wind
is the singing of the Sabbath.

And my heart's song
is an eternal Sabbath.

Jean Valentine

AND WHAT WILL HAPPEN

And what will happen
when the fliers come back
and say there is no heaven?

Where will I look then,
if not to the sky?

How will I bear the gray rain,
the dust of these stone streets?
How will I keep from turning my heart away?
And who will help with my poems,
if there's no one at all in the sky?

But I won't believe the fliers.
I won't believe them.

For I have seen an angel,
more than once,
and more than once he has saved me
from plagues that threatened.

I will not trust the fliers.
I will not trust them.

And what will happen if the fliers come back
and say there is no paradise,
home of the saints?

How will I walk across papery bridges
if we have no more saints?
How will I fly across chasms and ditches
if I can't hang on to their tails?
Who will keep my hungry soul?
Soothe my crying?

But I will not listen to the fliers.
I won't listen.

For I have seen the saints,
more than once.
They went in yoke and torment,
and carried the world on their backs.

So I will not look at the fliers.
Not notice them.

Heaven can be reached
by those who weave with its blue,
walk on miracles as on stairs,
and know the ways of the secret.

Jean Valentine

WHITE NIGHT

White night, my painful joy,
your light is brighter than the dawn.
A white ship is sailing from East Broadway
where I see no sail by day.

A quiet star hands me a ticket
open for all the seas.
I put on my time-worn jacket
and entrust myself to the night.

Where are you taking me, ship?
Who charted us on this course?
The hieroglyphs of the map escape me,
and the arrows of your compass.

I am the one who sees and does not see.
I go along on your deck of secrets,
squeeze shut my baggage on the wreath of sorrows
from all my plucked-out homes.

—Pack in all my blackened pots,
their split lids, the chipped crockeries,
pack in my chaos with its gold-encrusted buttons
since chaos will always be in fashion.

—Pack the letters stamped *Unknown at This Address*—
vanished addresses that sear my eyes,
postmarked with more than years and days;
sucked into my bones and marrow.

—Pack up my shadow that weighs more than my body,
that comes along with its endless exhortations.
Weekdays or holidays, time of flowers or withering,
my shadow is with me, muttering its troubles.

Find me a place of honey cakes and sweetness
where angels and children picnic together
(this is the dream I love best of all),
Where the sacred wine fizzes in bottles.

Let me have one sip, here on East Broadway,
for the sake of those old Jews crying in the dark.
I cry my heretic's tears with them,
their sobbing is my sobbing.

I'm a difficult passenger, my ship
is packed with the heavy horns, the *shofars* of grief.
Tighten the sails of night as far as you can,
for the daylight cannot carry me.

Take me somewhere to a place of rest,
of goats in belled hats playing on trombones—
to the Almighty's fresh white sheets
where the hunter's shadow cannot fall.

Take me . . . Yes, take me . . . But you know best
where the sea calmly opens its blue road.
I'm wearier than your oldest tower;
somewhere I've left my heart aside.

Adrienne Rich

GOD OF MERCY

O God of Mercy
For the time being
Choose another people.
We are tired of death, tired of corpses,

We have no more prayers.
For the time being
Choose another people.
We have run out of blood
For victims,
Our houses have been turned into desert,
The earth lacks space for tombstones,
There are no more lamentations
Nor songs of woe
In the ancient texts.

God of Mercy
Sanctify another land
Another Sinai.
We have covered every field and stone
With ashes and holiness.
With our crones
With our young
With our infants
We have paid for each letter in your Commandments.

God of Mercy
Lift up your fiery brow,
Look on the peoples of the world,
Let them have the prophecies and Holy Days
Who mumble your words in every tongue.
Teach them the Deeds
And the ways of temptation.

God of Mercy
To us give rough clothing
Of shepherds who tend sheep
Of blacksmiths at the hammer
Of washerwomen, cattle slaughterers
And lower still.
And O God of Mercy
Grant us one more blessing—
Take back the gift of our separateness.

Irving Howe

BERISH WEINSTEIN
(1905–1967)

HUNGER

Leaves under my footsteps break into yellow leaf meal and
    scatter into November.
Frost nibbles the nails of my mute fingers
And my hands hunger for a little shoe, for a wool shirt for
    a child.
Those warm doors with the smell of broiling meat are driving
    me crazy.
The hot steam of cooking insults my nostrils.
I can smell bread baking through frost-thick windows.

Now wild wet snowdrifts beat against my eyes,
Wind smashes my hair and the young snow turns it lighter.
Hands gelid with cold, clothes leaking with rain,
I'd rather be blind and tamp out with my feet
Some magical message on every threshold.
Someone might hand me something out of a door or a window.

I will find hoodlums willing to teach me how to break windows,
Teach me the craft of the dripping blade of the knife.
My eyes move fast like the heart of a robber
While over me clowns the half-torn tin of a gutter.
A drunken whore is shouting a curse at a car
Because her period has begun to flow.

I know the gnawing cities, the benches, the bums,
Vienna, Krakow, New York,

I regret my own house, though the child already crawls
Like a dumpling over the floor to play with a leaf
That has just now fallen from a friend's plant.
The latch is covered with dust, for no one opens our door.

Karl Shapiro and Selwyn Schwartz

SECOND SON

Late December night, leaves skipping down the walk,
Our steps are drawn by the moon on the nervous road
To the gate of the hospital.
The woman trembles on my arm,
The child in her belly pushes at the womb;
Her cries leap up to the dark belated windows

As she lurches downward with her heavy pain.
I curse myself for the hot nights,
For the searing marrow of my bones.
My incandescent tongue that smothered her eyes.

Now that you're born, your little eyes opening, son,
Seeking your mother's nipples on the pillow
Perhaps by instinct you will recognize my hands
And curse your father.
I'm not one to sing the lullaby of "The Golden Goat."
Your little hand will grasp such wicked, foolish hands as mine,
Leading me past the masculine city of birth.

You will point out beggars stumbling through frost with coal,
You will grow up, hair will appear on your breast,
And like every male you will gape at women,
Your lips will demand that hers will quench your lips
Until that hour when you lead her pregnant
In drowsy garments down the nervous road
To the dark belated windows.

Karl Shapiro and Selwyn Schwartz

SAILORS

The hearts of sailors yearn for railroads, cities and mobs.
Their eyes hold the wilds of the sea, the distance of landfalls.
Endlessly yearning, they hang harbors over their beds,
Pin-ups of girls wiser than mothers.
It's simple for sailors to daydream and stiffen
Over the image of flowing garters and vibrating knees
And girdles that grip a girl's body, breasty and ripe.

Somewhere on the sea on a holiday night
Their faces shine like silver in the moon.
In white blouses, seated on the deck,
With feet tucked under like Chinamen,
With flaming lips, embracing each other like women,
They pour out songs about mothers
Who wander about with heavy-laden baskets
In alien harbors, eyes raised to the sky
Seeking a son or a daughter in the slow smoke of the ships.

Meager and weak are the mothers of sailors,
Who fondle the earth with their tender steps.
Nevertheless they spawn strong sons and strapping daughters;
Their husbands are tall, broad-shouldered, with hairy hands,
Fleshy red noses, angry eyebrows and rough wild beards.

Sailors have hearts that yearn for railroads, cities and mobs.
In cities they promenade in round white collars,
Blue uniforms, and wide long trousers on narrow legs.
With the wildness of oceans they rush toward young girls
Who bashful-eyed sink deep into their laps
With legs crossed and with shaking knees.

Hands that moor boats lie heaving on their hips,
On heated shoulders of warm transparent silk.
Wild kisses gnaw their nipples and their hands
And cool themselves in nakedness of knees—
In the silken rustle of summer leaves
This cools the blood of the daughters of port cities.

                    Karl Shapiro and Selwyn Schwartz

ALEPH KATZ
(1898–1969)

BOXER

Storm wind,
Waiting blind in his arms,
Charges the ferocious lightning through his fists
That chase the sparks
Of his eyes.

Jungle nights, bleeding fountains of fire,
Burgeon up from the ring,
And light up an auto-da-fé to heaven
In a forest of eyes.

The woods are burning,
A cry bears itself forth—
An eternity,
And silences the last sob
Of the defeated, and sings forever the song
Of accidental strength,
The winner of nothing.

James Wright

BOWERY MOTIFS—I

Dust and dirt,
Bread begged for,
A dead life.

A cursed blessing,
Broken world,
Stink of money.

Man a mistake,
A ghost of lice,
Fear of mice.

An outraged city
Deafens a secret,
And laughs at God.

James Wright

BOWERY MOTIFS—II

The mountain is high,
And the avid merchant stingy:
The market is full of buyers,
And the diver brings back few pearls.

The shadow strangles,
The glance gulps down
and dies.
The way is forbidden,
Blocked.

Wishes are trampled;
The heart, a dead body.
Alone, one surrenders and waits, trembling,
For a miracle.

James Wright

BOWERY MOTIFS—III

Heart thrown into the garbage,
Its terrible burden too heavy,
The fields of the spirit lie desolate,
The mast of fortune broken.

Better to live this way,
A lone thorn in the field,
Than the golden way of the world
That charges a quick death
For its straw, its bread.

James Wright

ROSA GUTMAN-JASNY
(1903–)

I F

If another flood should come,
Let us, sisters all, from every land,
Say to God in his looming tower:

Whom are you hitting? Would you smite grasses
For their grassy sins? For the crooked paths
And dark tangles to which you destined them?
For their scanty roots which push toward earth,
Remote from your face?

If another flood should come,
We will take a dark view of it.
Let us, sisters all, from every land,
Say to God:
Turn back your punishing hand!

As a ravaged field cannot nourish seed,
So our deprived bodies will be sealed.
You'll conduct the Sabbath for desert winds
And smite the sea with thunder for its sins.

Etta Blum

THE FARAWAY MOON

The faraway moon, has she already heard
That any minute now
She's to become a world by herself?
No longer a lotus flower, tender and bemused—
Just an ordinary drab world.

Today she shows us half her face,
drawn and pale.
That blonde capricious moon—
What might she not do from rage?

Turn swiftly to her lords on high,
And scatter all dreams since time began,
Like dust into outer space?

Oh no, moon, don't.

Etta Blum

FOR YOU I AM

For you I am the one and only
As that street has remained the one and only
In that city, in that land, where long ago
I was your first love.

For you there are no wrinkles on my face,
It's only a veil covering my young countenance
As a cloud caresses the moon
While behind it, as in Genesis, her light radiates.

Not sister nor wife. I am for you the one and only
As the tremor of half-childish touch
Long since, on that street, at that door.

For tell me, is there anyone,
Ever, who's had two first loves?

Etta Blum

EPHRAIM AUERBACH
(1892–)

NEWS

The world vibrates in my fingers.
I am a net of wires,
a pulse of a thousand pulses,
a seismograph of the world's turmoil.
The sun that rises in the east rises in me,
the sun that sets in the west sets in me,
a hurricane destroys my fields of bread,
on Broome Street I dissolve in flames,
the black Hudson drags me to its bottom.
I ignite the world in fires of rebellion,
with bare and wounded breast, with naked eyes,
I assault the satisfied.
The world vibrates in my fingers.

I am become a dark insanity.
Dusty papers, smoky faces,
machines—pulsating hearts,
choked thoughts on hunched backs,
imps in tired eyes,
and fingers leaping as on wires.

The metal devourer over me
swallows the letters in his burning belly
and spits them out in lines;
the Moloch of emotions is not sated—
me, too, he would devour,
and spit out in metal rows.

The world in my fingers—
I in the boiling belly
of the linotype machine.

The world stops suddenly—
and my fingers rest
on the scattered, frozen keys.
Down toward the table sinks
my metal-heavy head.
The net of wires turns into bristling wings
enfolding me with blinding calm,
with cold, sharp pins.
The Moloch over me
tears at his belly,
his anger erupts in smoke,
hunger cramps his entrails,
out of his eyes
creep red worms.

And on the splayed, frozen keys
of the machine—
my fingers.

Robert Friend

TO THE ELECTRIC CHAIR

Today they take them to the electric chair.
After midnight.
Through corridors where shadows
of the truncated years
collapse.

There is only one direction now. The final one.
And the last look back is a look transcending time.

Today, two brothers go to the electric chair.
The Bowery swallows up its last bum,

who drags his destiny
toward the stony night.
Through the window peers the city
with blind and hollow eyes;
the teletype clicks nervously.
The minutes are numbered.

My drunken fingers dance
on the typewriter keys.
I write: the current has poured death
into their veins.
My every limb trembles,
achieving the sickly ecstasy
of holding in my hands pulsating life
and annihilating it.
I have created death.
The letters fire the paper.
The electric current streams
from my fingers.
My heart is empty.

I drag myself through the Bowery
in the shadow
of the last bum's faltering footsteps.

                                            Robert Friend

RACHEL H. KORN
(1898–)

THE HOUSEMAID

The orchards of her home
still blossom in her glances
and in her dreams great flocks
of geese are feathered;
she used to drive baby geese
to the pond every spring
and guard them from the
crows and owls but now
for days she walks around
bewildered and her whole
body greedily drinks in
the fragrance from the new-cut
wood piled up by the stove
ready for burning.

Her faraway home was so
beautiful but it was a small
farm poor and rocky and
there were seven mouths
to feed so she the oldest
came to the city and here
her two hands are now the oars
which row her life through
dark and steamy kitchens.

When she gets a letter
from the neighbor's son
she runs to strangers
hanging on their glances,
first she reads their faces
for goodwill then begs them
quietly to read her letter,
to tell her all they
must tell all   all that
he has written! Then she
sees their scornful smiles
at his loutish crudely formed
letters which for her contain
the alphabet of love,
and she blushes, hides her face
for shame.

All week long her heart
composes answers until
at last it's Sunday and
the words are put down
beside each other like
invalids on pink paper
decorated with doves
and wreaths of roses.
Her girl friend scribbles
the words in a hurry then
reads out whatever was
dictated ending with
kisses and respectfully
yours; she smiles fleetingly
and in the corners of her mouth
lurk the shy love words
she has nursed all week
and there they hover
captive and unspoken.

Sometimes in an hour of rest
she opens her old prayer book

with a gold cross embossed
on its black cover; with awkward
hands she caresses the strange
letters, words full of God
and love and mercy and her eyes
grow dreamy thinking about
the miraculous world of A B C.

The world she knows
is tied in a thousand knots,
even the world of her prayer book
with its circles and lassos
is like some Judas: treacherous:
ready to sell her in a minute
for thirty hard days
of labor in every month.

Miriam Waddington

GENERATIONS

FOR MY DAUGHTER

Loving another, yet she married my father.
That other portrait faded with the years.
From her album paged in musty velvet
Shimmered forth his paling, yellowing smile.

To watch her embroider a towel or tablecloth:
She pricked the vivid silk with her nostalgia.
The stitches flowed like narrow streams of blood.
The seams were silvered with her silent tears.

And my grandmother—how little I know of her life!—
Only her hands' tremor, and the blue seam of her lips.
How can I imagine my grandfather's love of her?
I can will myself to believe in her suffering.

No letter remains, no, not a scrap of paper
Did she will us; only old pots in the attic
Crudely patched: tangible maimed witnesses
To a dead life: the young widow, the mother of five.

So she planted a luxuriant garden
That would embrace the newly barren house
And her new barrenness. So the trees grew,
Obedient to her will, in perfect rows.

Now my daughter is just sixteen
As I was on that quiet day in May
When I became pregnant of a single word
Scented with lilac, the remote song of a bird.

A few letters, and what is called "a slender volume":
These are the relicts of my life. I lacked perspective
On happiness, so I ran ever faster
To escape the happy boundaries of my fate.

Listen, my daughter, never go in pursuit!
It all lies *there*, in the woven strands of blood.
How the straight trees whisper in grandmother's garden!
Only listen! These dim echoes in my poem . . .

But what can sixteen years conceive of sorrow?
And pensiveness? the tremor of old lives?
For her, only the eternal beginnings.

Where she goes, old shadows kiss her footprints.
Somewhere, in white lilac, the nightingale
Gasps out his fragile song

Which ends always with the note of eternal beginning.
Carolyn Kizer

KEEP HIDDEN FROM ME

Keep from me all that I might comprehend!
O God, I ripen toward you in my unknowing.

The barely burgeoning leaf on the roadside tree
Limns innocence: here endeth the first lesson.

Keep from me, God, all forms of certainty:
The steady tread that paces off the self

And forms it, seamless, ignorant of doubt
Or failure, hell-bent for fulfillment.

To know myself: Is not that the supreme disaster?
To know Thee, one must sink on trembling knees.

To hear Thee, only the terrified heart may truly listen;
To see Thee, only the gaze half-blind with dread.

Though the day darken, preserve my memory
From Your bright oblivion. Erase not my faulty traces.

If I aspire again to make four poor walls my house,
Let me pillow myself on the book of my peregrinations.

God, grant me strength to give over false happiness,
And the sense that suffering has earned us Your regard.

Elohim! Though sorrow fill me to the brim,
Let me carefully bear the cup of myself to Thee.

Carolyn Kizer

I FLED FROM DESOLATION

I fled from desolation
And now I perish
Each day anew
Under skies drawn with smoke.

Lord, let me not fall so low
As to have to count consumptive hours
And be unable to look the sun in the eyes.

Buttress my dreams
With a pillow of stone—
Engraved with sayings,
Incantations against woe.

And send down an angel, stern visaged,
So that I need not struggle with myself alone,
While a starless night becomes desert about me
And into the distance there sinks a human moan.

Etta Blum

ELIEZER GREENBERG

(1896–)

DIALOGUE AT NIGHT

—All right, the days don't belong to me.
But the nights do. The nights.
Why do I lie awake through nights drenched in sorrow
And toss from side to side
Until far into early tomorrow?

Why do I lie awake
And litigate
With all the unending complainants of day?
As a rule the talk gets under way
With Desire and Duty arguing.
The pair of them
Haul me off to court:
Each puts in the scales his claim upon me,
And Duty weighs more than Desire, inevitably.

The case has been continuing for years.
The nights have it all memorized by now,
This dialogue of accusations,
Charges, defenses, confrontations.
One side cries: "Abel!" and the other, "Cain!"
The courtroom cracks apart in pain.

When either party seems to be losing,
Each summons conscience to his side.
By now it's all for the best that the dawn breaks through

And the dialogue of night
Gets chopped in two.

John Hollander

LUCK TIPS THE BALANCE

Sadness is heavy at my heart;
Like a hulk after storms at sea,
After the pounding and all the losses,
I lie here, wracked with agony.

I lie awake late, late at night,
Hearing stars move, winds in the sky,
I hear, in heaven's wide blue womb,
Dripping through flames, a silent cry.

Sleep shuns my blurred and wearied eyes;
My hearing stays acute and clear.
I have weighed Luck against Misfortune—
Luck tips the balance with a tear.

John Hollander

FAME

Then finally the long-desired hand of fame
Reached him as well. A foaming cup, aflame
With sunlight touched his lips, and silently bade him:
"Taste!" whispering, "I remember when it came,

Your first word. And since then I have followed your long
And arduous way. I remember the stammer, the pain
Of your first line, then the late and ripened song;
Now for the harvest, the long-awaited gain."

As, after long nights, a beam of the morning spring
Through the thick darkness and the sun appears,

So did his bones commence in joy to sing;
Dispersed and vanished, all his doubts and fears.

But when a second time he was passed the same
Cup, he averted his lips, wry, silently.
He longed for the time that innocent first word came,
For the shivering delight of doubts, sweeter than fame.

John Hollander

MEETING

Her face: familiar and unfamiliar.
We once chanced to meet—where was the place?
I stood, and brooded for a space:
Yes, once we were together there;
Somehow, at the time, I couldn't
Manage to remember where.

Like having slept through a nightmare
When years spin backward into dream,
It was ... yes ... yes ... once ... and I saw
An image, mirrored in memory,
Of a long since extinguished gleam.

For a moment I stood speechless,
Then quietly asked if she were well,
And almost about something else.
But her face clouded over quickly
With the pain of old injuries opening up.
Regret and sorrow together fell
In a flash of light across her eyes.

I wanted to touch her
Once I had unchained my tongue.
But she turned her eyes away,
Without a word she left me there.

Alone, with my extended hand
Still warm, still reaching out in air.

John Hollander

MY HOME

What is left of you,
My Lipkan, home of mine?
Ruin inscribed in your few
Fractured walls of lime.

No fluttering of a wing,
No shuffle of human feet;
Dust, brickwork crumbling,
And emptiness of street.

Raving fall winds speaking
In a lamenting roar;
The loud, rusted creaking
Of a half burned-out door.

A chimney here and there;
Gravestones' unending tale.
Only deaf vacancies stare
Down this grievous vale.

John Hollander

VISITING SECOND AVENUE

I seldom come to see you, these days,
And except for a used-up old building
They have managed to leave alone—
Like some old souvenir—
I'd never recognize this neighborhood;
You have changed so much, Second Avenue!

But even these trinkets abandoned by the past
Remind me of the treasure here that was ours!

O closest of all these neighboring streets!
I said good-by to you long ago
And try to keep out of your way
—It's painful, now, to come across you,
For when I tread your ground
It's as though I were walking
On my nearest ones' graves.

But must we talk of loss,
Plunging hearts into mourning?
Whoever forgets these things
Has never remembered,
Nor ever shared our joy,
Nor sips of our sorrow now!

But if the woes of sacrifice are vast
They command neither memory nor imagination:
A true treasure can never be wasted!
There is a Great, One-Shot Festival
That burns all the weekdays in eternal flames.

More than just that one time
Its awakening breath
Can make dry bones live,
Raising them from the valley of death,
Giving them life, winged with faith, and hope.

John Hollander

FOUR-FOOTED POEMS

Giraffe, Nightingale, Owl and Rooster

Of all the animals the giraffe has the longest neck. The nightingale
Has song. The owl, who's blind except at night, sounds woebegone
At sunrise. Half-asleep, the rooster crows to hail
The coming of his murderer, the dawn.

Dog and Tiger

The dog is cousin to the wolf, but more acceptable.
He pays for it with a life of shame. For every gob of bread
He must kiss his master's hand. The tiger will not be tamed—
He would rather be stinking dead.

Bear, Cat and Dove

The bear is a slob. Sleep is his paradise
Till a wild hunger drags him to his prey.
The cat is a fathead, awarded claws, and the price
Is what the dove must pay.

Parrot, Fish, Tiger and Mule

The parrot runs at the mouth and has nothing to say.
The fish is mute and gets around, from bay to bay.
The paranoiac tiger is always ready for the kill.
The mule is a hard worker—and an imbecile.

Lion and Rabbit

The caged lion does not call for pity.
His royal mien belies the state he's in.
Pity rather the rabbit who even when free
Keeps trembling in his skin.

Adam—A Man

Helpless and strong, frightened and bold, he vows
To conquer earth and sky. Tied in a knot, he climbs toward
    higher views,
Leaving a mess behind. He prates of justice and lives by the
    sword.
And he was born to lose.

Stanley Kunitz

GOLDEN BIRDS

O golden birds of my drunken summer
Where have you gone?
The stars and the sun
Long to hear once more
Your song which, yet
Unfinished, came to a stop.

O golden birds,
Reappear: come back
With your little beaks full
Of comforting words:
Of how grief is a track
Leading joy back
To where it came to birth.
O golden birds.

John Hollander

ISRAEL EMIOT
(1909–)

AS LONG AS WE ARE NOT ALONE

THE AMERICAN GEORGE SMITH DISCOVERED IN 1961 THAT
WITH THE SOUNDS OF MUSIC FLOWERS GROW MORE
QUICKLY.

As long as we are not alone,
As long as we have somebody near,
Perhaps even a stone can hear.
We shall rejoice, we shall rejoice.
Amid the silence of the universe
From the soul straight up to God
A random bird unwinds its song.
But a bird does not compare
To the silence of God.
The city makes its noise,
And does the cosmos care?
But look: the flowers nod
And whisper to the air.
Why should not stones respond?
We shall rejoice, we shall rejoice.

Stanley Kunitz

FROM "SIBERIA"

My God, I believe in you so much,
Believe in me too a little.
How often you try me!
Toughen my spirit.

The curse that I must wear
Was never fitted to my stature;
Whether I rise or fall,
Let it be true to my measure.

I did not ask to be great,
Nor to be meanest in creation.
Yet you permit but one ray
To pierce the window of my prison.

You who made holy my mind,
Keep me from joining your betrayers.
After all, you cared when you assigned
Colors to the flowers.

And when you punished the night
With darkness, you did not overpour;
And when you cursed the sea with tempests
You also chained it to the shore.

Stanley Kunitz

WE GROW OLD

We are slowly becoming ancients, bit by bit.
We tap out with our fingers an agreeable air
Which we have heard a thousand times before.
We keep talking about the weather:
"Today the sun will shine."
We come back to Heine,

To Goethe.
And we say:
"Perhaps it was always meant to be this way."
Complaining a little about eyesight,
Looking for a soothing rinse,
And trying for a semblance
That will remain of us,
To leave a grandson
Who will be the remembering one.

Lenore Marshall

AARON ZEITLIN
(1898–)

BEING A JEW

Being a Jew means running forever to God
Even if you are His betrayer,
Means expecting to hear any day,
Even if you are a nay sayer,
The blare of Messiah's horn;

Means, even if you wish to,
You cannot escape His snares,
You cannot cease to pray—
Even after all the prayers,
Even after all the "evens."

Robert Friend

TEXT

All of us—
stones, people, broken glass in the sun,
tin cans, cats, trees—
are illustrations to a text.

Somewhere, we are superfluous.
There the text alone is read;
the pictures fall away like dead limbs.

When the wind of death breathes in the deep grass
and sweeps the west clean of all
the pictures raised by clouds—
Night comes and reads the stars.

Chana Faerstein

ODE ON THE LAST INTERNATIONAL

When some day all have work and abundance both
A Lenin of all the blind and the lamed
Will take up the cause of the man who is maimed
And become the great Singer of Justice and Truth.

Capital will have been slaughtered by then
But he'll lead the mobs against laboring
As now they are led against Capital.

And thus, the Last International—
International of Man, the Maimed,
Of all the blind and all the lamed,
Of poets who want not to sweat, but to sing,
As they count Sephira, ring by ring
Above unknown waters.

Hark! the Last International's song,
International of the multitudes
Who never yearn, and will never learn,
To be chained to laboring:
A premature anthem—but one could be wrong.

A Man will come at the end of days
The Foe of Toil and Care,
Firing up all those who wear
The gold, yet deserve smelting down themselves,
The Nonworkers of the World.
And thus the Last Leader will proclaim:

Work is the Daughter of Capital,
Work is no End; work is a Way,
Only, toward the ultimate Play,
The free, sublime Play for God.

And crowds will wander among the cities,
And among the cities the crowds will cry,
Give us happiness
Give us happiness
Give us happiness
Turn backward, turn backward, turn backward, yes,
All joys—hands, feet, eyes,
Paradise!
And the cry will rip through seas and skies
And God Himself must then descend
And assume some shape; in a splendid guise
Of starry and soul-studded robes
He reveals himself
To the Revolutionists.
And the cosmic Boaz will open his store
And of his riches
Give each that which is
His: To the blind, a flaming eye;
To the halting speaker, the sharpest tongue;
To the twisted, the straightness of the oak;
To the poet, the Song as yet unsung;
To every sterile woman, her Child;
To every Golem, his human Creator.

This is the song of the ultimate,
Highest and truly just,
International.

                                        John Hollander

I BELIEVE

I

Should I believe in Spinoza's geometric god?
A god that cannot change its own creation,
that snared by its own law must suffer its own rod,
a pitiful slave to its own situation;
a god without horror or miracle,
a god coldly heretical,
a distant relative
who won't acknowledge me as his relation;
who is incapable
of making it his concern
whether I die or live,
or burn
in every fire until
the final generation;
a god, a bookkeeper, to whom my cry
will not reach when I die;
a god with ciphers for his seraphim.
Rather than in him,
I'd willingly believe in Satan and damnation.

II

Or should I believe in the redeemer who never redeems,
the dreamed-up god who dangles on all the crosses,
whose religion forgives before commission
the sins of bloodshed and of fornication?
Should I
believe in the god of cloister bells
whom the dark dreams
of sadists bleed and kill
with the deliberate will
to torture my truth with his lie?

III

Not in the legend of a god become a man,
blood-legend of the crucified,
not in this resides men's guilt and not in this the mystery
of the nether world.
I know a truth six million times
more terrible, six million times
more inscrutable: the reality
of a devil who became a man,
who lived with us here upon earth,
lived and was seen, lived and was heard,
and—incinerating, gassing—crucified
a people.
The literary mystery of Christ,
what is that mystery
compared with the mystery
of this that actually took place?

IV

The would-be gods!
They—and those other shadows, ism and ism!
More hollow than ever their claims
After the all-destroying flames.
In whom can I believe if not in Him,
my living God of cataclysm,
God of naked revenge and secret consolation?
One is—what one is.
I am Jew as He is God.
Can I then choose not to believe
in that living God whose purposes
when He destroys, seeming to forsake me,
I cannot conceive;
choose not to believe in Him
Who having turned my body to fine ash
begins once more to wake me?
If I become a storm, or if I blaze

in rebellion against Him,
is He not still the One who bleeding in my wounds,
my cries still praise?
For even my pain confirms Him.
Who would rebel against pale Jesuses?
And who would rage
against a Spinozan god,
a nonbeing being?

V

And once again I ask:
Can I then choose, even now,
not to believe in Him,
God of the Psalms and of the books of prayer?
For only to Him, only to Him
can I cry out the cry
of every vein and limb.
Because He lives and wills,
because He does not sleep in rigid law,
I cannot understand His deeds.
(But even my lack of understanding proves
that He exists.)
At His feet my ashes lie.

VI

I believe God gives
His inconceivable hells
because somewhere else
His eye surmises
inconceivable paradises
for his slaughtered fugitives.

VII

I believe:
He suffers with me;
if I cry out against Him,

with me He cries;
He wishes for me
the pain that purifies;
He who commands the destroyer
to set my house on fire
wishes to reward and crown me
with His most dazzling crown.
He will raise me above the great ones in His heaven
because I believe in Him, yes, even
after the millions—fed to the flames,
sacrifices without angels and without lambs.

VIII

The God of the Psalms, the Inconceivable
turns day to night,
permits my slaughter;
and then commands me to rise up again;
with or without my consent
conducts each experiment
through me,
who burn eternally.
He lets no one go under,
as He lets me go under,
lets no one be
so utterly
a paradigm in fire.
There is no one He will equally desire
to find, to lose.
And I for my part find and lose Him, too,
lose Him and find Him,
an interchange of beatitude and law,
lamentations and the Song of Songs.

IX

Who so volcanic as my God?
If He is Sinai to me,
He is Maidenek as well.

No matter how much I rebel,
no matter how much I grow
weary, I must be Jew.
We cannot let go
of each other,
not He of me, nor I of Him.
You say "Israel" when you say "Elohim."
If I have fallen into His hands,
the dream of the End of Days
sings me consolation.
It is nearer than farther now,
and you already on the way
to the day
of His last experiment.

X

I believe in the consolation,
believe that the experiments on me,
experiments in fire
will yield Him His desire,
a second genesis.

XI

I believe in this,
this is my trust,
that the God of the Jewish nation
because of me—the remnant of the nation—
will smite, when the End of Days begins,
the nonexisting law
and re-create creation.
He will seat me at His right hand,
my Redeemer,
and trample the false gods
into the dust.

Robert Friend

JACOB GLATSTEIN
(1896–)

COME NOW, LET'S

Come, let's secure ourselves
with a bit of fence.
Not a ghetto, God forbid,
just a quiet wall.
Let's sit here, by ourselves,
and with common sense
let's find a way to mend
our wasted hands.

This wretched interim of ours,
like a *succah* clapped together,
falls to bits.
Everything is hunchbacked, worn with weather,
full of years.
We don't want to fall asleep—but they
are rocking us with drastic lullabies.
Come, let's find a way out.

Chana Faerstein

TWO MOUNDS

The mother of all that lives has died.
But she does not complain.
For all that lives she takes with her.
This is the secret of the end.
To join one's mother is not punishment.

The whole pitiful squabble
Shot up into a tiny, smiling flame
And with thanks stretched out to me its
Five-fingered hand:
You have performed a good deed;
More than visiting the sick:
Visiting death while he blossoms
Like a sapling. It is well that the leave-taking
At least has a tongue, and speaks.
Tomorrow or the day after I shall lie
Near my mother.

To be gathered in,
That means to accept with love,
Unlamenting,
Even with praise,
This grassy eternity,
This crumbling into dust
Of my firm, massive, characteristic self—
God save the mark!

He held me in a bony handshake:
This means homecoming,
In peace, in goodwill, not at odds.
To lie near one's mother means
To be cradled to sleep.
I no longer have the strength for heavy thinking,
Not even the desire for the last tottering step
Toward God.

My thoughts kindle like fireflies,
A flicker and a falling into blackness.
There waits for me, foreordained,
Warm sanctity,
Holy earth.
How can a man be so vile
As to begrudge his life
When his own mother has died?
There is your purpose in death,
To die for your mother's death.

Two little mounds, a shining of grace.
You understand it well,
God of Compassion.
Last pains torment
The rebellious flesh.
To all, greeting,
L'hitraot,
You and you and you.

Ingathered to merited rest.

Maurice Samuel

AT FIFTY

Indeed overnight
I grew a little Confucius beard
and began to babble
about the meaning of life.
What has happened
to my clever little sword
with which I used
to learn how to fence?
Can it be that only yesterday
I gave it away?
Let him keep it, he
on whom I bestowed it!
It is years already
since I've longed for my childhood.
I think that it would be
both audacious and rude
to be young
in such haggish times.

I am precisely as old as one should be
this very moment.
On the one hand,

just enough days consumed;
on the other, still a few
of what I'm worth
for a restless stroll
on this searing earth.

Do I believe in the future, in humanity?
I imagine *yes*—
but I've been believing that for a good many years.
And I am tired,
as I am a Jew,
of wading through blood.
I no longer have the hardihood
to immerse myself in faith.
New believers are maturing,
and new thieves;
and even of the living remnant,
seeded and scattered,
new Jews are emerging
for a fresh cycle—
beginning, middle, almost-end.
Here it is! *almost-end.*
Punishment without reward,
darkness and salvation—accounted?
How many have remained,
farther driven, farther fled?
I am tired
Of the constant hunt and hurry
As, or because,
I am a Jew.

See with what dexterity I knew
when to be born!
I could have sworn
I am now exactly as old
as a young man of my years
ought to be.
Exactly as old

as is that distant spot
of my childhood's ravaged home
from which, upon a time,
without longing
but with childish temerity I rode away.
How foolishly!
I've caught a reminiscent glance thereon
in my later years
and ought youthfully to give
one saddened look at least
upon a piece of burned-
out future life.

Etta Blum

WAGONS

With quiet signs of faraway
At dusk the mournful wagons come.
Doors stand ajar,
But no one waits to meet them.
The town is peaceful, bells of silence toll.
Every blade of grass pricks up
In the heady cool.
A few sickly Jews climb down from the wagons,
And a clever word falters
In every brooding head.
God, on your scale of good and bad,
Set a dish of warm porridge,
Toss some oats, at least, for the skinny mules.
The deadness of the town grows dark.
A cruel silence afflicts the Jewish beards,
And each sees in the other's eyes
A prayer of fear:
When death comes,
Let me not remain the only one,
Do not pass over me with my thin bones.

Chana Faerstein

SMOKE

From the crematory flue
A Jew aspires to the Holy One.
And when the smoke of him is gone,
His wife and children filter through.

Above us, in the height of sky,
Saintly billows weep and wait.
God, wherever you may be,
There all of us are also not.

Chana Faerstein

WITHOUT JEWS

Without Jews there is no Jewish God.
If we leave this world
The light will go out in your tent.
Since Abraham knew you in a cloud,
You have burned in every Jewish face,
You have glowed in every Jewish eye,
And we made you in our image.
In each city, each land,
The Jewish God
Was also a stranger.
A broken Jewish head
Is a fragment of divinity.
We, your radiant vessel,
A palpable sign of your miracle.

Now the lifeless skulls
Add up into millions.
The stars are going out around you.
The memory of you is dimming,
Your kingdom will soon be over.
Jewish seed and flower

Are embers.
The dew cries in the dead grass!

The Jewish dream and reality are ravished,
They die together.
Your witnesses are sleeping:
Infants, women,
Young men, old.
Even the Thirty-six,
Your saints, Pillars of your World,
Have fallen into a dead, an everlasting sleep.

Who will dream you?
Who will remember you?
Who deny you?
Who yearn for you?
Who, on a lonely bridge,
Will leave you—in order to return?

The night is endless when a race is dead.
Earth and heaven are wiped bare.
The light is fading in your shabby tent.
The Jewish hour is guttering.
Jewish God!
You are almost gone.

Nathan Halper

GHETTO SONG

On your little bones my song
Drifts like early snow;
In your eyes remembered joy
Shines as long ago.
Laugh again, my child,
Sing, my grief, my all;
Seven suns will rise
On an old, old wall.

The shamed Sabbath weeps
From the treetops high;
On the blackened streets
The dead beggars lie.
Hush and hush, my child.
Sleep; a golden fish
Will be dancing brightly
In your empty dish.

Stars light up the way
Where your father fares
In the hunted night
With the moon for wares.
Go to sleep, my child,
Close and close your eyes;
Over the dark ruins
A white dove flies.

You are that white dove,
Your small hands are wings;
Where your hungry cradle rocks
Your mother sits and sings.
Lullaby, my child,
Hush and hush, my fate:
Your father's sturdy arm
Will unlock the gate.

Marie Syrkin

GOOD NIGHT, WIDE WORLD

Good night, wide world
Big stinking world!
Not you but I slam shut the door.
With my long gabardine,
My fiery, yellow patch,
With head erect,
And at my sole command,
I go back into the ghetto.

Wipe off all markings of apostasy!
I roll my body in your grime;
Glory, glory, glory to you,
Crippled Jewish life!
I cast out all your unclean cultures, world!
Though all has been laid waste,
I burrow in your dust,
Sorrowing Jewish life.

Swinish German, hostile Polack,
Thievish Amalekite—land of swill and guzzle,
Slobbering democracy,
With your cold compress of sympathy,
Good night, brash world with your electric glare.

Back to my kerosene, my shadowed tallow candles,
Endless October and faint stars,
To my twisting streets and crooked lantern,
To my sacred scrolls and holy books,
To tough Talmudic riddles and lucid Yiddish speech,
To law, to duty, and to justice,
To what is deeply mine.
World, joyously I stride
Toward the quiet ghetto lights.

Good night, I give you in good measure
All my redeemers;
Take your Jesus Marxes; choke on their daring
Burst with each drop of our baptized blood.

And still I trust that though He tarry,
My waiting will spring newly day by day.
Green leaves again will rustle
On our withered tree.
I need no comforting.
I walk again my straight and narrow way:
From Wagner's heathen blare to Hebrew chant
And the hummed melody.

I kiss you, cankered Jewish life,
The joy of homecoming weeps in me.

Marie Syrkin

THE BEGINNING

I

Shall we perhaps begin anew, small and toddling,
with a small folk?
We two, homeless wandering among the nations.
Laborers of the soil will bow before you,
for you will have become a drowsy idol
subsisting upon sacrifices of scorched flour.
I shall stroll about reciting the wisdom of the people,
my words never finding their way
outside our borders, and the least child
will greet me with a good morning.
Shall we perhaps go home now, you and I,
to begin again, small from the beginning?

Begin once more! Be the small God of a small people!
Transparent Jehovah, how largely you grew,
spreading over the seven skies and continents
to become that universal God of steel,
with vast churches and synagogues.
You abandoned the field and the stable;
I, the circumscribed love of my people.
Alas, we both ended by becoming universal.
Go back, beloved God, go back to a small people!

Begin once more with idolatry!
Become ours again and wholly.
And I shall stroll about,
speaking plain words that
will be mulled over in the dwellings.
Let us be provincial, you and I,

God and the poet,
which will be more to our liking perhaps.
You will begin with the small truth,
and no longer promise multiple joys:

You will keep in mind the man,
his flesh, his bone, his vices,
the wine enrapturing his spirit,
the body's joyousness.
And in those moments when his heart
invokes you, believing,
you will love him simply.
From blood and from the ax and from murder shall you be
    estranged,
having chosen to be the achieved God of our *minyan*
rather than the powerful God of cutthroats.
You will become closer to us,
and together we shall spin new laws,
more suitable for you and for us.

Shall we perhaps begin anew,
small and toddling,
to grow with the growing borders
of a blessèd land?
Children will confront us with laughter,
seeing that we are poor and without guile.
Your godly blessing will be entirely adequate
for a kindly and peaceful people.
And my words will be treasured
as in the bosom of one's family.
Your nostrils will begin to sense
the first burned offerings of a people
just beginning to cherish its God
with all that is truly precious.
I, too, shall be protected and caressed like a child
and cradled into a narrow, comfortable fame.
For outside of these borders
none will heed—
neither your name nor mine.

Shall we perhaps go home, you and I?
Shall we perhaps, unconquering, go home?

II

Us did you choose.
You have chosen us.
A small God. A small people.
They have acclaimed us both as great,
in order to scatter us as dust
and undo us completely.
With you have they bestarred a whole universe.
It is too much for your strength!
Are such multitudinous nations for such as you
who have but recently
left the workbench of Abraham?
Silent and sated with pride,
you are ours entirely.
Why did you abandon your tabernacle
and your small tent,
faring forth to become the God of the universe?
Therefore, we became your disobedient children,
shakers of pillars, starters of world fires.

It was you who first became the Jewish International,
and into the world we followed you
and were nauseated with your world.
Save yourself! Together with the pilgrims, return,
return to a small land.
Become once more the small God
of a small people.

Etta Blum

CHAIM GRADE
(1910–   )

THE COAT

A coat pursues me—its collar high,
two empty sleeves raised to choke.
Clothes without a body. Like old sarcophagi
dug up in shards that broke
their marble gods to footless frieze
and armless trunk, so from the dead
a monument accompanies
my step: collar without a head.

In the ghetto, my mother grieves—
the coat soaks up her cries,
I see her kiss the very sleeves
good-by, and fondle eyes
sunk frozen in the thread
like staring fish in ice.
The two sleeves whip my dread:
—Why did you leave us in the ghetto of the dead?

Through seven streets the ghetto spread
its carrion, while a cloud of black
rode on my back,
the rain's eyes riding dead.
My coat and I run there alone,
and if I kick a cobblestone
I see a skull—heads smooth, faces
seeping sand, weeds in the spaces.

The rain washes, it cannot wash away the slain,
the rain washes, eyes live in the drops of rain.
Hairy and hard as hide the prickly thing
that pillowed my head in my wandering.
The rain washes the blood of the kill,
but the dying mouth is shrill.
I'll cover him up with my coat, I said,
and run from home. And fled.

Since then my coat harasses me:
—I am the last of what is not.
Was it memories you meant to flee
when you left me in those seven streets to rot?
Stripped tree, die without your bark!
Specter! your looking glass shows dark.
Amid the rubbled ghetto's carrion
I, your coat, live on.

Cynthia Ozick

ELEGY FOR THE SOVIET YIDDISH WRITERS

I

I weep for you with all the letters of the alphabet
that made your hopeful songs. I saw how reason spent
itself in vain for hope, how you strove against regret—
and all the while your hearts were rent
to bits, like ragged prayer books. Wanderer, I slept
in your beds, knew you as liberal hosts;
yet every night heard sighs of ancient ghosts:
Jews converted by force. My memory kept
it all, your hospitality, and all that Russian land
that fed me, broad as its plains and confining as a cell,
with its songs on the Volga, and the anchor sunk in sand;
homeland all gone down in blood. And so I tell
your merits, have always looked to your defense, not to justify

for pity of your deaths, but for what you were when all the space
of Russia sustained you still, and you lived your deathly lie:
Marranos—your deepest self denies your face.

II

I saw you, stunned and dumb,
Yiddish poets of Minsk, Moscow, Kiev, when they brought home
Job's heavy hurt, the few whom fate had spared. Agonized,
you saw the credo you had catechized
in holy Hebrew—*Ani m'amin*
b'emunah shlomah—fall dead in the ravine
at Kiev, among the hidden slain: "With full faith I believe
in Friendship of Peoples!"—faith even faith could not retrieve
from Babi Yar.
              "Are you asleep?" David Bergelson came to me in
     the night:
"No sleep for me, Chaim. My bed is all nails from fright
of what we hoped for—the New Enlightened Man!
And I have lived to know him in my own life's span."
I can see his noose hanging down like lead,
and his canny eyes, quick to find.
From the way he bites on the knot of his thoughts with teeth set
     askew in his head
I can tell no one knows better the maze of his mind.

III

Aaron Kushnirov fought in the Civil War:
Communist, gray-haired captain, he fought with his own disillu-
     sionment even more.
In the vastness of victory at Vilna, the smashed synagogue
shook him out of his fog.
His son fell in the fighting, the father with wet eyes
came: "My son was your age—should it surprise
you, little brother, that I talk to you tenderly? Don't take offense!
Teach me Scripture. In Yiddish, so I can feel the sense."
On an old violin David Hofstein played a Yiddish air,
and often David Bergelson played with him—a fiddling pair.

Both covered me with mourning: no fiddles' cries
went with them to the sacrifice.
Hofstein came to see Tel Aviv building;
the Russian fields, unyielding,
drew him home. Home sentenced him to die
a traitor; he laughed, with a madman's eye.

IV

Mikhoels, tragedian of Tevye and King Lear!
The milkman's faith, the king's despair—
your very fingers speak the lines,
while double-dealing fate plays on.
They call you Solomon, and Moscow crowns
you King. I myself would rather shun
Mikhoels; I fear nothing in him throbs
for Solomon's Song, or Israel's sobs.
But one New Year's night when a blizzard beat,
and partied and vodka'd all Moscow went mad,
and both of us drunk we pitched through the sleet,
he groaned out the grief that stuck in his blood:
"I play the King with my hands, Susskin the Fool with his feet.
The audience knows no Yiddish; we bleat
to an ignorant hall." The nation trembled at his death
when tyranny snuffed the guiltless breath.

V

I sat on the springs of a faded chair,
and, leaning on his cane, with wild gray hair,
Dobrushin stood prophetic. The place was cold and in need of a
    broom.
Spiders walked on the books and webbed the air.
Between mountain peaks, in the middle of the room,
as if beside Mount Ebal and Mount Gerizim,
Dobrushin speaks: "The world is all Hitler! Cursed, a snare!
Blessed be our Soviet land, and sacred Socialism!"
Only the Nistar warned: "Children, beware,
run away!" He alone ran off, old man, into the ground.

On the last of my Moscow nights I found
Leib Kvitko guzzling *schnapps.* I guzzled with him.
The village cow was in his clothes, he smelled of milk and bread,
the steppe stuck to his ears.
"Don't talk ill of Russia!"—his kiss was thick with beers.
"Don't talk ill of Russia!"—he chased me down the stairs.
Murdered poet! —What would you call after me now?

VI

Smelling of summer, a stag with belly sated,
charming as a child, Kvitko smiled and prated.
But Bergelson bellowed, "A third eye's what you'll need
for all the tears you've yet to lose if you run
away, Chaim—you'll only run to weep!" Feffer gave his creed
with outstretched arm: "The days of the trials are done."
Posters on walls could thrill us then—but he forgot
the walls of the cellars where the prisoners were shot.
The day of his trial—let me be mute:
praise God I wasn't there. I feel my own head crack
with the bullet aimed at Colonel Itzik Feffer's back
in cold murder. Hard for me to speak of him, and then
hard not to. Still let me deliver
his name from evil repute. *Ani ha-gever!*
I am the man!—When we met to remember the slain
I saw his tear, and heard his hallowed Amen.

VII

Murdered poets! no vengeance for your blood.
Turned into a crowd of ghosts. What stood
watch over you—gates, guards, bars—gone:
till it seems you are skimming my window under the moon.
Sometimes you are the wind and the fog up from the sea,
sometimes a shadow. In a dove's flash
I see you; or you flame up like an ash
in my face; or your tears fly free
from a cloud. Like a chorus of birds on a single steeple,
brightly you sang the Oneness of People.

Leaf-gold that credo: as leaves that fall
to their dun death after all.
You were not meant for larks who sing while they stray—
yet like Bedouin birds, from day to day,
you wander about unredeemed, and drag
tears to the full in your water jug.

VIII

Peretz Markish flies into my room with the storm,
flies out again with the lightning's flare,
his grave grown scant for his giant's form,
his arms spread wide with wing-like whirr.
Stormy poet, enchanting silhouette,
how the style of your step bewitched!
But when you ranted a great bird twitched,
and your poems were rant caught up in a net,
thickets of words. You boomed like a wind,
all gusto and gladness— "Why does everyone fret?"
The storm in your song was thinned
for the doomed Siberian dead.
"Am free, am free, am free!" you said;
wild as your poems, you shook out your wild hair.
Already the rifle was cocked to tear
Apollo's wreathed and lovely head.

IX

Remember the poet who had no legs!
The Germans hurled his wooden pegs
after him, onto the pile of dead. Vilna townsmen both,
Gradzenski and I. They threw his legs with a jeer. And I am loath,
Markish, mourning you, to pierce your pride with grisly metaphor
made to mourn your song: but it was a god of wood
flung after you into the grave—that poem where with a roar
of rage you paid violent tribute to the dead.
"Who can sleep? The horror!" you used to gasp. "The German
    dregs,
hangmen! To throw at a legless man his legs!"

Since then your mouth is numb and dumb. And since you fell,
I have no sleep or praise for God for any miracle,
though I came safe away. The miracle you waited for—
that the Revolution's poets might not become its prey—
vanished with the verdict on that fearful day:
"Slay the Jewish poet, slay his Lenin medal, slay slay slay!"

X

I weep for your beauty, gone to dust,
comely as Adam on his first day.
Your glance silenced me to awe.
A god made your mouth, your face, your hands.
As David mourned his friend in a bound of trust,
Mount Gilboa's battle-fallen prince,
so I mourn you, Peretz Markish. Your wound, long stilled,
oozes in my heart. O you whom the rule of Stalin killed,
my brothers, poets!—no one knows your burial place
in the land where you were sentenced to disgrace
even after death. Your language, your repute,
were trampled underfoot.
Then let this song be your monument and rest.
In every phrase I cache your being, lest,
blundering birds, you wearily go
after death's black ship, to and fro.

XI

Sacrifice of my Yiddish tongue, peace to your dust!
Pockmarked Father of Peoples with a hangman's lust,
whose celebrants sang in tens of tongues,
demon escaped from the Flood—was it on him your muse
bestowed her Yiddish songs?
I was in that hell and I know the cause!
The Jew in the chorus made you rejoice;
where terror goes, love pursues.
Sing or die was your choice:
in the West they were killing Jews.
So you sang your festival airs, and shook with fear

of a knock in the night at your door.
I don't judge your neighbor the Slav; he proved to be
—himself. But may the riffraff that counseled me to hide
your anguish from the world outside
drop like rotted branches from our tree.

XII

Ghosts justify my despair, phantom faces
smile their lost mute shame.
Through nights of fever and dream
you razed your palaces
to glimmering ruin. In your poems you were
like a pond—crooked mirror
for the world of truth. The young
have forgotten you and me and the hour
of our grief. Your widows receive their dower
of blood money. But your darkly murdered tongue,
silenced by the hangman's noose,
is no longer heard, though the muse
again sings in the land. You left
me your language, lilted with joy. But oh, I am bereft—
I wear your Yiddish like a drowned man's shirt,
wearing out the hurt.

Cynthia Ozick

VI

YIDDISH
POETS
IN ISRAEL

ISAIAH SPIEGEL
(1906–)

MY FATHER'S BOOTS

Patched
And cleated
My father's boots
Are lying in the sand
Of the Auschwitz hill.

Shiny
And white
The cleats
Are glittering in the sand
Of the Auschwitz hill.

From your holy patched boots,
From your holy shining cleats,
I hear you say in me:
My son, with these patched boots
And these shining cleats
I can even go to meet the Messiah.

Irving Feldman

THE SACRIFICIAL KNIFE

His face is a twisted red knife
And a heavy fist
Hunting someone's face
In the dark.

I sit across him—I say nothing.
The knife unbinds itself from his face,
Falls to the floor.

He wants me
To pick the knife up
And put it in his outspread fist—
Together with my offered throat.

For two millennia the knife lies on the floor.
Let it.
And I shall always live
Beside the knife.

Irving Feldman

MERCIFUL HEAVEN

Heaven, merciful heaven,
Why do I stammer in my prayers?
Why do I fall on your steps?
Why do the dead braids choke me?
Why is my bread brine?
And my tongue lame
And my word?
Have you forgotten to sow
Delight at my doorstep?

I should not, I think, name you
Heaven, merciful heaven.
I will say, You, You, You,
I stammer, pity me,
Pity me, I fall.

Irving Feldman

ABRAHAM SUTZKEVER
(1913-   )

FROM "SPIRITUAL SOIL"

I.1

The earth still wheels about; and Time has still
No power over lasting memory.
With freight of years and years upon its waves
That ocean measures out my odyssey.
Where do I sail? I never conquered Troy
But *Trauer,* island of my wanderings.
The waves lie back—blue tips of eagle wings—
Then puff themselves erect as if to buoy
The whole expanse of sea! But it is plain
Their sorrow weighs as mine, and they collapse, disarmed, in vain.

I.2

My monosyllable: O sea! How can
A syllable ensnare your element?
A sound, that is the child of your own sounds,
Born in the sunset's orchestra? Not I
Am singing hymns to you—not I, but wounds
Like sea shells that can still recall the deeps.
For there is not a sign of Ashmedai
In all your kingdom—he who was hell-bent
At setting human beings like pitch afire.
Why could you not have risen then and flooded his Empire?

I.4

The *Patria's* nothing but gleam and rust;
A patch of motley coloring, its sails.
One could compare it to a centaur that
Had bolted down the passengers and crew.
Boxed and camouflaged, like contraband,
They lie in steamy cabins down below.
A naked sailor balanced on the mast
Plucks at a mandolin to please the gulls.
They thank him with their wheeling saraband
Until the sun goes down and then, shalom! back to their land.

I.12

Day is the denial of all dreams.
Day comes to wipe the bloody parchments clean.
The sea is sea. A chimney's just a chimney.
The human spirit pares its outer skin.
A fallen wave no longer is a wave.
A dead man does not even seem a corpse.
It's all chimera. Shores of Italy
Peel off. A sea of roses gleams.
I love the birth of light, the pure fantastic
Of the naked and the real. Without bombastic.

II.17

The sun has made a wager: it will melt
The iciness that's gelled about my bones.
As if an overcoat could ever warm
A world gone dead. The streets of Tel Aviv
Bustle with life. A hullaballoo. Look: each
Minute grows old. An "extra" down the drain.
A Yemenite Messiah holds a speech.
And as a beehive magnified—a swarm
Of faces. Strange, these are the very ones
That Vilna, Kovna, Grodna burned to ashes in their kilns.

II.41

My hand droops helpless as an autumn stalk:
Can it bring produce worthy of the crop?
We've crossed the Jaffa Gate, and now we walk
To the Old City. Sing, my hand, I am
Your master! Crumbling walls are forged
With cries of generations. It defies
Belief. But next to David's Tower lies—
A market. On both sides are narrow shops
With linen awnings, rolled out so the cunning
End-of-summer sun won't set this gaudy palette running.

II.43

Nearby, in a gray headgear that rides
High on his skull, a crazy Berber sits,
Babbling his noisy prophecies for brides
Who listen to him safe behind their veils.
A bowl of sand, whiter than alabaster,
Lies at his feet. Snakes dance round the rim.
A happy fortune costs you half a piaster;
You never have to ask this prophet twice.
An officer with lobster-red mustaches
Strolls whistling round the market, buying pins and sashes.

II.44

The scent of perfume, vinegar and dung.
A cinnamon potion to seduce a lover.
Pistachios—from faraway Damascus.
Earthnuts from the banks of the Nile
And coconuts as hairy as baboons
From Africa. Red poppies and a pill
To light your dream with seven rosy suns.
And jars of herbs, tucked neatly in a basket,
To make men potent, to help women bear—
Sold by the daring mothers who are scarcely sixteen years.

II.46

Where am I, here? Get out, and quick, if you care
To save your skin. This market is pure lies.
Leading his goats, an Arab bars my way
And offers me a rose of Jericho.
"Jew, buy a rose, this flower is unique,
Just water it, this rose will live for aye,
One could compare it to your eternal folk . . . "
What does he mean by that? Is he taunting me?
The goats are laughing, laughing to their death,
And magic traps the customer with webs of spider breath.

II.47

And suddenly, a stately, grave old man,
A Jew who lived in Lodz, reincarnate,
Gazing straight before him, blind to the crowd.
The shadowy black velvet of his hat
Makes his skin whiter still. And with a cane
He parts the market place as Moses once
The waters. Soon there will appear the Wall.
A long way off, he glimpses it, within,
Brooding, prayer book in hand, a Jew alone
Going to chant the noonday prayers before the ancient stones.

II.52

My heart is full of apple wine. Romance?
No word for it. If one of you should blame—
The stairway stones are blue and squared. Look: I
A European, grave imposing name,
Am trembling as a willow twig, and small.
The blue contortions of the stairs grow tight.
The ground drops down. An alleyway. And all
My thoughts are drawn deep, deep into a cave.
The blueness is a well that's blossomed blue
And suddenly a different blue: the cave is lopped in two.

II.54

How can the stillness carry such a weight
Of blueness on its back? How do I dare
Speak, where the very soil is blue with prayer
And grasses in their charity turned blue?
A candle man, made out of wick and wax,
Comes near to me, and asks if I would light
A candle here. His voice is dead, but two
Small eyes are jutting at me blue as waves.
My dear Jew, I don't know, if but you can—
Then kindle a million lights at the Wall for me, good man!

II.55

I sob my longing out to him: the past
Is ground away like kernels ground to meal.
My vision shrugs its husk aside, and speaks:
A million candles set in lamps of blue,
A burning candlewood! Its spiky peaks
Support a chariot of gold. The tall
Among the trees are guarding younger ones.
A wood of candles now: the Wailing Wall.
And where am I? Burning to purity
Upon my stake with thee, till I can see eternity!

II.57

The days burn out from steady heat, and shrink;
Their stubble glares like buckwheat after dark
Between dark grasses growing from the brink.
By dawn they have sucked out their final food.
And somewhere on a mountain, like a brood
Of huddled eagles, poised for days, the rain
Lurks, waiting. Branches feel its fanning breath.
At plowing, raw earth shows a different shine.
Withered leaves sigh out their stale putrescence
Before the coming rain, before its veiling iridescence.

II.60

Checkered violet and ruled in greens,
The earth, silent with pleasure, veils her flesh.
Blue flames of alcohol incense the air.
An olive tree sips at a hookah, steams.
Orange trees have leaves as black as ravens;
The damp sun hasn't fed their narrowness.
That blackness is a sign of health—the leaves
Have nursed and sucked out every drop of green
That streaked the callow fruit. And in the sun
The oranges are glowing amber-gold. They're nearly done.

III.10

Acacia, you're a scent of violins,
The taste of the first kiss. How I go wild
At evening's rain of spices in the spring.
Each branch becomes a gaudy parakeet
That our Lord himself taught how to sing
Its primal language: sounds of mint and myrrh
And ginger rhymes—till a taste of Paradise
Pushes its way out of my tiny room,
Out of my breast. And all my yesterdays
I sense among the blossoms of the blood-flecked lilac sprays.

Chana Faerstein

RICUDAH POTASH
(1903–1965)

JERUSALEM BEGGARS

On a fine spring morning
beggars sit in Jerusalem,
beggars sit, blind, lame,
come from the earth's four corners.

The beggars talk among themselves:
—Has the Messiah put on his shoes yet?
—Has the Messiah put on his clothes?
—No! says someone,

No, he still can't go.
His coat's got millions of buttons.
He hasn't even gotten to
the hundredth button yet.

Another beggar
shakes his white head:
—Has the Messiah
harnessed his white horse yet?

—No! says someone,
No, first that white horse
must be led to a quiet stream,
it must be bathed there and brushed carefully,
so the Messiah should not be late.

Jean Valentine

ODE FOR MY FATHER'S
EIGHTIETH BIRTHDAY

With the psalm you bring every morning
to the Yemenite synagogue,

take along my newest song,
purify it in the holy light
that trembles on the wall there.

I know you don't hold with my Yiddish songs, I know
your song is the Song of Songs.

But I am your child,
come too soon.

I wouldn't on any account give up my own way,
which glistens with dew: light and water
trembling in the raw daybreak.

Jean Valentine

ANONYMOUS

I go out into the day, anyone,
no one. My face the face of the librarian,
carefully keeping the lists of books,
keeping the names of the great painters, sculptors,
cartoonists, illustrators.

Sometimes it happens I come across
curved Stone Age oxen, thin
stiff primeval men.
Then my throat strains with the cry
of the first day's sun,
the first night's sorrow,
the first tearing of the first wind.

Still bent over some picture, my eyes flare
with the first fire of the world.
Later, a swollen moon floats up,
sorrowful as I am,
knowing she is growing smaller every hour.

Jean Valentine

MIRROR

Dreamed-up clown,
your tin-foil crown is worn out: queen
out of an old deck of cards!
Idle, ghastly queen, without a country.

Dreamed-up clown,
why do you do everything I do?
If I lift my hand,
you lift yours; if I cry, you cry;

if I open the door to my heart,
you open yours.
My sorrow steps out,
sits in the corner: your sorrow steps out, and shimmers.

Dreamed-up clown, I live in you.
You are the sixth lake
of those lakes
where I saw my poems stare back.

Jean Valentine

ARYEH SHAMRI
(1907–)

WOUND AND DREAM

Belief and doubt, tenderness, hostility—
I never spoiled anyone like a first-born child.
I am wound and dream, a well, a conflagration,
Like the rest of my generation.

William Merwin

GRAPES

Seven years after the planting
I came to the vineyard.
And there were grapes: ripe,
Gleaming with sunlight.

I have seen wounds, too:
Deep carvings, set in.
They burned more fiercely, leaving
My thirst and questions unslaked.

With what trembling fingers
I snatched the grapes!
Don't be afraid to smile
At the flash of this rare joy.

Don't be ashamed to tell
Of this miracle as it really is,
Plump grapes to give away
After seven wounded years.

Take a bunch in your palm
And go out on the road.
Hang it on stars in honor
Of the eighth year.

Let the grapes make the desert's
Hard substance glitter.
In my corner of the world
I will pull the bunch to my mouth.

William Merwin

SEEDS ON COBBLESTONES

Wherever, wherever
I arrive, I will have with me
the fields' dusk, the fields' dawn,
knees chalked with lime, and your sky
on my shoulders. And here
in tumult and noise,
I bless each flake of bread,
your sheaves, the seeds on your loaves,
and I breathe with your grasses,
with your leaves, with the wind,
as I am, alone, estranged,
standing out in my rough linen shirt
in this place, before the temples
of the stony gods.

William Merwin

HOUR OF MEMORIES

To me also comes the hour of memories.
Thus says the lord of the years:
All that is young and beautiful, and a dream,
Must become memory.

What does that mean?
    Little stag, enough of your prancing.
    Peacock, enough of your brilliance.
Another day, another hour,
It is growing late,
And shadows fall on the doorsill of my room.

That's what you mean:
The darkness is growing,
It's better to be alone.
That's what you want:
As a hermit
I shall withdraw into the shell
Like a turtle,
And make an end to drifting
Between the steps of God
And the fluttering souls
Of people
And things.

You say that everything vanishes, dries up,
Every wave falls back,
Its strength nothing but foam.
I look to sea,
You show me a sail leaning in the wind.

Oh, it is the hour of memories approaching.

I who am in love with the present,
The fields, the children,

And in every smile find my reward
And in each blade of grass my crown,
How shall I enter the shell
To weave memories?

William Merwin

A PRAYER

What have you prepared
For my last years?
I know. A black coffin.
A bright star is what I ask for.

One that does not go out
With the candles.
But when I am sunk deep
Deadens my death.

William Merwin

M. YUNGMAN
(1922–)

POEM

From anywhere
And everywhere.

Never known before,
Yet old acquaintances.

The same green faces,
The same black beards.

Jews from graves,
Saintly Jews.

Murmur of prayer,
The prayer after midnight.

They come from Gerba.
They come from Meknes.
They come from the caves of Adam.
A thousand years they gathered stars in the desert,
A thousand years they dried moons on mountains.
Tall men, with burnooses on their heads,
They hewed out a god,
Who was never known to smile.

They saw him in the thorns,
They saw him in sacred amulets and earrings.

Dark, with a wife and child,
He sat on the humps of the camels
And beat out a path in the sand.
They followed this path.

Through desert winds they followed.
Through eclipses of the sun they followed.
Arabic mosques behind them
Held up the heavens
So that he should not fall—
He was so low.

Miriam Hershenson

POEM

I will ring in the day with a donkey and gourds,
Big-boned, in sun, with a chuckle of wheels,
Sparrow's chirp and wetness of grass.

To the rabbit-like tents, baby clothes in the wind,
Huts of shiny tin, white doors curving,
To these native hills, these fields—good morning!

I have taken the light of a different world.
Spread in the potbellied jugs,
With donkey, bell and sun, I carry it to you.

Drink, glowing huts and ripening fields!
Children of Cochin, Iraq, India.
Drink—eyes of gazelle and lips of Yemen.

Nathan Halper

NEW CITY

In the dark skies, still the ancient stars.
But under them, blooming young walls.
A new city, a silver one, is our investment,
The songs sung to her, the interest.

Our fortune grows. We are now men of wealth
Who can indulge ourselves, in unison,
To count windowpanes, add up doors,
Becoming entangled, not knowing their total.

Our fortune grows. No matter the measure or boundary,
No matter how many stories high, or how high the roof.
The smallest nail adds a new indication,
The lightest stone, a simple thing, will be a city.

One doesn't calculate. May the street run freely,
And let one's legs lead where they will,
And let each one feel, each in his own way,
That the conclusion is the same.

Miriam Hershenson

JACOB FRIEDMAN
(1910–)

POEM

I am David, I cry, David the shepherd.
They laugh at me, the boys and girls whisper tales about me,
They make fun of me.

I lower my eyes and begin chanting Psalms:
"Be to me a breastplate and a fortress, Creator."
And I soothe myself with fine white skins of the sheep:
—Sisters, I say, there's so much compassion in the world
So much endless grace.

The harvesters rise with song in the vineyards
And among them I recognize—Shulamith.
She is slender like a cypress.
Turtledoves in her eyes.
O God watch over her and protect her!
I take my pipe and sing for her:
The Song of Songs.

She lowers her eyes, and her black braids
Fall over her shoulders.
To me she is a small sailboat
On the waters of my song.

Frederick Plotkin

POEM

I call the red-haired shepherdess Eve.
—Adam, she replies, laughing in the hills.
—Loved one, I say, it is as the first day,
The first day of creation.

She looks at me with wide eyes:
—You're demented, she says, but I am fond of you.
—See there, pointing to a swallow flying by,
The day kisses her with the first drop of gold.

Demented one, she smiles, I love your raving,
—It's Sabbath in the middle of the week.
—Look, I say, how silence
Undresses us with mothers' hands, to relieve our burden,

Burden of time, of place, of all the ages,
We come from nowhere, not from time, but from dream.
If you but wish it, we can ride to Jerusalem,
Or become two monkeys on a tree.

Frederick Plotkin

POEM

I am living in my dream
(dream, too, can be a home . . .)
It's twilight,
I'm returning home from the pasture.

Today I'm Jacob.
At Laban's tent.
Rachel is milking the white goats,
Near the almond tree in the field.

Uncle Laban approaches.
I'm frightened out of my wits,
Rachel hides her head among the goats,
Her eyes filling with tears.

Frederick Plotkin

GLOSSARY

Chumish—the Pentateuch, the five books of the Torah.

Gemorah—second part of the Talmud, consists of commentaries on its first and basic part, the Mishnah.

Golem—a human creature without a soul, a dummy; an automaton created by magical means.

Haggadah—prayers and songs recited on the first two nights of Passover.

Hasidism—pietistic and mystical Jewish sect flourishing in Eastern Europe during eighteenth and nineteenth centuries.

Havdalah—benediction over wine at the conclusion of the Sabbath.

Kaddish—mourner's prayer for a deceased close relative, usually said by the son.

Landsman—one who comes from the same town in the old country.

L'chayim—a toast to health.

Minyan—a quorum of ten males for religious services.

Natura Karta—literally, watchers of the city; an extreme religious group in Israel, with sympathizers elsewhere, who reject the state of Israel and await the return of the Messiah.

Payes—sideburns worn by religious Jews.

Shekhina—Divine Presence.

Shofar—ram's horn sounded on Yom Kippur.

Shtetl—a Jewish small town.

Shul—synagogue.

Succah—tabernacle, a wooden hut with thatched roof covered with green twigs, used for observance of Succoth holiday.

Tallis—prayer shawl.

Tefillin—phylacteries.

Torah—Mosaic law.

Tsimmis—desert or stew; colloquially, making a fuss.

Yisgadal—first word of the Kaddish: may He be glorified.

Zmires—Sabbath songs, sung during the Sabbath meal.

INDEX OF POETS

INDEX OF TITLES